NAIS

Journal of the NATIVE AMERICAN *and* INDIGENOUS STUDIES ASSOCIATION

VOLUME 2.2

2015

COVER PHOTOGRAPH: Richard Throssel, circa 1910. Courtesy of the National Anthropological Archives, Washington, D.C.

NAIS (ISSN 2332-1261) is published two times a year by the University of Minnesota Press, 111 Third Avenue South, Suite 290, Minneapolis, MN 55401–2520. http://www.upress.umn.edu

Copyright 2015 by the Regents of the University of Minnesota

All rights reserved. With the exception of fair use, no part of this publication may be reproduced, stored in a retrieval system, or transmitted, in any form or by any means, electronic, mechanical, photocopying, recording, or otherwise, without a license or authorization from the Copyright Clearance Center (CCC), or the prior written permission of the University of Minnesota Press.

Postmaster: Send address changes to NAIS, University of Minnesota Press, 111 Third Avenue South, Suite 290, Minneapolis, MN 55401–2520.

Information about manuscript submissions can be found at naisa.org, or inquiries can be sent to journal@naisa.org.

Books and other materials for review should be addressed to NAIS Reviews, American Indian Studies, 1204 West Nevada Street, University of Illinois, Urbana, Illinois 61801.

Send address subscription orders, changes of address, and business correspondence (including requests for permission and advertising orders) to NAIS, University of Minnesota Press, 111 Third Avenue South, Suite 290, Minneapolis, MN 55401–2520.

SUBSCRIPTIONS

- **Individual subscriptions to NAIS** are a benefit of membership in the Native American and Indigenous Studies Association. NAISA membership is $50 annually. To become a member, visit http://naisa.org/.
- **Institutional subscriptions to NAIS** are $100 inside the U.S.A., $105 outside the U.S. Checks should be made payable to the University of Minnesota Press and sent to NAIS, University of Minnesota Press, 111 Third Avenue South, Suite 290, Minneapolis, MN 55401–2520.
- **Back issues of NAIS** are $25 for individuals (plus $6 shipping for the first copy, $1.25 for each additional copy inside the U.S.A.; $9.50 shipping for the first copy, $6 for each additional copy, outside the U.S.A.).
- **Digital subscriptions to NAIS for institutions** are available online through the JSTOR Current Scholarship Program at http://www.jstor.org/r/umnpress.

JEAN M. O'BRIEN COEDITOR
    (*White Earth Ojibwe*) University of Minnesota
ROBERT WARRIOR COEDITOR
    (*Osage*) University of Illinois, Urbana–Champaign
KYLE MAYS MANAGING EDITOR
    (*Saginaw Chippewa*) University of Illinois, Urbana–Champaign
JAMESON R. SWEET MANAGING EDITOR
    (*Lakota/Dakota*) University of Minnesota

EDITORIAL BOARD

JENNIFER ADESE
    (*Otipemisiwak/Métis*)
    Carleton University
KIM ANDERSON
    (*Cree/Métis*)
    Wilfrid Laurier University
KATHLEEN A. BROWN-PÉREZ
    (*Brothertown Indian Nation*)
    University of Massachusetts Amherst
LUIS CÁRCAMO-HUECHANTE
    (*Mapuche*)
    University of Texas and Communidad de Historia Mapuche
VICENTE M. DIAZ
    (*Pohnpeian*)
    University of Minnesota
CHAD HAMILL
    (*Spokan*)
    Northern Arizona University
SUZI HUTCHINGS
    (*Central Arrernte*)
    University of Adelaide
BETH LEONARD
    (*Deg Xit'an Athabascan*)
    University of Alaska, Fairbanks
K. TSIANINA LOMAWAIMA
    (*Muscogee*)
    Arizona Sate University
KELLY McDONOUGH
    (*White Earth Ojibwe Heritage*)
    University of Texas

MAY-BRITT ÖHMAN
    (*Lule/Forest Sámi*)
    Uppsala University
JACKI THOMPSON RAND
    (*Choctaw Nation of Oklahoma*)
    University of Iowa
DYLAN ROBINSON
    (*Stó:lō*)
    Queen's University
PHILLIP ROUND
    University of Iowa
MAUREEN TRUDELLE SCHWARZ
    Syracuse University
NOENOE SILVA
    (*Kanaka Maoli*)
    University of Hawai'i, Mānoa
ALICE TE PUNGA SOMERVILLE
    (*Māori*)
    University of Hawai'i, Mānoa
COLL THRUSH
    University of British Columbia
KIARA VIGIL
    (*Dakota and Apache heritage*)
    Amherst College
MAGGIE WALTER
    (*trawlwoolway palawa of the northeastern nation of Tasmania*)
    University of Tasmania

Articles

JONATHAN GOLDBERG-HILLER and **NOENOE K. SILVA**
1   The Botany of Emergence: Kanaka Ontology and Biocolonialism in Hawaiʻi

MAILE ARVIN
27   The Polynesian Problem and Its Genomic Solutions

ANGELA PARKER
57   Photographing the Places of Citizenship: The 1922 Crow Industrial Survey

MARGOT FRANCIS
87   "Bending the Light" toward Survivance: Anishinaabec-Led Youth Theater on Residential Schools

ERIC STEVEN ZIMMER
106   Building the Red Earth Nation: The Civilian Conservation Corps—Indian Division on the Meskwaki Settlement

JENNIFER ANDREWS
134   The Erotic in Contemporary Native Women's Poetry in Canada

Reviews

BOOKS

JILL DOERFLER
157 *Métis: Race, Recognition, and the Struggle for Indigenous Peoplehood* by Chris Andersen

STEVEN WILLIAMS
159 *The Death and Afterlife of the North American Martyrs* by Emma Anderson

ERICA NEEGANAGWEDGIN
161 *The Students of Sherman Indian School: Education and Native Identity since 1892* by Diana Meyers Bahr

DAN TAULAPAPA McMULLIN
163 *Robert Davidson: Abstract Impulse* by Barbara Brotherton, Sheila Farr, and John Haworth

M. ARÁNZAZU ROBLES SANTANA
165 *Feminismos desde Abya Yala: Ideas y proposiciones de las mujeres de 607 pueblos en Nuestra América* by Francesca Gargallo Celentani (review in Spanish)

M. ARÁNZAZU ROBLES SANTANA
168 *Feminisms from Abya Yala: Women's Ideas and Propositions of 607 Peoples in Our America* by Francesca Gargallo Celentani (review in English)

C. JOSEPH GENETIN-PILAWA
172 *Remembering the Modoc War: Redemptive Violence and the Making of American Innocence* by Boyd Cothran

LORENZO VERACINI
174 *Red Skin, White Masks: Rejecting the Colonial Politics of Recognition* by Glen Sean Coulthard

CURTIS F. FOXLEY
176 *Fort Marion Prisoners and the Trauma of Native Education* by Diane Glancy

GREGORY ROSENTHAL

178 *A Nation Rising: Hawaiian Movements for Life, Land, and Sovereignty*, edited by Noelani Goodyear-Kaʻōpua, Ikaika Hussey, and Erin Kahunawaikaʻala Wright

JESSICA CAREY-WEBB

181 *Native and National in Brazil: Indigeneity after Independence* by Tracy Devine Guzmán

HEIDI KIIWETINEPINESIIK STARK

184 *Elder Brother and the Law of the People: Contemporary Kinship and Cowessess First Nation* by Robert Alexander Innes

JESSICA LESLIE ARNETT

187 *Yupik Transitions: Change and Survival at Bering Strait, 1900–1960* by Igor Krupnik and Michael Chlenov

JOHN P. BOWES

189 *Gathering Together: The Shawnee People through Diaspora and Nationhood, 1600–1870* by Sami Lakomäki

BETH LEONARD

191 *A Dangerous Idea: The Alaska Native Brotherhood and the Struggle for Indigenous Rights* by Peter Metcalfe with Kathy Kolkhorst Ruddy

JENNY TONE-PAH-HOTE

193 *For a Love of His People: The Photography of Horace Poolaw*, edited by Nancy Marie Mithlo

KATHLEEN CARTY

195 *That Dream Shall Have a Name: Native Americans Rewriting America* by David L. Moore

NICHOLAS A. TIMMERMAN

197 *Choctaw Resurgence in Mississippi: Race, Class, and Nation Building in the Jim Crow South, 1830–1977* by Katherine M. B. Osburn

PENELOPE KELSEY

199 *Sacred Wilderness* by Susan Power

KATHIE BEEBE
202 *The Power of the Talking Stick: Indigenous Politics and the World Ecological Crisis* by Sharon J. Ridgeway and Peter J. Jacques

ARTURO ALDAMA
204 *Our Sacred Maíz Is Our Mother: Indigeneity and Belonging in the Americas* by Roberto Cintli Rodriguez

ROBERT PAHRE
206 *Indigenous Peoples, National Parks, and Protected Areas: A New Paradigm Linking Conversation, Culture, and Rights*, edited by Stan Stevens

KIARA M. VIGIL
209 *American Indians and the American Imaginary: Cultural Representation across the Centuries* by Pauline Turner Strong

CORTNEY SMITH
211 *The Gift of the Face: Portraiture and Time in Edward S. Curtis's "The North American Indian"* by Shamoon Zamir

WEBSITE

MARISA ELENA DUARTE
213 *American Indian Histories and Cultures*, Adam Matthew Digital

JONATHAN GOLDBERG-HILLER AND NOENOE K. SILVA

The Botany of Emergence:
Kanaka Ontology
and Biocolonialism in Hawai'i

> *The Biotechnology Industry ... in Hawai'i cannot succeed without the manipulation and ownership of our Mana or biodiversity and related traditional, Indigenous knowledge. They have taken our lands and now they come to take our Mana, our very soul.*
> —WALTER RITTE AND LE'A KANEHE

> *Though the plant is distinguished from the animal by fixity and insensibility, movement and consciousness sleep in it as recollections which may waken.*
> —HENRI BERGSON

> *He poʻo ulu ko nā mea kanu. (Plants have heads that can grow again.)*
> —MARY KAWENA PUKUI

THIS ESSAY HAS TWO PURPOSES and proceeds in two voices. The first is to observe the steadily growing resurgence among Kanaka Maoli (Native Hawaiians) of a Native Hawaiian world and to argue for a more elaborated recognition of the spiritual and familial dimension of plants (as well as animals and other elements of nature) within it. The second is to analyze the ongoing colonial/imperial efforts of the state and global corporations to use Hawai'i's land to propagate genetically modified organisms, especially seed corn, replacing our Native life on the land, despite the continual protest of Native Hawaiians and environmentalists. We argue in this essay that plants provoke and organize necessarily incommensurate colonial and Indigenous ways of thought and practice. We therefore ask, what are the effects of contemporary and past biocolonial labors on the efforts toward resurgence of a Maoli[1] world, and vice versa?

Our argument proceeds historically and philosophically in order to examine Kanaka struggles against the biocolonial genomic industrialization of corn in Hawai'i, whose roots we discover in the European encounters with 'ulu (breadfruit), and the plantation colonialism of pineapple. We present, first, a brief theoretical inquiry into the political and philosophical meaning of plants in the colonial and settler-colonial contexts of the Pacific, and introduce our concept of emergence for comprehending the distinctiveness of Kanaka ontologies. We then discuss the colonial investment in botany—comprising multiple specialized forms of knowledge about plants—that has ordered many of the political theories, scientific institutions, and laws underlying settler colonialism in Hawai'i. Finally, we turn to a discussion of genomic corn production and Kanaka resistance, seeking to understand what is currently emergent in this struggle.

Emergence

What does it mean to restore a meaningful Kanaka life amid ongoing colonial occupation? Jeff Corntassel and Taiaiake Alfred suggest that one answer for similarly situated Indigenous peoples can be found in the maintenance of interconnection: "There are new faces of empire that are attempting to strip Indigenous peoples of their very spirit as nations and of all that is held sacred, threatening their sources of connection to their distinct existences and the sources of their spiritual power: relationships to each other, communities, homelands, ceremonial life, languages, histories.... These connections are crucial to living a meaningful life for any human being" (2005, 559). For Kanaka Maoli, I (Silva) argue that living a meaningful life should also include reviving and maintaining our interconnections with divine spirits embodied in trees, herbs, water, fish, animals, clouds, winds, sunlight, rain, and so on. Let's imagine the thought world or ontology of my Kanaka ancestors. They live/d in a "honua ola," a living earth (Kanahele 2011). In this world, many plants, animals, birds, and other beings precede/d humans in our cosmogonic genealogies. Thus, as Kaleomanu'iwa Wong often comments, they, too, are our (Kanaka Hawai'i's) kupuna (ancestors).[2] The deities of our ancestors took many forms, inhabiting many bodies, a concept called kino lau. Pukui and Elbert (1986, 153) describe kino lau as "many forms taken by a supernatural body, as Pele, who could at will become a flame of fire, a young girl, or an old hag" (see also Goldberg-Hiller and Silva 2011). Kino lau means that many plants, animals, birds, clouds, and so on are the bodies of deities, either the powerful akua nui (major akua) like Kāne, Kū, Pele, Haumea, and others, or less powerful but just as meaningful 'aumākua, family spirits. In the Hawaiian world, then, plants (and many other elements) are considered to be animate beings capable of acting on the world. This divine world, its beings integrated through kino lau, exists in an ontology that is historically grounded but not bound to the past, already and always emerging, generation after generation.

Previous to colonial capitalism, our 'āina was replete with these ancestors, 'aumākua, and akua, plants, animals, and elements of nature, many brought with us on our arrival voyages. For various reasons including mass death caused by foreigner-introduced epidemic diseases, many Kānaka converted to Christianity in the nineteenth century, which devalued these ancestors (Kameʻeleihiwa 1992). Other foreign pressures, desires and debt, led many aliʻi to treat some plants, notably ʻiliahi (sandalwood), as commodities. Others later agreed to change the mode of land tenure to the Western real estate model, which opened the way for plantation capitalism based on monocropping (Kameʻeleihiwa 1992; Perkins 2013). The first monocrop was sugar, and the plantation corporations succeeded in diverting water from loʻi kalo (wetland taro farms)—models of diverse cropping—to grow cane in previously arid lands (Wilcox 1998). In the twentieth century, more lands became monocropped with pineapple. Now that both sugar and pineapple have become unprofitable because of gains by unionized labor, we see some of these same lands monocropped in genetically modified seed corn. What remains constant and constantly morphing in this history is the practice of monocropping, with its attendant removal and refusal of our Native ancestral plants, efforts that threaten to steal "the very soul" of Indigenous peoples, in Ritte and Kanehe's epigraph.

Today, however, one may easily observe Kānaka Hawaiʻi ʻŌiwi dedicating themselves to opening or reopening loʻi and planting kalo with other Native plants in diverse cropping as our ancestors did; replanting land with Native plants; rebuilding our ancestors' fishponds; regaining and defending our rights to fresh water; as well as many other forms of cultural resurgence such as learning, speaking, and teaching ʻōants Hawaiʻi (Hawaiian); writing master's theses, dissertations, books, and newspaper columns in ʻōlelo Hawaiʻi; building, consecrating, and voyaging on waʻa (vessels often misnamed canoes) inspired by ancient forms; learning, dancing, and teaching hula and its associated art forms; and many other activities too numerous to list. All these efforts are evidence of our people's insistence on re/creating our own world and taking back as many of our lands and waters as possible, restoring them to health and carrying out our kuleana to our ancestors, ʻaumākua, and akua. Jeff Corntassel (2008, 107) has pointed out how colonial inducements to participate in settler ways of self-assertion, such as rights-claiming, have "deemphasized the cultural responsibilities and relationships that indigenous peoples have with their families and the natural world (homelands, plant life, animal life, etc.) that are critical for their well-being and the well-being of future generations." Many of our people seem to be sidestepping this rights-based, entitlement-based discourse, and proceeding with these projects motivated by their sense of kuleana, genealogy, and spirituality. Our kalo farmers, fishpond builders, ʻōlelo teachers, and so forth, engage in their work despite the lack of structural support or even the undermining of their efforts by the political powers that be. They may or may not speak of their rights to do so, but continue perpetuating this Hawaiian world despite the discourses of colonial governance.

Along with Leanne Simpson and others who have argued for a resurgence based in the Indigenous apprehension of the natural world (Simpson 2011, 88, 91; see also Geniusz 2009), we choose to conceptualize these activities as *emergence,* an idea expressing Kanaka ontology that we derive from culturally significant plants such as kalo, ʻulu, maiʻa (banana) and others that naturally propagate themselves by budding, moving underground, and arising again in new foliage, alongside themselves. Emergence expresses this biological advantage for reproduction in thin tropical soil, and thus recognizes cultural continuity and creation even in the context of thin political and material resources. The plant-based image of emergence is more than metaphor: it is the materialization of knowledges and ways of becoming in a world that is, and in some ways is not yet still, one's own. Another way of conceptualizing this is as an aspect of a moʻokūʻauhau (genealogically) oriented way of life. In the great cosmogonic moʻokūʻauhau, the Kumulipo, one aspect of Papahānaumoku, Haumea, is said to be reborn over and over again, having children with her own male children and grandchildren. We understand this story to express a complex temporal ethics, which never loses the ideas and practices of past generations while creatively interpreting them in order to care for people and the ʻāina in the present, and anticipate the needs of future generations.

Emergence, as one means of conceptualizing Indigenous sovereignty, is materially incompatible with monocropping and the meanings of plants for the institutions of empire. The destruction of Indigenous agriculture and the appropriation of Indigenous crops were essential tasks for the weakening of resistance to early settlement and the seizure of land, the institution of slavery in the Caribbean and the Americas (Sivasundaram 2001; Bligh 1988), the installation of markets and the creation of a proletariat (Marx 1992), and the production of commodities such as sugar, copra, pineapple, and coffee in Hawaiʻi and elsewhere (Mintz 1985; Abbott 2011). The taking and transplantation of new world and tropical plants filled eighteenth-century British gardens that signified the cultivated, civilized man (Darian-Smith 1999, 51ff.; Casteel 2003; Drayton 2000) and metaphorically constituted his discursive abject, the "savage": a human etymologically linked to both undomesticated animals and uncultivated plants. Gardens became vital to early Christian missionizing and Pacific colonization (Sivasundaram 2001; Merry 2000). According to Elizabeth DeLoughrey (2007, 6), "Plants provide[d] organic metaphors for civilization," and they later offered "a means of naturalizing the nation and/or ethnicity through the grammar of 'roots' and genealogical 'branches'" (see also Glissant 1997, 11ff.). This metaphor of rootedness is vital to settler colonialism today.

We find the concept of emergence, embedded in Kanaka knowledge of plant life, preferable to that of the rhizome, which has been deployed in some critical philosophy to challenge this sense of the root. Rhizome, which is deployed separately by Edouard Glissant (1997) and Gilles Deleuze and Felix Guattari (1987) to challenge the imperial character of some Western forms of thought, suggests to them an ethical relation outside the dynamics of capitalism and colonialism. In Glissant's words, the image of the rhizome "prompt[s] the knowledge that identity is no longer completely within the root but also in Relation" (1997, 18), potentially opening the colonial divide between colonizer and colonized to dialogue and encounter. We note, following an important critique by Chickasaw scholar Jodi Byrd, that the ethical mobility of the rhizome made by these philosophers facilitates this reordering of Western knowledge through a misrecognition and misrepresentation of the experiences of many Indigenous peoples. Thus the association of rhizomatic thinking with the "Indian" is an ethical position that represents Indigenous peoples as rootless in their own lands. Byrd (2011, 13) writes, "U.S. lines of flight across treaties with indigenous nations were always rhizomatic and fluid rather than hierarchical, linear, and coherent," implying that the important claims for Indigenous land (an unwanted territorialization in Deleuze and Guattari's terminology) are both unacknowledged by colonial power and imputed as a (false) value within rhizomatic thought. Emergence, at times subterranean, at times visible, better captures the development of Native ontology that does not depend on dialogue and ethical relation with colonial powers, while it avoids the impossible demand for a historical and ethnological authenticity (a demand for Indigenous rootedness) inherent in the colonial politics of recognition (Simpson 2014; Coulthard 2006; Bhandar 2011; Borrows 1997).

In this essay, we emphasize Indigenous, Hawaiian ways of living with plants and other beings, and the value of this relatedness and interconnection for thinking and working toward the restoration of Indigenous ways of life. These Hawaiian ontologies and epistemologies, rooted in cosmogonic genealogies of the 'āina (land), hold the potential to counter what we see as an unstable colonial grammar of rootedness and scientific genealogy that derive from and inform the authority and practices of botany (including Native and foreign agricultural practices). We examine this critical language of plants in three colonial *dispositifs*[3] (the assembled institutions and discourses that govern, study, and cohere the environments of colonialism) with four plants: 'ulu or breadfruit, which dominated early colonial ambitions in the Pacific and provided support to the imperial doctrine of discovery; pineapple, around which the multicultural governance within and identity for a more permanent settler colony of the United States was created; and GMO corn seed, a crop that now somewhat stealthily dominates agricultural production in Hawai'i and raises new legal issues. We juxtapose the massive planting of corn seed with the resurgence of kalo (taro) farming. Kalo is a plant whose history long predating colonial intervention we find particularly important as we observe Hawaiians nurturing their native world in the face of and despite advanced settler colonialism. In our study of these plants, the 'ulu as a gateway to colonial value, and kalo, a target of colonial plantation capitalism, we are attentive to the ways in which capitalist ambitions intersect with colonial concerns for biology and language, what Kaushik Sunder Rajan (2006, 14) has called "a grammar of life." We understand Indigenous ontologies (in one way) to have mana with which to challenge colonial biopower in the interest of Native peoples because of different grammars of life.

'Ulu

While Kānaka Hawai'i often speak of kalo as our older sibling, 'Ulu, too, is among the important ancestral spirits living on in kino lau. A famous long-distance voyager named Kaha'i, in one version the grandson of Mō'īkeha, and the third generation to sail to Kahiki[4] and back (starting with Mō'īkeha), is said to have brought the 'ulu to Hawai'i. S. M. Kamakau (1865), the eminent nineteenth-century historian says in a genealogy:

> O Kahai keia nana i kanu ka ulu i Puuloa, nana no i holo i Kahiki, a me na aina ma ka hema o Wawau, o Upolu, o Sawaii, nolaila mai ka ulu.

> (This is the Kaha'i who planted the 'ulu at Pu'uloa, who sailed to Kahiki, and to the lands to the south, Wawau, Upolu, and Sawai'i, which is where the 'ulu came from.)[5]

Wawau is recognizable as Vavau on the island of Upolu, and Sawai'i as Savai'i, all places in Sāmoa.

The 'ulu is very difficult to transplant, much less transport and then transplant, for it requires the root sucker to be maintained within the very soil in which it was growing (Handy, Handy, and Pukui 1991, 152). Kaha'i is accordingly considered a folk hero for having successfully transported 'ulu across approximately 2,600 miles of open ocean. 'Ulu's importance to Hawaiian thought extends far beyond the historical remembrance of its perilous journey. Mary Kawena Pukui relates a folktale in which Kū, a major male akua, was the source of the 'ulu. In a time of famine, he stood on his head and sank into the ground headfirst. From the spot grew the 'ulu tree, whose fruit fed his family, and whose progeny, suckers that grew up from the ground, fed the other people in the neighborhood. A note following the tale reads, "The Hawaiians have another story attributing the tree to Haumea. The low-lying breadfruit is called *kino o Haumea*, 'body of Haumea,' and *nā ʻulu hua i ka hāpapa*, 'low-lying like a bush.' It is thought of as female. The ordinary upright tree is called male and named *ʻulu kū*, or 'upright breadfruit'" (Pukui 1995, 8). From this we can see that one variety of ʻulu is thought of as the kino lau of Kū, whose name itself can be glossed as "upright." Another variety is the kino lau of Haumea, a major deity who is female. The translation of *nā ʻulu hua i ka hāpapa* above is a loose one. It might also be glossed as follows: The ʻulu trees that fruit in the hāpapa. According to the Pukui–Elbert dictionary, hāpapa is "1. n. Rock stratum covered with thin earth; shoal; shoal water, coral flat; shallow. *Fig.*, superficial. 2. vt. To grope, feel the way, reach for, extend out; to experience, feel" (Pukui and Elbert 1986, 59). This set of meanings evokes a sense that, while the tree requires much care in transplanting, it reproduces well on its own, feeling its way underground, then emerging, and, importantly, it can grow in thin soil or a shoal. This aligns well with other attributes of Haumea, who is associated with birth in the Kumulipo, manifesting in kino (lau) of various women and giving birth one generation after another.

In a separate moʻolelo, Haumea takes the ʻulu tree as a new kino lau when she rescues her mate, Wākea, from a rival aliʻi named Kumuhonua. Kumuhonua had Wākea tied to an ʻulu tree, waiting to be killed in an imu (underground oven). Haumea pretended to be saying good-bye to him and instead forcefully struck the tree, which opened and allowed her to push Wākea inside, thus effecting Wākea's escape. In the same blow, the ʻulu tree is transformed into the kino lau of Haumea called Kāmehaʻikana (Poepoe 1906),[6] who becomes an important deity of war and government.

The ʻulu tree said to be the very one that Haumea struck lived a very long life in Nuʻuanu, Oʻahu. Joseph M. Poepoe noted its location when he wrote down the moʻolelo in 1906. Silva's own great-aunt remembered having seen the tree in the mid-twentieth century. When and for what reason it died or was destroyed is unknown. The long life of this tree and the persistence of its memory suggests the importance of history that the ʻulu embodies. Moreover, the recollection of its provenance from Kahiki was, perhaps, strengthened by the use of its wood in pale (gunwales) on the waʻa on which it was once carefully carried over thousands of miles of the Pacific. Its complex gendering also reinforces its association with motion and movement.

ʻUlu, which they enterprisingly named breadfruit, captivated the imaginations of Captain James Cook and Joseph Banks on their Pacific voyages in the late eighteenth century to discover commercial opportunities for, and threats to, empire (Pratt 1992, 37). At the time of Captain Bligh's voyages to take and transport breadfruit to feed slaves in the Caribbean in 1789, Erasmus Darwin had popularized Linnaeus's botanical classifications based on the reproductive parts of plants, and the British were absorbing and debating his moral lessons for the boudoir and domestic life, linking the lives of plants to a vibrant pre-Victorian sexuality and its moral limits (Darwin 1806; see also Browne 1989 and 1996). Tropical plants, in particular, were associated with sultry heat, wanton growth, and rapid decay, which eroticized them and rendered them dangerous (Allewaert 2013, chaps. 1 and 2; Teute 2000; Pratt 1992; Browne 1996). Thus the potential imperial value of the breadfruit tree demanded a different history, gendering, and sense of movement than that given by its Pacific cultivators. The asexual cultivation of 'ulu, along with its bland taste, helped insulate it from concerns of sexual immorality back in England (Newell 2010, 151; see also Browne 1996; Fara 2003), and its renaming as breadfruit also helped to domesticate the Islanders in the popular metropolitan imagination. Despite the care and knowledge that Tahitians, Hawaiians, and others applied to the cultivation, oceanic transportation, and transplantation of 'ulu, Europeans imagined the same tree to provide these people with a labor-free life, projecting Native gardeners as passive and feminine (Smith 2006, 57; Banks 1896, 135; Moloney 2005, 263).

The juxtaposition of bread and fruit in the renaming of 'ulu was politically and culturally fecund. It reinforced an Edenic metaphor for Tahiti and Hawai'i, while contradictorily retemporalizing the Genesis story making the divine edict to toil by the sweat of one's brow (symbolized by the production of wheat and baking of bread) an integral aspect of the fruit of this prelapsarian tree (Newell 2010, 151). This metaphoric (con)fusion of bread and fruit legitimated colonial power, serving as benevolent cover for the transplantation of breadfruit to feed slaves. Bread, whose high costs in Britain led to working-class riots at the time of the European discovery of 'ulu, inflated the ideological value of breadfruit for doing the "good" work of empire and the slowing of abolition efforts (Spary and White 2004, 76; DeLoughrey 2007).

This demonstration of plants' political power helped integrate the science of botany into the structure of empire and colonialism. As Foucault (1982) and Sunder Rajan (2006) each suggest, the scientific abstraction of botany increasingly played an essential role in developing the political grammar useful for imperial economy and nation. The possibility of monocropping that defines modern forms of agriculture, that made imperialism profitable, and that altered the shape of colonial governance (Lafuente and Valverde 2007; Bassett 1988) was dependent on the uprooting of the Indigenous knowledge of emergence, and re-rooting plants through the mutually reinforcing abstractions of science and politics.

Pineapple

Pineapple, in contrast to ʻulu, does not have deep roots in Kanaka moʻolelo or cosmogonic genealogies. By the mid-twentieth century the pineapple had become a significant export crop in Hawaiʻi, where nearly 90 percent of the world's fresh and canned pineapple was grown (Bartholomew, Hawkins, and Lopez 2012). Pineapple was crucial for creating Hawaiʻi's supposedly paradisiacal multicultural society, rooting itself within the colonial image of Hawaiʻi as exotic, delicious, and available to Americans as their own (Okihiro 2009; Lyons 2010; Suryanata 2000). This process depended on an assemblage of politics, law, science, and economy which make up this historical colonial *dispositif* that in turn made the identification of pineapple with Hawaiʻi seem utterly natural. This *dispositif* included public and private scientific study in Hawaiʻi of the pineapple and its growth patterns, including the discovery of chemicals whose application could manipulate the timing of its flowering, permitting intensive monocropping. The development of canning techniques that retained pineapple's sweetness allowed inexpensive shipping and marketing of the fruit by 1882, long before the invention of refrigerated transport (Hawkins 2011). The *dispositif* also involved techniques for recruiting a plantation labor force, which drew heavily from Asian contract laborers brought in by the sugar industry.

The application of sovereign power contributed to the *dispositif* in several ways. Access to arable land was made possible by a legal system of private property institutionalized in the Māhele of 1845 through 1855 that eventually led to the dispossession of most Hawaiian farmers. It thus led to the consolidation of plantation lands in the hands of missionary families, which "became the source of ʻĀina, replacing the traditional function of the *Mōʻī* and *Aliʻi Nui*" (Kameʻeleihiwa 1992, 287ff.; see also Osorio 2002, 44–56; Banner 2005; Stauffer 2003). Despite a long history of Hawaiian resistance (Silva 2004), Sanford Dole, relative of James Dole, whose pineapple company would come to lead and define the industry, led the coup that overthrew Queen Liliuʻokalani and the Hawaiian Kingdom government in 1893 and headed the provisional government that sought annexation to the United States. The illegitimate annexation in 1898 permitted sugar and pineapples to be exported to the United States without tariffs; this enabled the industry to grow rapidly, displacing other experimental crops such as corn, whose value was premised on nationalist doctrines of economic self-sufficiency rather than profit (Duensing 2008, 171). The purchase of the entire island of Lānaʻi in 1922 and its conversion into a pineapple plantation, along with the displacement of Hawaiians living there, was perhaps the apex of the sovereign political and legal power essential to make pineapple so successful.

As an exotic and somewhat unknown fruit in the nineteenth century, pineapple could not succeed economically without a huge cultural investment, one that also reflected the dynamics of colonial power. Pineapple's commodity value was not found just in its intrinsic taste; it was uniquely identified with Hawai'i and the accessibility to tropical paradise that Hawai'i symbolized, a colonial relationship that created desire before the first juicy bite. The fruit itself had been associated with sovereign power from its earliest discovery by Columbus, who took it back to Spain as a gift for Isabella and Ferdinand, and its body could be read to hold this trace, as Gary Okihiro (2009, 89) has noted: "The 'princess of all fruits' came to symbolize the tropics, the Orient in opulence, leisure, a terrestrial paradise.... The fruit's top, or 'crown,' though manifestly regal, terminated in sharp thorns along with the plant's spiny leaves . . . disclosing that it was at core, like America's natives and flora and fauna, 'very wild.' Paradise . . . was indeed both civil and savage." One way the savagery of the fruit was civilized was to code it (and certainly Hawai'i along with it) as feminine. As tourism thrived on advertisements and ideology depicting the native Hawaiian culture as a sexually available woman (Trask 1993), so, too, would pineapple's imagery fuse with this parallel construction of Hawai'i's accessible exoticism.[7] To develop the taste for pineapple was to enact a possession that was political in every sense. It played on the contradictory themes articulated for statehood: that Hawai'i was simultaneously unique and fully assimilable (Meller 1960; see also Lyons 2010, 87).

The political roots that pineapple sowed grew in tandem with the expanding plantation fields. Solidarity among ethnically segregated workers grew in the second iteration of the plantation where Hawaiians were few, because many or most Hawaiians disliked plantation work. Labor unions fought throughout the twentieth century to build on a linguistic localism among workers that grew across language barriers. But language and localism were not enough for unions to break through. The success of the International Longshore and Warehouse Union in winning contracts for the pineapple workers after World War II partly depended on thinking with the pineapple and its growing seasons. The significant 1947 strike for an industry-wide contract on Maui collapsed when the strategy of striking during harvest season encountered too many contract workers, hired only for the summer harvest, who had no interest in union membership (Beechert 1985, 302). Strikes during planting season later became the norm.

Unionization of the plantations was a critical step in the construction of a multicultural norm of citizenship in Hawai'i, one that stressed civil rights and "equality" as a means to envision citizenship without the overt legacy of ethnic hierarchy and white supremacy. Civil and labor rights promised to manage the chaos of broader participation by turning social and economic grievances into public forms of recognition. This was an ecological politics, one that integrated plants and persons in a politically and scientifically regulated plantation society (Manganaro 2012, esp. chap. 5).

However, the refusal of most Hawaiians to enter plantation life facilitated the ability of foreigners to recast what "Hawaiian" meant to them and to the United States. Hawai'i had long posed problems to North American ideals of nationalism, threatening Asian inclusion at the time of "yellow peril," and native inclusion at a time of increasing repression of Indians (Rowland 1943; Basson 2005; Sneider 2008). Plantation life, with its legal and scientific supports, was represented as a civilizing process that cultivated exotic plants, as well as citizens who didn't look thoroughly American but who could be appreciated and domesticated through the sweetness of the iconic pineapple. Perhaps no image captures this process better than that reproduced in Figure 1. Hiram Fong, the first U.S. Asian American senator, is shown celebrating his place in Washington, D.C., with a pineapple held up to its image carved in the ceiling relief outside the U.S. Senate chamber. Fong later ran for the Republican nomination for president, sometimes relying on a pineapple motif. Pineapple citizenship promoted public recognition of Hawai'i's diversity within the islands, and within the nation, in a manner that did not threaten an America still in the throes of Jim Crow.

This was the beginning of that idealized multiculturalized world for the Asian immigrant plantation workers striving to become American settlers (Fujikane and Okamura 2008), but the whole project depended, and continues to depend, on erasing Indigenous Hawaiians from history and the present (not to mention the land itself). Patrick Wolfe (2006) has argued that settler colonies, such as Hawai'i, operate through a logic of elimination of the Native, designed to secure and control Native lands. Elimination occurs sometimes through genocide, but most often through cultural displacement. Pineapple citizenship made settlers the natural inhabitants of Hawai'i by integrating Native and settler alike into commensurate relations of equality via civil rights.

Kalo and Corn

In this section we intertwine the discussion of two plants, kalo and genetically modified corn grown for seed. This textual intercropping follows the political logic of Native Hawaiian activists whose opposition to GMO corn has highlighted the significance of kalo, a plant that challenges the colonial *dispositif*. We ask what the contrast between these two plants means and what Hawaiian knowledge about kalo provides for Indigenous resurgence.

The moʻolelo of Hāloa, the kalo, is well known. Briefly, the progenitors

FIGURE 1. Pineapple citizenship. Senator Hiram Fong showing a live pineapple to one carved into the woodwork in Washington, D.C., circa 1959. Fong was the first Asian American senator. Photograph courtesy of the U.S. Senate Historical Office, Washington, D.C.

Papahānaumoku (Papa, who gives birth to islands) and Wākea, after having some island progeny, have Hoʻohōkūkalani, a girl child. When she is grown, Wākea sleeps with her and she gives birth to Hāloa, a premature or malformed fetus. He is kanu ʻia (the phrase means both buried and planted) and from the site grew the first kalo. The next child of Wākea and Hoʻohōkūkalani is a male named for his older sibling, Hāloa. He is the first aliʻi from whom all Kanaka descend. Hāloa the kalo is therefore the older sibling of Kanaka (Kameʻeleihiwa 1992, 25–26; Handy, Handy, and Pukui 1991, 74). Almost everyone in our Native communities knows the moʻolelo related above and takes seriously its implications that we, as the younger siblings, have responsibility to care for the ʻāina (symbolized by Hāloa) and to propagate Hāloa, the kalo.

In a less well-known set of moʻolelo, Hiʻiakaikapoliopele, the younger sister of Pele the volcano deity, goes on a journey across the archipelago from Hawaiʻi in the east to Kauaʻi in the west and back again. We learn in the version by a writer named Hoʻoulumāhiehie that Hiʻiaka eats only lūʻau, the leaf of the kalo. She says, "ua laa iho la kuu kino i ka lau o Haloa i puka i ke ao" (My body is consecrated to the leaf of Hāloa who emerged into the realm of ao [daylight, realm of human life])[8] (Hoʻoulumāhiehie 1905–6, 4). The last phrase is a reference to the Kumulipo, where the story of Hāloa is poetically recounted. It ends with these lines:

| Kanu ia Haloa ulu hahaloa | Hāloa is buried/planted, grows with tall stalks |
| O ka lau o Haloa i ke ao la, Pu—ka— | The leaf of Hāloa in the ao, Emerges. |

(He Pule Hoolaa Alii 1889, 58)

The phrase "ulu hahaloa" is, first, a play on the name Hāloa, long stalk and long breath. But it also brings to mind the word hāhā, to grope or feel around, just as in the saying about the ʻulu, "nā ʻulu hua i ka hāpapa." Hāloa also grows, not only with tall or long stalks, but also via shoots under the ground, which then emerge (puka) into the daylight. In this and other versions, Hiʻiaka often refers to eating lūʻau or to others eating poi as ʻai Hāloa, or eating Hāloa. To take up this practice of referring to our poi and lūʻau as Hāloa would remind us that we do not just consume a plant, we eat the kino lau of a divine being, our cosmogonical older brother.

In contrast, the *dispositif* of genomic corn production suggests to us an extension of the logic of multicultural governance built around the pineapple, a logic that is, however, vulnerable to Hawaiian veneration of kalo. Our idea is that there is something uncanny between the modification, on the one hand, of the constitutional code giving rights to the legal subject that takes place in a multiculturalist society, and on the other, the modification of DNA in the patented organism. This is a similarity that has made gene splicing "a uniquely compelling cultural metaphor" (Pottage 2007, 322), at least for settlers in the colony. Both these political and biological processes intimate that nature, both human and biological, is modifiable by legal culture that protects both persons and (intellectual) property. But as with all experiences of the uncanny, the two do not always sit easily with each other. As Alain

Pottage (2007, 321–22) argues, "Legal form has acquired the anthropological function of conditioning and delimiting individual existences; legal institutions inscribe each individual into a logic of kinship, sexual division, and chronology in such a way as to deny fantasies of individual self-creation or self-sovereignty. These are precisely the institutional coordinates that biotechnology threatens to dissolve." The permeability between the cultural and natural boundaries (between what is made versus what is grown, between property and person) (Pottage 1998, 61; Strathern 1992 and 1999) is unsettling, threatening the various ways in which the legal form of multiculturalism helps to naturalize a sense of rooted belonging after colonialism. The Kanaka insistence on planting and eating Hāloa and fighting to regain the ʻāina to do so constantly challenges this naturalization with a different sense of time and history. While Monsanto and the other seed companies take advantage of Hawaiʻi's corporate governmentality, Kānaka keep on planting more and more ʻāina in Hāloa, ignoring and working around these structures, as well as overtly contesting legal and discursive multiculturalism.

Corn for seed, most of it genetically modified, is now Hawaiʻi's largest (legitimate) agricultural crop, having eclipsed the value of pineapple in 2006. Pineapple rivaled corn—called "Indian corn" in the nineteenth century as a trace of its Indigenous origins elsewhere—at the turn of the twentieth century, successfully competing for arable land. The decline of corn indicated changing political relationships as well as economic circumstances. Nineteenth-century missionaries encouraged the planting of corn as a useful crop for civilizing Hawaiian farmers (despite acknowledging the fact that kalo fed more people), and later the Hawaiian Kingdom government promoted corn for cattle feed and human consumption as essential to national self-sufficiency (Duensing 2008). The corn crop also diminished because of poor farming techniques that depleted topsoil on Maui, a present concern as well. Today, biotechnology companies such as Pioneer Hi-Bred, Monsanto, and Syngenta have developed and patented varieties of corn for seed, planting as many as four crops per year. More than 4,600 acres total are planted in Hawaiʻi on Maui, Oʻahu, Kauaʻi, and Molokai, which alone has more than 2,300 acres, some on the Maunaloa pineapple plantation lands that Norbeck studied fifty-six years ago (Norbeck 1959).

Despite the premier economic role of this agricultural enterprise, the industry has tried to operate quietly and surreptitiously. Pineapple was once celebrated as uniquely Hawaiian, and tourists today still flock to the Dole Plantation on Oʻahu to taste pineapple and tour the gardens that show the plant at various stages of development, atavistically enjoying an association between fruit and island long economically dissolved. In contrast, corn is relatively low-key, sometimes grown behind hedgerows, the fields almost always lacking signage, the tourists oblivious to this new agricultural engine. That the economic value of GMO seed production needs fewer cultural investments suggests that corn requires another dimension of abstraction, one that is geometrically distant from that which grew from colonial botany in the eighteenth century and was refined in the production of pineapple and the extolling of the pineapple's delectable body. As Nikolas Rose (2001, 13) reminds us, biology was already rethinking the scale of life during the reign of the pineapple: "In the 1930s, biology came to visualize life phenomena at the submicroscopic region—between 10^{-6} and 10^{-7} cm. . . . Life, that is to say, was molecularized. . . . This molecularization was not merely a matter of the framing of explanations at the molecular level. Nor was it simply a matter of the use of artifacts fabricated at the molecular level. It was a reorganization of the gaze of the life sciences, their institutions, procedures, instruments, spaces of operation and forms of capitalization" (see also Braun 2007). This gaze of the life sciences captures what Rose (2006) has subsequently called a "style of thought," which we think, especially in the case of GMO seed production, is distinctively antihistorical. While nineteenth-century settlers and the Kingdom imagined corn to be key to civilizing the Hawaiian farmer and thus legitimating the nation (Duensing 2008, 160), today corn is stripped of these imaginative roots by the corporations that exploit and the state government that fosters its profitability.

Some Kānaka, however, do remember and are concerned about the desecration and exploitation of a plant that is sacred to many other Indigenous peoples in North America. Corn constitutes the bodies of some Indigenous peoples in an analogous manner to Hāloa being the sibling of Kānaka (Rodriguez 2008; Awiakta 1994). The cultivation of this distorted, even monstrous, version of the sacred plant on Hawaiians' 'āina puts Kanaka Hawai'i in the terrible position of being unwilling hosts to a practice that damages other Indigenous peoples.

GMO corn seed gains its value within a risk economy, one with a particularly spatial and temporal character that makes this history and this cultural damage less relevant and accessible. The value of patents on genomic materials is time-bound, and biotechnology companies essentially speculate on the future value of their agricultural and pharmacological inventions in the limited time before their patents expire (Pottage 2007, 332–33; Sunder Rajan 2006, 143). This orientation toward risk is not only economic. Risk circulates as a general concern about the dangers to human health that GMO products may entail. Recent efforts to legislate a labeling requirement for foods containing GMO products both in Hawai'i and nationally stem from concerns that risks to health associated with this new technology are essentially unknown and that consumers should be allowed to choose whether they ingest genomic products. Public concerns over the dangers to health of pesticides used in the production of corn seed were the overwhelming rationale behind protests in 2013 that led Kaua'i, Hawai'i, and Maui counties to pass legislation regulating GMO production (Yap 2013; Bernardo 2014; Lichtenstein 2014; Hofschnieder 2013). As a consequence of a scientific exceptionalism, where the state cedes to scientists and corporations the authority to act on sovereign matters, the burden of proof to establish danger rests on the protesters rather than those who profit from this farming.

One public response by the genomic industry to regulatory efforts has been to again stress risk by highlighting the importance of food security. Yet where this security was seen in the nineteenth century as the responsibility of the state that promoted corn production for the local ranching industry, today this security is depicted in global terms. As one GMO supporter wrote in the opinion page of the *Honolulu Star-Advertiser* in early 2014, "When we consciously decide to close the door on a technology that has the potential to improve the quality of life for tens of millions of our fellow travelers in this world, then that is a tragic loss of aloha" (McHugh 2014). Invoking aloha, this argument strives to cover corporate activities with a veneer of Hawaiian values, but even this camouflage is rare for the corporate interests heavily invested in Hawai'i. Monsanto's efforts to help farmers "grow more, conserve more" is a response to an imputed global need for intensified agriculture that only genomic science can provide. Yet while Monsanto and other companies farm seeds in Hawai'i ostensibly to feed the world, they fail to feed Hawaiians or anyone else in Hawai'i in any substantial way; their plantations preclude both the replanting of Kanaka ancestors, akua, and 'aumākua, and taking proper care of our 'āina.

The emergence of these concerns thrust kalo into the ongoing Kanaka challenge to corn. One set of struggles in 2005 has played a galvanizing role in this conflict. That year, Hawaiian activists discovered that the University of Hawai'i patented, three years previously, several varieties of kalo that had been genetically engineered. University scientists had claimed they were motivated to eliminate diseases in the crop that might crash what limited production remained, and they hadn't consulted Hawaiian farmers because patenting the engineered hybrids was necessary under their union contract in order to apportion the value of the intellectual property between the university and the scientists (Schlais 2006).

Once the patents became public knowledge, protests erupted on campus, drawing attention to the theft of cultural knowledge that these legal instruments signified. In addition, the manipulation of genes was identified as genocidal rather than the infusion of (future) life to kalo that the scientists claimed: "Hawaiians have expressed their deep concern about genetic engineering by referring to this technology as *mana mahele,* which means owning and selling our *mana* or life force. Mana is the spiritual force that comes from our knowledge and intricate relationship with nature. Part of mana is what westerners call 'biodiversity'" (Ritte and Freese 2006, 11). While biodiversity has been a key concept justifying the scientific management of state resources—often in the name of Hawaiian values without inviting Native Hawaiian control over those resources—it also draws negative attention to what the growing industrial commitment to GMO technology means for Hawaiian survival.

The response of the university to these protests was to propose granting the patents to a Hawaiian entity to do with as it pleased (Schlais 2006, 600). But the protestors who refused a legal relationship to kalo rejected this solution: "Hawaiians are saying that kalo cannot be owned, so why would the Hawaiians want to own it?" (Walter Ritte quoted in Schlais, 602). "Hawaiians would never dream of patenting kalo. Kalo is a gift handed down to us by our ancestors. We have a Kuleana or responsibility to honor, respect, and protect Haloa, so he in turn will sustain us" (Le'a Kanehe quoted in Schlais, 602). In a virtually unprecedented action, the university agreed to allow the patents to be ceremonially and legally destroyed, while the legislature debated whether to restrict further genetic experimentation and cultivation of kalo.[9]

Why not accept the patents? Marxist theorists of the legal form argue that the capacity to enter into commodity relations defines the abstract legal subject (Pashukanis 1978; Balbus 1977). At some level, the activists' rejection of ownership rights is a denial of commensurability and this very abstraction. The ownership of the patents and the opportunity to exploit them on behalf of a Native Hawaiian entity proposed a hypothetical form of recognition based on property relations that could lead to community control over the technology. The activists' rejection is nonetheless ambivalent. It was not a denunciation of ownership per se, but rather a repudiation of its terms. The ceremony in which the patents were destroyed made this apparent: the patents were publicly received by three representatives and then torn in half. Ownership continued through an assertion of the cultural impropriety of intellectual property rights in kalo, a point that the state conceded in ceasing its research. And it was strengthened in the metamorphic claim that kalo was an ancestor.

This ancestral claim challenged the technical manipulation of genes in several ways. Metonymically, it contested the idea that a Hawaiian individual (e.g., kalo as elder sibling) could be technically created, and by analogy, that the extension of legal rights to this individual—or to an Indigenous people within a multicultural scheme of governance (a "pineapple politics")—could cause a politically relevant metamorphosis. Since bioengineering is also a speculative capitalist venture oriented toward the mitigation and control of future risk—a risk that underwrote the value for the patent holders—opposition to kalo's genetic manipulation also served to reorient kinship within different temporal frames signified by emergence. Hawaiian kalo farming depends on replanting the huli, or the green sprout, after harvesting the corm. Thus Hawaiian kalo is reproduced as a clone, the self-same being that lives at once as ancestor and again as the following generation (in some ways also echoing the story of Haumea and ʻulu, above).

The French philosopher Catherine Malabou (2012, 32–33) argues that clones should not be seen as identical replicas, and as such they challenge some aspects of genomic thinking and value:

> The fact that it's possible to become daughter of your daughter, to be simultaneously older and younger than yourself, to auto-clone yourself in some way, effectively . . . produces difference not in the sense to which we've become accustomed by good old DNA and other such kinds of code—a difference between individuals—but a difference *between code and message*. . . . We might not ask ourselves anymore if clones are really twins, but instead how the phenomenon of cloning allows us to take twinness as the model of truth. Plasticity, from the perspective of such an investigation, [would be linked] to the eruption of a reversibility between before and after that modernizes posterity by giving new forms to atomized, nuclear sameness. (See also Franklin 2007, 41)[10]

Replanting kalo intervenes in the plant's lifecycle in order to assure a clone that also moves from loʻi (paddy) to loʻi, identical yet different, creating the semantic possibilities of new messages based on an ancient lineage. With some affinity to Malabou's notion of plasticity, this is one Hawaiian sense of rootedness, emergence, and reemergence.

The kalo patents and the fights against genetically modified kalo galvanized Hawaiian activism against GMO agriculture generally, in part because kalo provides a plant body to think with in Hawaiian ways. In the genealogical understanding of kino lau—kalo as transformed body and as ancestor to Hawaiians—the Hawaiian ontological refusal of the distinction between nature and culture can be seen. In what ways does this differ from the *dispositifs* surrounding genomics that have demonstrated the vulnerability of nature to biochemistry, law, economics, and colonial dispossession? One important difference can be found in the preservation of history. Kalo production clones the body of the plant, extending the life of the living organism without break from ancestry: this kalo *is* Hāloa. The budding power of the kalo is also a conduit for social and political metaphor persisting beneath the veneer of colonial power: the word ʻohana (or family) has etymological roots in kalo, and kalo provides enduring political metaphors as well.[11] Ancient Hawaiians hybridized kalo strains, preserving this history and integrating Pacific peoples in an alternative political framework than those imposed by settler colonial multiculturalism and neoliberal globalization. Walter Ritte and Leʻa Kanehe (2007, 133), referencing the kalo patent controversy, complicated the jurisdictional issue of patent ownership by relaying this history:

> Maui Lehua is one of 300 Hawaiian varieties that has been developed over centuries by extensive breeding by Hawaiians to suit differing micro environmental and cultivation conditions, for special qualities of color and taste, and for different cultural, social, medicinal, and ceremonial purposes. . . . The three patented lines carrying within them the traits that Hawaiians and other Pacific islanders have bred for over millennia [sic]. . . . Given that the male parent for these hybrids is a Palauan variety, the indigenous peoples of Palau who are responsible for the Ngeruuch variety, should also be involved with the rightful repatriation and stewardship and custodianship of these new varieties. In any case, UH does not have a right to claim ownership.

These historical memories emphasize the responsibility for, and the precarity of, significant plants, linking kalo to the memories of ʻulu and its swaddled voyage from Tahiti to Hawaiʻi hundreds of years ago.

Historical knowledge of plants and their voyages challenges the state's rhetorical (though often empty) commitment to biodiversity. Biodiversity has a strong affinity to the multicultural valorization of diversity, and as we have argued elsewhere (Goldberg-Hiller and Silva 2011), legislation that protects the environment frequently invokes Indigenous ontologies and Hawaiian stewardship for the land for its legitimation. The goal of protecting biodiversity also draws from ecological theory that erases the significance of Indigenous peoples and their historical and ongoing reliance on plants and animals for subsistence. In Hawaiʻi, for example, the pig is represented as a scientifically assessed pest without any acknowledgment that ancient Hawaiians intentionally introduced the pig and rooted it in culture, and that some Hawaiians continue to live from its flesh. As keepers of this human and natural history, Hawaiian ontologies do more than express an assimilable notion of "personhood" that can reorient critical ecologists toward a new humanism and a new ethics. We argue that this idea of personhood as it becomes universalized may be vulnerable to colonial *dispositifs* such as civil rights that infuse the settler colony and re-create Indigenous marginality and destruction (see Hall 2011, especially chap. 5; see also Allewaert 2013). In contrast, Hawaiian ontologies help perpetuate a Hawaiian world where Hawaiian history and human, plant, animal, rock, and other bodies are rooted and continually reemerge.

Conclusion

Our concept of emergence, for Kānaka linked to a moʻokūʻauhau orientation to the world, emphasizes the vital reproductive energies of valued tropical plants. It is designed to foreground cultural and political efforts to firmly root Hawaiian ontology and expand its significance for the struggles against biocolonialism and genomic agriculture. Emergence depicts the manner in which native plants such as kalo, ʻulu, and maiʻa (as well as pineapple) propagate by budding, dividing, and arising again from subterranean exuberance as well as visible stems, expressing new forms of the same living being whose Indigenous history is manifest in the flesh. Emergence occurs neither through code and its technical manipulation, nor through sex and its colonial implications for hierarchy, nor does it depend on the exclusion of other budding plants. We think current efforts to plant and defend kalo, and the proliferating festivals on several islands celebrating ʻulu and its care and replanting, reveal some of the ways that Hawaiians are firmly acting in accordance with principles of moʻokūʻauhau thinking—that is, that we are researching and then reviving planting practices of our ancestors while establishing new, healthy, Native food sources for coming generations.

JONATHAN GOLDBERG-HILLER is professor of political science at the University of Hawaiʻi at Mānoa. He is the author of *The Limits to Union: Same-Sex Marriage and the Politics of Civil Rights* and the coeditor of *Plastic Materialities: Politics, Legality, and Metamorphosis in the Work of Catherine Malabou*.

NOENOE K. SILVA is professor of Indigenous and Hawaiian politics at the University of Hawaiʻi at Mānoa. She is the author of *Aloha Betrayed: Native Hawaiian Resistance to American Colonialism*.

Notes

We extend our thanks to Tony Lucero and colleagues at the University of Washington, whose invitation precipitated this research, participants in our department colloquium, Eve Darian-Smith, J. Kēhaulani Kauanui, Renisa Mawani, Kim TallBear, and the reviewers, all of whom offered helpful advice.

    1. We do not italicize Hawaiian words because they are not foreign to us and we are located in Hawaiʻi.

    2. Kaleomanuʻiwa Wong, personal communication, 2012.

    3. Michel Foucault (1980, 194) writes that a *dispositif* is "a thoroughly heterogeneous ensemble consisting of discourses, institutions, architectural forms, regulatory decisions, laws, administrative measures, scientific state-

ments, philosophical, moral and philanthropic propositions—in short, the said as much as the unsaid.... The [*dispositif*] itself is the system of relations that can be established between these elements."

4. Kahiki refers to all places outside of Hawai'i, thus not necessarily Tahiti.

5. Silva's translation.

6. Note the relationship of the name of this kino lau deity, Kāmeha'ikana, and the epithet that Handy, Handy, and Pukui (1991) record for the 'ulu, 'ai kāmeha'i. The word kāmeha'i, wondrous, refers not only to the tree's ability to reproduce itself in an amazing manner, but also to the powers of Haumea and her kino lau. See also Pukui and Elbert (1986, 126).

7. The rise of pineapple and its association with tourism in Hawai'i led to the filling of the kalo lo'i (paddies) in Waikīkī in 1928 under the guise of a health emergency, another sign of the decline of native Hawaiian ways of life.

8. Silva's translation.

9. S.B. 958, S.D.1, & H.D. 1 (2007) ("Imposes a 10-year moratorium on developing, testing, propagating, cultivating, growing, and raising genetically engineered taro in the State"); H.B. 1663, H.D. 1, & S.D. 2 (2009) ("Prohibits the development, testing, propagation, release, importation, planting, or growing of genetically engineered Hawaiian taro in the State of Hawai'i"). The legislature did pass an act making kalo the state plant. Hawai'i Revised Statutes Div. 1, Tit. 1, Ch. 5 (Pursuant to 2007 Haw. Sess. Laws, Act 36, §2, as amended by 2008 Haw. Sess. Laws, Act 71, §1).

10. Michael Marder (2013, 95) has provocatively suggested that "the meaning of vegetal being is time."

11. 'Ohana stems from 'ohā, which is a shoot or sucker from the base of kalo that is frequently replanted. "Twelve taro patches, one taro plant" is the translation of an 'ōlelo no'eau, indicating Kamehameha and the unification of the twelve Hawaiian islands (Handy, Handy, and Pukui 1991, 76).

Bibliography

Abbott, Elizabeth. 2011. *Sugar: A Bittersweet History*. Toronto: Penguin Canada.

Alfred, Taiaiake, and Jeff Corntassel. 2005. "Being Indigenous: Resurgences against Contemporary Colonialism." *Government and Opposition* 40, no. 4: 597–614.

Allewaert, Monique. 2013. *Ariel's Ecology: Plantations, Personhood, and Colonialism in the American Tropics*. Minneapolis: University of Minnesota Press.

Awiakta, Marilou. 1994. *Selu: Seeking the Corn-Mother's Wisdom*. Golden, Colo.: Fulcrum Publishing.

Balbus, Isaac. 1977. "Commodity Form and Legal Form: An Essay on the 'Relative Autonomy' of the Law." *Law and Society Review* 11: 571–88.

Banks, Joseph. 1896. *Journal of the Right Hon. Sir Joseph Banks... : During Captain Cook's First Voyage in H.M.S. Endeavour in 1768–71 to Terra Del Fuego, Otahite, New Zealand, Australia, the Dutch East Indies, Etc.* New York: Macmillan.

Banner, Stuart. 2005. "Preparing to Be Colonized: Land Tenure and Legal Strategy in Nineteenth-Century Hawaii." *Law and Society Review* 39, no. 2: 273–314.

Bartholomew, Duane P., Richard A. Hawkins, and Johnny A. Lopez. 2012. "Hawaii Pineapple: The Rise and Fall of an Industry." *HortScience* 47, no. 10: 1390–98.

Bassett, Thomas J. 1988. "The Development of Cotton in Northern Ivory Coast, 1910–1965." *Journal of African History* 29, no. 2: 267–84.

Basson, Lauren L. 2005. "Fit for Annexation but Unfit to Vote? Debating Hawaiian Suffrage Qualifications at the Turn of the Twentieth Century." *Social Science History* 29, no. 4: 575–98.

Beechert, Edward D. 1985. *Working in Hawaii: A Labor History*. Honolulu: University of Hawai'i Press.

Bergson, Henri. 1944. *Creative Evolution*. New York: Modern Library.

Bernardo, Rosemarie. 2014. "Maui Petition Pushes to Get Anti-GMO Initiative on Ballot." *Honolulu Star-Advertiser*. March 3.

Bhandar, Brenna. 2011. "Plasticity and Post-Colonial Recognition: 'Owning, Knowing and Being.'" *Law and Critique* 22, no. 3: 227–49.

Bligh, William. 1988. *Return to Tahiti: Bligh's Second Breadfruit Voyage*. Edited by Douglas L. Oliver. Honolulu: University of Hawai'i Press.

Borrows, John. 1997. "Frozen Rights in Canada: Constitutional Interpretation and the Trickster." *American Indian Law Review* 22, no. 1: 37–64.

Braun, Bruce. 2007. "Biopolitics and the Molecularization of Life." *Cultural Geographies* 14, no. 1: 6–28.

Browne, Janet. 1989. "Botany for Gentlemen: Erasmus Darwin and 'The Loves of the Plants.'" *Isis* 80, no. 4: 593–621.

———. 1996. "Botany in the Boudoir and Garden: The Banksian Context." In *Visions of Empire: Voyages, Botany, and Representations of Nature*, edited by David Miller and Peter Riell, 153–72. Cambridge, U.K.: Cambridge University Press.

Byrd, Jodi A. 2011. *Transit of Empire: Indigenous Critiques of Colonialism*. Minneapolis: University of Minnesota Press.

Casteel, Sarah Phillips. 2003. "New World Pastoral." *Interventions* 5, no. 1: 12–28.

Corntassel, Jeff. 2008. "Toward Sustainable Self-Determination: Rethinking the Contemporary Indigenous-Rights Discourse." *Alternatives: Global, Local, Political* 33, no. 1: 105–32.

Coulthard, G. 2006. "Indigenous Peoples and 'the Politics of Recognition.'" *New Socialist* 58: 9–12.

Darian-Smith, Eve. 1999. *Bridging Divides: The Channel Tunnel and English Legal Identity in the New Europe*. Berkeley: University of California Press.

Darwin, Erasmus. 1806. *The Loves of the Plants*. Vol. 2. London: J. Johnson.

Deleuze, Gilles, and Felix Guattari. 1987. *A Thousand Plateaus: Capitalism and Schizophrenia*. Minneapolis: University of Minnesota Press.

DeLoughrey, Elizabeth M. 2007. "Globalizing the Routes of Breadfruit and Other Bounties." *Journal of Colonialism and Colonial History* 8, no. 3. Muse.jhu.edu.

Drayton, Richard Harry. 2000. *Nature's Government: Science, Imperial Britain, and the "Improvement" of the World*. New Haven, Conn.: Yale University Press.

Duensing, Dawn E. 2008. "Hawai'i's Forgotten Crop: Corn on Maui, 1851–1951." *Hawaiian Journal of History* 42: 159–75.

Fara, Patricia. 2003. *Sex, Botany, and Empire: The Story of Carl Linnaeus and Joseph Banks*. New York: Columbia University Press.

Foucault, Michel. 1980. "The Confession of the Flesh." In *Power/Knowledge: Selected Writings and Other Interviews, 1972–1977*, 194–228. New York: Pantheon.

———. 1982. *The Archaeology of Knowledge and the Discourse on Language*. New York: Pantheon.

Franklin, Sarah. 2007. *Dolly Mixtures: The Remaking of Genealogy*. Durham, N.C.: Duke University Press.

Fujikane, Candace, and Jonathan Okamura. 2008. *Asian Settler Colonialism: From Local Governance to the Habits of Everyday Life in Hawai'i*. Honolulu: University of Hawai'i Press.

Geniusz, Wendy M. 2009. *Our Knowledge Is Not Primitive: Decolonizing Botanical Anishinaabe Teachings*. Syracuse, N.Y: Syracuse University Press.

Glissant, Edouard. 1997. *The Poetics of Relation*. Translated by Betsy Wing. Ann Arbor: University of Michigan Press.

Goldberg-Hiller, Jonathan, and Noenoe Silva. 2011. "Sharks and Pigs: Animating Hawaiian Sovereignty against the Anthropological Machine." *South Atlantic Quarterly* 110, no. 2: 429–46.

Hall, Matthew. 2011. *Plants as Persons: A Philosophical Botany*. Edited by Harold Coward. Albany: State University of New York Press.

Handy, E. S. Craighill, Elizabeth Green Handy, and Mary Kawena Pukui. 1991. *Native Planters in Old Hawaii: Their Life, Lore, and Environment*. Rev. ed. Bernice P. Bishop Museum Bulletin 233. Honolulu: Bishop Museum Press.

Hawkins, Richard A. 2011. *A Pacific Industry: The History of Pineapple Canning in Hawaii*. London: I. B. Tauris.

He Pule Hoolaa Alii: He Kumulipo No Ka-I-Imamao, a Ia Alapai Wahine. 1889. Honolulu: Pa'iia e ka Hui Pa'ipalapala Elele.

Hofschnieder, Anita. 2013. "Environmentalists Push for GMO Labeling in Hawaii." *Honolulu Star-Advertiser*. February 4.

Hooulumahiehie. 1905–6. "Ka Moolelo o Hiiaka-i-ka-poli-o-Pele." *Ka Na'i Aupuni*. January 17.

Kamakau, S. M. 1865. "Ka Moolelo o Hawaii Nei." *Ka Nupepa Kuokoa*. September 30.

Kame'eleihiwa, Lilikalā. 1992. *Native Land and Foreign Desires: How Shall We Live in Harmony* [*Ko Hawai'i 'Āina a Me Nā Koi Pu'umake a Ka Po'e Haole: Pehea Lā E Pono Ai?*]. Honolulu: Bishop Museum Press.

Kanahele, Pualani Kanakaole. 2011. *Ka Honua Ola: 'Eli'eli Kau Mai* [*The Living Earth: Descend, Deepen the Revelation*]. Honolulu: Kamehameha Publishing.

Lafuente, Antonio, and Nuria Valverde. 2007. "Linnean Botany and Spanish Imperial Biopolitics." In *Colonial Botany: Science, Commerce, and Politics in the Early Modern World*, edited by Londa Schiebinger and Claudia Swan, 134–47. Philadelphia: University of Pennsylvania Press. Available online at http://digital.csic.es/handle/10261/32575.

Lichtenstein, David. 2014. "Food Fight: The Safety of Growing GMO Crops." *Molokai News*. May 5. TheMolokaiNews.com.

Lyons, Laura E. 2010. "Dole, Hawaiʻi, and the Question of Land under Globalization." In *Cultural Critique and the Global Corporation*, edited by Purnima Bose and Laura E. Lyons, 64–101. Bloomington: Indiana University Press.

Malabou, Catherine. 2012. "Following Generation." Translated by S. Porzak. *Qui Parle: Critical Humanities and Social Sciences* 20, no. 2: 19–33.

Manganaro, Christine Leah. 2012. "Assimilating Hawaiʻi: Racial Research in a Colonial 'Laboratory,' 1919–1939." PhD diss., University of Minnesota. http://search.proquest.com.eres.library.manoa.hawaii.edu/pqdtglobal/docview/1037992264/abstract/E3DD0C42C72A495CPQ/1?accountid=27140.

Marder, Michael. 2013. *Plant-Thinking: A Philosophy of Vegetal Life*. New York: Columbia University Press.

Marx, Karl. 1992. *Capital: Volume 1: A Critique of Political Economy*. London: Penguin Classics.

McHugh, John. 2014. Letter to the Editor. *Honolulu Star-Advertiser*. January 30.

Meller, Norman. 1960. "Hawaii: The Fiftieth State." *Parliamentary Affairs* 13 (1960): 489–508.

Merry, Sally Engle. 2000. *Colonizing Hawaiʻi: The Cultural Power of Law*. Princeton, N.J.: Princeton University Press.

Mintz, Sidney Wilfred. 1985. *Sweetness and Power*. New York: Viking.

Moloney, Pat. 2005. "Savages in the Scottish Enlightenment's History of Desire." *Journal of the History of Sexuality* 14, no. 3: 237–65.

Newell, Jennifer. 2010. *Trading Nature: Tahitians, Europeans, and Ecological Exchange*. Honolulu: University of Hawaiʻi Press.

Norbeck, Edward. 1959. *Pineapple Town: Hawaii*. Berkeley: University of California Press.

Okihiro, Gary Y. 2009. *Pineapple Culture: A History of the Tropical and Temperate Zones*. The California World History Library 10. Berkeley: University of California Press.

Osorio, Jon Kamakawiwoʻole. 2002. *Dismembering Lāhui: A History of the Hawaiian Nation to 1887*. Honolulu: University of Hawaiʻi Press.

Pashukanis, Evgeni i Bronislavovich. 1978. *Law and Marxism: A General Theory*. Translated by C. J. Arthur. London: Ink Links.

Perkins, Mark ʻUmi. 2013. Kuleana: A Genealogy of Native Tenant Rights." PhD diss. University of Hawaiʻi.

Poepoe, J. M. 1906. "Ka Moolelo Hawaii Kahiko." *Ka Naʻi Aupuni*. May 18, November 1.

Pottage, Alain. 1998. "The Inscription of Life in Law: Genes, Patents, and Bio-Politics." *Modern Law Review* 61, no. 5: 740–65.

———. 2007. "The Socio-Legal Implications of the New Biotechnologies." *Annual Review of Law and Social Science* 3, no. 1: 321–44.

Pratt, Mary Louise. 1992. *Imperial Eyes: Travel Writing and Transculturation*. New York: Routledge.

Pukui, Mary Kawena. 1983. *ʻŌlelo Noʻeau: Hawaiian Proverbs and Poetical Sayings*. Honolulu: Bishop Museum Press.

———. 1995. *Folktales of Hawai'i He Mau Ka'ao Hawai'i*. Bishop Museum Special Publication 87. Honolulu: Bishop Museum Press.
Pukui, Mary Kawena, and Samuel H. Elbert. 1986. *Hawaiian Dictionary: Hawaiian–English, English–Hawaiian*. Rev. ed. Honolulu: University of Hawaii Press.
Ritte, Walter, and Bill Freese. 2006. "Haloa." *Seedling*. October, 11–14.
Ritte, Walter, and Le'a Malia Kanehe. 2007. "Kuleana No Haloa (Responsibility for Taro): Protecting the Sacred Ancestor from Ownership and Genetic Modification." In *Pacific Genes and Life Patents: Pacific Indigenous Experiences and Analysis of the Commodification and Ownership of Life*, edited by Aroha Te Pareake Mead and Steven Ratuva, 130–37. Wellington, N.Z.: Call of the Earth Llamado de la Tierra and the United Nations University of Advanced Studies.
Rodriguez, Roberto Garcia. 2008. "Centeotzintli: Sacred Maize: A 7,000-Year Ceremonial Discourse." PhD diss., University of Wisconsin–Madison.
Rose, Nikolas. 2001. "The Politics of Life Itself." *Theory, Culture, and Society* 18, no. 6: 1–30.
———. 2006. *The Politics of Life Itself: Biomedicine, Power, and Subjectivity in the Twenty-First Century*. Princeton, N.J.: Princeton University Press.
Rowland, Donald. 1943. "Orientals and the Suffrage in Hawaii." *Pacific Historical Review* 12, no. 1: 11–21.
Schlais, Gregory K. 2006. "The Patenting of Sacred Biological Resources, the Taro Patent Controversy in Hawai'i: A Soft Law Proposal." *University of Hawai'i Law Review* 29: 581–618.
Silva, Noenoe K. 2004. *Aloha Betrayed: Native Hawaiian Resistance to American Colonialism*. American Encounters/Global Interactions. Durham, N.C.: Duke University Press.
Simpson, Audra. 2014. *Mohawk Interruptus: Political Life across the Borders of Settler States*. Durham, N.C.: Duke University Press.
Simpson, Leanne. 2011. *Dancing on Our Turtle's Back: Stories of Nishnaabeg Re-creation, Resurgence and a New Emergence*. Winnipeg, Can.: Arbeiter Ring Publishing.
Sivasundaram, Sujit. 2001. "Natural History Spiritualized: Civilizing Islanders, Cultivating Breadfruit, and Collecting Souls." *History of Science* 39: 417–43.
Smith, Vanessa. 2006. "Give Us Our Daily Breadfruit: Bread Substitution in the Pacific in the Eighteenth Century." *Studies in Eighteenth Century Culture* 35, no. 1: 53–75.
Sneider, Allison L. 2008. *Suffragists in an Imperial Age: U.S. Expansion and the Woman Question, 1870–1929*. New York: Oxford University Press.
Spary, Emma, and Paul White. 2004. "Food of Paradise: Tahitian Breadfruit and the Autocritique of European Consumption." *Endeavour* 28, no. 2: 75–80.
Stauffer, Robert H. 2003. *Kahana: How the Land Was Lost*. Honolulu: University of Hawai'i Press.
Strathern, Marilyn. 1992. *After Nature: English Kinship in the Late Twentieth Century*. Lewis Henry Morgan Lectures, 1989. Cambridge, U.K.: Cambridge University Press.

———. 1999. *Property, Substance, and Effect: Anthropological Essays on Persons and Things*. New Brunswick, N.J.: Athlone Press.

Sunder Rajan, Kaushik. 2006. *Biocapital: The Constitution of Postgenomic Life*. Durham, N.C.: Duke University Press.

Suryanata, Krisnawati. 2000. "Products from Paradise: The Social Construction of Hawaii Crops." *Agriculture and Human Values* 17, no. 2: 181–89.

Teute, Fredrika J. 2000. "The Loves of the Plants; or, The Cross-Fertilization of Science and Desire at the End of the Eighteenth Century." *Huntington Library Quarterly* 63, no. 3: 319–45.

Trask, Haunani-Kay. 1993. "'Lovely Hula Hands': Corporate Tourism and the Prostitution of Hawaiian Culture." In *From a Native Daughter: Colonialism and Sovereignty in Hawaiʻi*, 136–47. Monroe, Maine: Common Courage Press.

Wilcox, Carol. 1998. *Sugar Water: Hawaii's Plantation Ditches*. Honolulu: University of Hawaiʻi Press.

Wolfe, Patrick. 2006. "Settler Colonialism and the Elimination of the Native." *Journal of Genocide Research* 8, no. 4: 387–409.

Yap, Britt. 2013. "Against the Grain? Kamehameha Schools Finds Itself at the Center of Hawaiʻi's GMO Controversy." *MANA Magazine*, July–August, 26–35.

MAILE ARVIN

The Polynesian Problem and Its Genomic Solutions

> *In what consists the ever constant interest in the handful of people that comprises the Polynesian race? . . . The answer is, no doubt, the mystery that surrounds their origin, their intelligence, their charming personality, and—one likes to think—their common source with ourselves from the Caucasian branch of humanity, which induces in us a feeling of sympathy and affection above that felt toward any other colored race.*
>
> —S. PERCY SMITH, "POLYNESIAN WANDERINGS"

MARTINICAN POSTCOLONIAL THEORIST Edouard Glissant has reminded us that the "West is not in the West. It is a project, not a place."[1] This essay can be similarly described as a study of how Polynesia is a project, not a place, in the eyes of Western scientists. As a project of the West, Polynesia's origins can be traced to the imaginations of European imperialists and scientists conveniently dividing the "almost white," friendly Polynesians from the decidedly more savage and hostile "black" Melanesians.[2] The French writer Charles des Brosses has been credited with the first use of the term "Polynesia" in 1756 (in French, "Polynésie"), having derived it from the Greek "polloi," meaning "many."[3] For des Brosses, "many" signified many islands. While Micronesia marked a geographic contrast to Polynesia (signifying in Greek "the area of small islands"), and was at times understood linguistically and ethnologically as a related subset of Polynesia, the division between Polynesians and Melanesians was explicitly racial.[4] Indeed, the label Melanesian derived from "melas," meaning "black" in Greek.[5]

Today, the term "Polynesian" holds a debatable value to scholars and Indigenous Pacific Islanders themselves, especially as it has been used alongside the labels "Micronesian" and "Melanesian" to mark what are now understood to be rather spurious ethnic/racial divisions between Indigenous Pacific Islanders.[6] Yet, the "ever constant interest" in (and white identification with) "the Polynesian race," as put in 1911 by S. Percy Smith in the epigraph above, then president of the Polynesian Society (a New Zealand–based "learned society" focused on the study of Māori and other Pacific Island peoples), continues to fuel Western scientific knowledge production about Polynesia and Polynesians today.[7] While this abiding interest is often naturalized and depoliticized, it is actually an articulation of settler colonial power. In particular, this power, what I term "possession through whiteness," is manifest as feelings and practices on the part of white settlers of entitlement to Polynesian resources and identities, because of an assumed racial identification between white settlers and Indigenous Polynesians. As I explain below, possession through whiteness is a framework within which to understand that the goal of settler colonialism is to make whiteness Indigenous. In this process, Indigenous peoples are not made white exactly, but they become possessed by whiteness. This means that white settlers are able to claim that their whiteness is Indigenous to a place, while Indigenous peoples, who are interpellated as almost white, become the feminized, exotic possessions *of* whiteness, rather than gaining a secure power to possess whiteness or identify as white themselves.

This essay uses the framework of possession through whiteness to conceptually link the "Polynesian Problem"—the historical nickname given to social scientific studies of that interesting "mystery" of Polynesian origin, intelligence, and charm, as S. Percy Smith put it—to understandings of race and Indigeneity in contemporary genomics. As I show in the second part of this essay, contemporary scientific interest in Polynesians replicates some of the same problems embedded in the historical Polynesian Problem and its underlying concern with racial classification and the construction of Man as that universal, transcendent subject of the European Enlightenment.[8] Attention to the history of the Polynesian Problem is therefore instructive and important for those scholars interested in engaging issues of race and Indigeneity in the Pacific.[9] Indigeneity in my usage, as particularly informed by the Kanaka Maoli context, refers to the condition of being genealogically related to specific lands/oceans, which determines particular kinds of relationships between a people and a place, where the place is often understood as an ancestor for whose welfare the people are responsible.[10] Settler colonialism often disrupts the abilities of an Indigenous people to fulfill such responsibilities or *kuleana*. This happens in part through the production of Indigenous peoples as a race, rather than as a sovereign people, and the production of settlers as the native, natural owners/residents of a place (though without the same genealogical relationships and responsibilities to that place that Indigenous peoples have).[11] At stake in understanding the history of the Western construction of the Polynesian race, then, is gaining a better grasp of how categories of race and Indigeneity (both the genealogical relationships valued by Indigenous peoples and the claims settlers make to being native) operate in structures of settler colonialism both in Oceania (of which Polynesia is only part) and globally. While the structures and categories operative in Polynesia may differ significantly from those that are familiar within Native American or First Nation contexts, this essay offers a starting point from which Indigenous studies might flesh out how attention to such differences may enrich our broader theorizations of settler colonialism everywhere.

Part 1 of this essay provides a grounding of the framework of possession through whiteness in historical studies of the Polynesian Problem. I use the work of nineteenth-century writer Abraham Fornander as an example of how the Polynesian race was constructed as a possession of whiteness, and engage with theorists of whiteness, race, and Indigeneity to articulate some of the particularities of possession through whiteness in the Polynesian context, in contrast to the Native American context. Part 2 uses the analysis in the previous section as a basis for understanding and critiquing some of the foundational logics of contemporary genomics, specifically the proposed Hawaiian Genome Project. This study drew significant protests from the Native Hawaiian community, some of whom resisted not only the sequencing of a "Hawaiian genome" but also the genomic definition of Man itself. I examine how the protests are regenerative for Native Hawaiians, despite scientists' surprise and confusion at the refusal to participate in potentially medically and financially beneficial studies. Ultimately, this essay's analysis demonstrates that short of substantial decolonization of Western scientific epistemologies, knowledge used to prove the universality of Man will continue to entrench rather than eradicate the underlying colonial logics of the Polynesian Problem.

The Aryan Polynesian in Abraham Fornander's An Account of the Polynesian Race

Many of the earliest Europeans to travel through the Pacific Islands, including Captain James Cook and his crews in the eighteenth century, observed that many Polynesian peoples seemed white.[12] Tahitians in particular seemed to represent an idealized "natural man" and Tahitian women were constructed as the sexually desirable objects of the male European gaze.[13] Yet, this did not mean that Polynesians were seen as identical to Europeans. Cultural studies scholar Jeffrey Geiger argues that Polynesians were elevated over other colonized peoples, but inhabited a space of a cultural and racial ambiguity rather than being seen as equal.[14] He suggests, "Arguably this ambiguity, rather than disappearing under the weight of nineteenth-century racial taxonomies, was to become a formative feature of Polynesian representations."[15]

Certainly, the ambiguity of Polynesians' seeming proximity to the white race would animate numerous studies through at least the early twentieth century. Ethnologists John Dunmore Lang, Edward Treagar, W. D. Alexander, and William Churchill were some of the notable writers publishing on the Polynesian Problem in the late 1800s and early 1900s.[16] Many novelists would echo these scientific accounts as they created "almost white" Polynesian characters, including perhaps most notably the romantic portrait of Fayaway, a Native woman from the Marquesas, in Herman Melville's *Typee*.[17] While cultural studies scholars like Geiger have examined Polynesian almost whiteness in literature and film, in this essay I focus largely on the impact of the scientific representation of Polynesians as almost white on Native Hawaiians, and in this section I specifically analyze the work of Abraham Fornander, an ethnologist and folklorist who resided in Hawai'i in the late nineteenth century. He was a respected judge and "Knight of the Royal Order of Kalākaua."[18] In 1878 he published a three-volume work, *An Account of the Polynesian Race: Its Origin and Migrations and the Ancient History of the Hawaiian People to the Times of Kamehameha I*. In this work, Fornander made detailed observations about the racial provenance and character of Indigenous Pacific Islanders, under the rubric of analyzing Hawaiian "folklore." In the introduction of the text, Fornander stated his belief that his well-known reputation in Hawai'i allowed him "to speak on behalf of the Polynesian people, to unravel the past of their national life."[19] He further stated that it was his goal in *An Account of the Polynesian Race* to use the "folklore" of the Native Hawaiian people themselves to prove that Polynesians were "fundamentally Arian of a pre-Vedic type."[20]

As ku'ualoha ho'omanawanui has shown, Fornander was one of many haole settlers who, by "publishing Hawaiian legends, myths, and folklore under their own names . . . claimed an authority (kuleana) over the mo'olelo [narrative, story, history] they did have, and reframed mo'olelo to forward settler agendas."[21] ho'omanawanui, like many other Hawaiian studies scholars, has shown that analyzing writing from this period by Native Hawaiians in Hawaiian-language sources offers rich reclamations of Native Hawaiian *mo'olelo*, and importantly destabilizes the authority of those like Fornander over Native Hawaiian histories and cosmologies.[22] In this essay I analyze Fornander's *An Account of the Polynesian Race* not as an authority on Native Hawaiian *mo'olelo*, but as a text revealing of the settler colonial discourse of possession through whiteness. In particular, *An Account of the Polynesian Race*'s fascination with Polynesian Aryanism and Fornander's sense of himself as an ally of Native Hawaiians demonstrate the settler colonial violence that is possible through white settler efforts of inclusion of Indigenous peoples and histories into settler societies and imaginaries, rather than only overt, racist exclusion.

Today, popular understandings of Aryanism are deeply entwined with the histories of the Holocaust, Nazism and neo-Nazism, and eugenics. While Aryanism certainly informed the Holocaust in particular ways, it was applied in distinctly different ways in Polynesia. In order to understand the different histories and legacies, a brief contextualization of the history of Aryanism as an intellectual discipline is necessary. Aryanism first arose as a matter of linguistics. Sir William Jones is credited with the earliest Western study of Sanskritic tradition in India, and for first establishing a common linguistic and cultural heritage between northern India and Europe, in the 1780s (incidentally, at nearly the very same time that the West would begin to explore and colonize the Pacific).[23] Tony Ballantyne notes that the concept of an Aryan people was not originally European, but Indian: "It was deeply embedded in Vedic tradition. The *Rig Veda,* composed around 1500 BCE, recorded the incursion of tribes of pastoralists who identified themselves as 'Arya' (lit. noble) into India."[24] Thus Aryanism was fundamentally an Orientalist appropriation, born particularly in knowledge requisitioned by the British East India Company—what Ballantyne refers to as "Company Orientalism."[25] The linguistic discipline of Aryanism also informed Fornander's work, even though it was published an entire century after Jones's original studies on Aryanism. The discourse on Aryanism in Fornander's work must be understood in the context of two other highly influential scholars, namely, biologist Charles Darwin, who published his groundbreaking *On the Origin of Species* in 1859, and Max Müller, a Sanskrit scholar and philologist (the study of the structure of a language and/or relationships between languages) in the tradition of William Jones, who published prolifically from the 1860s through the 1890s.

While the reception of Darwin's *On the Origin of the Species* spurred the notion of positive, human evolution, ideas about degeneration (largely intertwined with Christian discourses) maintained an important place within ideas of progress in the late nineteenth and early twentieth centuries. Except now, degeneration was thought of as being a potential *biological,* as opposed to being a primarily historical, social, or individual moral, fate. Historian Gregory Moore describes the fears of degeneration in Europe as more than social paranoia or pessimism. Rather, it was understood as an "empirically demonstrable medical fact, as symptomatic of a more fundamental degenerative process within the European races."[26] Fears about "biological collapse" and "social pathologies" were enabled by Darwin's theories of evolution and natural selection (and his cousin Francis Galton's extrapolations of Social Darwinism) as well as a renewed passion for studying antiquity, brought about by other timely revolutions in geology and archaeology.[27] Geology had revealed that the Earth was much older than previous biblical understandings had held, and archaeology flourished as scientists attempted to piece together a better understanding of the various epochs of antiquity.[28]

The popularity of new ideas about human antiquity would come to shape more than just archaeology, however. For example, practitioners of anthropology also understood their task as "a sort of living archaeology."[29] Science studies scholar Cathy Gere evocatively describes this epistemology of science at the turn of the century as one of, in Thomas Huxley's terms, "retrospective prophecy."[30] For Huxley, this meant "that while the 'foreteller' informs the listener about the future and the 'clairvoyant' informs the listener about events at a distance, the retrospective prophet bears witness to events in the deep past. What unites them all is 'the seeing of that which, to the natural sense of the seer, is invisible.'" Gere notes that while the "effect was magical ... the method was eminently rational."[31] This retrospective prophecy could also be described as deductive reasoning, in the mode made classic by that Victorian fictional hero (and still popular) Sherlock Holmes. Yet this technique would also characterize innovations in fields such as criminology—in Francis Galton's invention of fingerprinting, for example—and psychoanalysis—such as Freud's insistence on recovering and coming to terms with one's past, pre-Oedipal layers.[32]

The scholarship of Max Müller should also be understood within the context of this turn toward "retrospective prophecy." Müller's views on the significance of studying ancient India within a liberal education is particularly clear in a series of lectures he delivered in 1883 to Cambridge University students about to enter the British Indian Civil Service. He argued that such study had "not only widened our views of man, and taught us to embrace millions of strangers and barbarians as members of one family, but it has imparted to the whole ancient history of man a reality which it never possessed before."[33] Though he maintained a strict differentiation between the ancient Aryan race who produced the Vedas and contemporary Indians, he asked the young men about to travel to India to consider their work as part of determining "a history of the human mind": "Is there not an inward and intellectual world also which has to be studied in its historical development, from the first appearance of predicative and demonstrative roots, their combination and differentiation, leading up to the beginning of rational thought in its steady progress from the lowest to the highest stages? And in that study of the history of the human mind, in that study of ourselves, of our true selves, India occupies a place second to no other country."[34] It is clear that Müller was interested in what critical race scholar Denise Ferreira da Silva would term transcendence—in other words, how Europeans as the epitome of Man had progressed inwardly, how they had realized their "true selves" from a long development over time.[35] While this kind of thinking may seem blatantly racist by today's standards, Müller clearly understood his work as both worldly and liberal. Gere notes that Müller attempted to distance himself and his scholarship on Sanskrit and Aryanism from more explicitly political attempts to shore up the purity of the white race.[36] Yet, understanding the Vedas as primarily the heritage of Europeans, rather than the heritage of contemporary Indians, was a colonial logic that persists in the Western study of other peoples and their "cultures" and resources.

As an ethnologist, Fornander was deeply influenced by Müller, and precisely understood his work as a kind of "living archaeology." He described his research as an intrepid, pioneering effort to tame and interpret the "almost impenetrable jungle of traditions, legends, genealogies, and chants" of Native Hawaiians.[37] What he found in that "jungle" convinced him of their fundamental descent from the "Arian" race, for "their own undoubted folklore, their legends and chants, gave no warrant for stopping there [in Malaysia]. They spoke of continents, and not of islands, as their birthplace."[38] Like the contemporary Indians in Müller's account, for Fornander the Polynesian race would almost certainly never retain their former place within the Aryan family. Nevertheless, contemporary Native Hawaiians were important repositories of Aryan knowledge and culture: "Throughout the grosser idolatry and the cruel practices springing from it in subsequent ages, these shreds of a purer culte [sic] were still preserved, soiled in appearance and obscured in sense by the contact, it may be, yet standing on the traditional records as heirlooms of the past, as witnesses of a better creed, and as specimens of the archaic simplicity of the language, hardly intelligible to the present Hawaiians."[39] In this description, "the present Hawaiians" are "hardly intelligible" of the "heirlooms of the past" they hold within their "Polynesian race." Aryan-ness was something that was biologically part of Hawaiians, but microscopic and presently inaccessible to them (anticipating, in an important sense, modern understandings of DNA). Their Aryan heritage was thus "soiled" and "obscured" but capable of being rescued by and for Man. Fornander understood his own task in writing his three volumes on Native Hawaiian "antiquities" and "folklore" in exactly these terms.

This understanding of obscure, ancient, civilized "specimens" trapped within Hawaiian language and Hawaiians themselves also endowed an extra significance on the understanding of Polynesians as a "mixed race." While Polynesians had long been spoken of as an essentially hybrid race of Asian and/or Malay mixture, Aryanism gave this mixture a more substantial hint of whiteness. Fornander argued that in Polynesian myth, "the body of the first man was made of red earth and the head of white clay" which indicated to him "a lingering reminiscence of a mixed origin, in which the white element occupied a superior position."[40] Note that marking the head as "white," whereas the "body" is red, played directly into notions of the distinction of white men as having "reason" and "self-determination." Thus, in Fornander's reading, Polynesians were originally mentally capable of being white, despite how they appeared as colored bodies. Not incidentally, Fornander was also one of many scholars who argued that Polynesians had not "mixed" or significantly "intermarried" with Papuans, thus preserving a distinction between the "almost white" Polynesian, not destined to be permanently "colored," and the indelibly black Papuan or Melanesian.[41]

Fornander's understanding of Polynesian folklore as a field ripe for a kind of "living" (if endangered) archaeology was common for American anthropologists at this time. Scholars including Yael Ben-zvi, Jenny Reardon, and Kim TallBear have shown that "redness" has long been understood as belonging to whiteness (often through understanding Native Americans as the ancestors of white people) in the United States, an idea that was especially prominent in nineteenth-century American anthropology.[42] Henry Lewis Morgan, one of the most influential American anthropologists of the time, is exemplary of such discourses for Reardon and TallBear, who note, "In these representations, white people did not violently colonize Native peoples. Instead, whites represented a more evolved form of the same people: Americans. Indeed, Morgan went further. He believed that American Indians represented all of 'mankind' in an early stage of evolution."[43]

Certainly, Morgan's construction of "American Indians" as the representatives of all humankind in an earlier stage of evolution is echoed in many Western constructions of Indigenous peoples globally. Thus, in one important sense, I see Jodi Byrd's formulation of the transit of empire at play in the extension of Morgan's ideas about American Indians as the ancestors of all (white) humanity, via Fornander's work, to ideas about Polynesians as "fundamentally Arian of the pre-Vedic type."[44] In other words, the idea of Indigenous peoples being almost white was not necessarily new or specific to Polynesia, and certainly drew from ideas developed about Native Americans on the American continents. However, in the interest of contributing to both Pacific Islander scholarship and Indigenous studies as a comparative field, it is worth noting some of the differences between the settler colonial deployments of whiteness in Polynesia and in the continental United States. Whereas with Morgan's work the emphasis was often on American Indians (as a race) as ancestors of present-day white Americans, in Fornander's work the characterization was most frequently that Polynesians (as a race) had white ancestry. Thus Fornander's construction deviated from Morgan's thesis. It was not that Polynesians were necessarily thought of as the direct (if metaphorical) ancestors of white settlers of Polynesia, in the manner that Morgan argued for seeing Native Americans as the ancestors of (white) Americans. Rather, Polynesians used to be white, and were descended from the same ancient Aryan ancestors as the white settlers of Polynesia. From northern India, the Polynesian branch had simply split out through the East whereas the European branch had gone west.[45]

Fornander, like Morgan, saw Polynesians as less civilized and less advanced than white Americans and Europeans. But the emphasis on Polynesians' common Aryan ancestry with white settlers, in contrast to Morgan's argument that Native Americans were ancestors of white people, fostered a settler narrative that not only did white settlers in Hawai'i have their own kind of ancestral claims to Hawaiian lands, but also that Polynesians were racially suitable as (or even destined to be) the sexual partners of white settlers. This lent a different valence to narratives about whiteness in Polynesia—representations of whiteness in Polynesia (and Polynesians) promised not just an evolved, civilized future (although it was this, too) but also seemed to prove that whiteness had always been a part of Polynesians. In this sense, Fornander was arguing not just that Polynesians were destined to evolve into white people, but that this was right and good because whiteness itself was Indigenous to Polynesia.

Considering the complexity of such a representation of whiteness in/as Polynesia, Aryanism as applied to Polynesia should not be understood, as Tony Ballantyne argues, simply as a "whitening" discourse. Rather, Aryanism as applied to Polynesians was an extension of "long-established Orientalist and ethnological traditions that developed out of the British encounter with South Asia."[46] For Ballantyne, historians who assume that Aryanism "naturally legitimized colonization" neglect the ways that "Aryan theories could just as easily subvert colonial authority and racial hierarchies as reinforce them. Tregear [author of *Aryan Maori* (1885)] himself argued that any European or settler who considered themselves superior to Maori had 'travelled little' and no European should 'blush' to recognize their affinity with the 'Bengalee' or the Maori 'heroes of Orakau.'"[47] Ballantyne points out here that the discourse of Aryanism in Polynesia was not overtly racist, and at times those who wrote about Aryanism understood their actions as disrupting rather than reinforcing commonly accepted Western racial hierarchies. Similarly, Fornander cannot easily be dismissed as an anti-Native Hawaiian racist—indeed, he was a longtime editor of the *Polynesian*, a pro-Hawaiian government newspaper, and was married to a Kanaka Maoli woman. He was viewed as an ally to Kanaka Maoli.[48] Nonetheless, Noenoe Silva notes that "Kanaka Maoli share with other Pacific Islanders theories about the migrations around the Pacific that are significantly different from those proposed by scholars such as Abraham Fornander."[49]

Although the discourse of Aryanism as used by Fornander did not legitimize the colonial domination of white settlers over Polynesians per se, it did legitimize the presence of white settlers in Polynesia and their vision of a white future for Polynesia. It was not whitening of actual Indigenous Polynesians that really mattered, but rather the white possession of Polynesian identities and resources that would justify various settler projects of nation/

empire building. Ballantyne goes on to explain this in terms of the work of Edward Tregear, a writer whose analysis mirrored Fornander's in many ways, though his focus was on New Zealand instead of Hawai'i. By (selectively) writing Māori and South Asians alongside the British into one Aryan family, Tregear was able, in Ballantyne's words, to:

> erase the conflict and violence of colonialism to imagine British imperialism in India and Pakeha power in New Zealand as reunions of long-lost Aryan siblings. Such an argument was neither "whitening" nor "assimilationist" for Tregear believed that, as fellow Aryans, Maori (or South Asians) were part of the same racial stock as Britons. Thus, rather than using assimilationist arguments to legitimate colonialism, Tregear instead naturalized the settler presence by denying racial difference and viewing the British empire not as a series of highly unequal power relations but as the product of a new wave of Aryan migration.[50]

In other words, Polynesians were not white, but their ancestry made them potentially compatible subjects of the British empire or, in the case of Hawai'i, citizens of the United States. This potential compatibility was at once racial and sexual, as the "reunion" would often be staged as "racial amalgamation" between whites and Polynesians, specifically through the sexual encounters and liaisons between white settler men and Indigenous women.

Pacific Studies scholar Damon Salesa has provided a rich historical analysis of "racial amalgamation" in New Zealand as a British settler colonial policy.[51] Racial amalgamation was promoted as a more "tender" form of colonialism because it did not depend (only) on killing off the natives, but rather encouraged intermarriage, especially between British settler men and landowning Tangata Whenu women (because under British colonial law, men automatically assumed their wives' land titles).[52] The children of such marriages were understood as "half-caste": not quite British, but on their way to becoming British. Thus, Salesa argues, "It was not just land that was being transferred from the 'native' to the 'European' categories, but people too."[53]

This "tender" form of settler colonialism was no less violent, as it was often profoundly effective in dispossessing Indigenous peoples. Scholar Lorenzo Veracini has defined colonialism as "a demand for labour," whereas settler colonialism, and its attendant exploitation of land, is "a demand to go away."[54] Yet, these oppositional definitions obscure the ways that exploitation of labor and land are in fact intertwined in settler colonialism. There is, as Indigenous studies scholar Scott Morgensen notes, a promised consanguinity between settler and native that is often eclipsed in formulations that focus only on settler colonial "vanishing" and "extinction."[55] This consanguinity enables constant (sexual, economic, juridical) exploitation, by producing the image of a future universal "raceless" race just over the settler colonial horizon.

As seen in Fornander's accounts of Aryanism as applied to Polynesians, the "tender" side of settler colonialism does not demand Indigenous peoples to "go away," but rather assumes the natural demise of the Indigenous "race," and the ultimate unification of settlers and Indigenous peoples in one settler nation and one white race. In addition to the slave, immigrant, and/or Indigenous labor required to turn land into profit, then, settler colonialism also requires the sexual and reproductive labor of Indigenous women, who are expected to birth the new, successively less "raced" generations, through coupling with white, settler men. Keeping an analytical eye on gender and sexuality in places where settler colonialism appears to be "tender" reveals that those "tender" spots are just as deserving of critical analysis as the more striking (because more "masculine") forms of violence such as war. For the management of gender and sexuality, like race and Indigeneity, is central to the structure of settler colonialism, not oppressions that merely added on or compounded for Indigenous women.[56]

Overall, my understanding of possession through whiteness as a central logic of settler colonialism in Polynesia emerges from the logics found in Polynesian Problem literature, exemplified here in Fornander's *An Account of the Polynesian Race*. Yet I also see this framework as holding the potential to help theorize settler colonialism, in its many iterations, more broadly. I see whiteness as a key ideological formation in all conventional settler colonial contexts (Australia, New Zealand, Canada, and the United States). Indeed, if only by default (in the way that those four countries are often cited as the primary examples of settler colonial nations), the settler–national investment in whiteness may be one of the most important features distinguishing settler colonialism from other forms of colonialism where "other" national subjects cannot be fully represented as white (e.g., the mestizo subject of Mexico and other parts of Latin America).[57] This is not to say that whiteness in Australia, New Zealand, Canada, and the United States is exactly the same. In fact, it is a call to better interrogate whiteness *in concert with how Indigenous peoples have been racially constructed* (something whiteness studies usually fails to do) in each of these places, precisely because they are different.[58]

Whiteness, as many scholars remind us, must be understood as a historically and geographically specific concept.[59] Yet it is nonetheless possible to track in the many variations and transformations of whiteness in the context of a place Cheryl Harris calls a "conceptual nucleus."[60] In settler colonial contexts, after Rey Chow's description, whiteness is an "ascendant" ideology, folding peoples into it, encouraging peoples to identify with the power/knowledge of whiteness even when they are individually excluded from identifying as white.[61] Indeed, it is important to note that whiteness in my analysis is not reducible to a set of phenotypes or group identity label. Even those

Polynesians who "looked white" to European observers were not automatically or securely extended the privileges of whiteness. Geiger has written of the European perception of Polynesian "whiteness" that "at least as significant as this desire to project whiteness onto a Polynesian canvas is the fact that Polynesians are, ultimately, never quite white enough. Polynesians may appear to be a white 'race,' but they never enter into what theories of whiteness have called the 'unmarked' or normalizing realms of whiteness itself."[62] Indeed, even for Fornander, who was invested in proving that Polynesians were Aryan, the whiteness of Polynesians remained a source of great intellectual curiosity. Polynesian whiteness was not, and would not for the foreseeable future ever be, "unmarked," even for those who were experts on the topic. However, even as individual Native Hawaiians were "never quite white enough," as Geiger notes, this ideology of Polynesian whiteness had powerful implications for U.S. settlement in Hawai'i—for example, it may have helped justify the inclusion of Hawai'i as one of the new "possessions" of the United States at the time of annexation, against racist fears about adding another dark race to the U.S. populous.[63]

This is not to say that Western knowledge about Polynesian whiteness was a magic bullet for any settler who wanted to employ this ideology. After all, the whiteness of Hawai'i was contested before, during, and after hearings on its annexation to the United States.[64] Nonetheless, this ideology played, and continues to play, a role in the U.S. occupation of Hawai'i. In short, my framework of possession through whiteness does not assume that the political and economic ends of settler colonialism in Polynesia have always been perfectly served by Western scientific knowledge, or that scientific knowledge is necessarily predetermined by settler colonial aims. Rather, this framework actually seeks to illuminate the specific conditions under which scientific theories have been appropriated for political ends, guided by my own sense that the ways knowledge about race shapes settler colonialism in Hawai'i and Polynesia has been under-theorized and under-studied. As Patrick Wolfe writes, through such attention to the historical conditions and convergences, "we need not detain ourselves with talk of colonial handmaidens or with trying to decide whether particular anthropologists were good guys or bad guys."[65] Similarly, in my framing, possession through whiteness is not simply furthered by individual white people, whether in the form of the white settler and/or white social scientist such as Abraham Fornander himself, but knowledge itself—particularly scientific and social scientific knowledge constructed about racial (physical, moral, and intellectual) difference. The second part of this essay continues this approach in analyzing medical genomics projects targeting Native Hawaiians, attempting not to identify "good" and "bad" scientists but rather how Western scientific knowledge works to incorporate Indigenous peoples within the post-Enlightenment model of Man, and how some decolonization efforts work against such incorporation.

The Hawaiian Genome Project and Regenerating Kanaka Maoli Concepts of Humanity

In the nineteenth century, the Polynesian Problem literature used linguistics and ethnology to formulate the relationship between Polynesians and Man. In the twenty-first century, this relationship is now often investigated through genomics. Jenny Reardon and Kim TallBear make this connection in their previously cited article, "Your DNA Is Our History," noting that just as anthropologist Henry Morgan understood Native Americans as representing an earlier stage of human civilization, and thus in his view, Native Americans and all their resources were the true inheritance of (white) Americans and indeed all (white) humanity, "In recent decades, Native American DNA has emerged as a new natural resource that Native peoples possess but that the modern subject—the self-identified European—has the desire and ability to develop into knowledge that is of value and use to all humans."[66] TallBear has further written about Native American DNA as a rather recently invented but highly desired and fetishized "object of knowledge." Her incisive book critiques the scientific construction of Native American DNA as a kind of "molecule-made-transcendent" for further confusing the often already poorly understood historical and political complexities of Native American tribal belonging.[67]

In the context of Polynesia, Indigenous DNA has similarly been a much desired and sought-after "object of knowledge" in recent years. Almost daily it seems there is a news article proclaiming new discoveries about the Māori having a "warrior gene," or Pacific Islanders being genetically ingrained to be football players.[68] Such discourses combine with sobering statistics about Polynesians' genetic susceptibility to obesity and diseases such as diabetes to propagate rather fatalistic community understandings of what it means to be Polynesian. As Lena Rodriguez and James Rimumutu George argue in their sociological study of Polynesian communities living in Australia, "The inflammatory language surrounding 'high risk' populations for diabetes has arguably had the effect of paralyzing rather than motivating the population to be tested. This has contributed to an idea pervasive among Polynesians that such ailments are genetically 'inevitable.'"[69] As Rodriguez and George point out, diabetes should not be a fatal disease, as it has been shown to be treatable through proper management of diet and exercise.[70] Yet, Rodriguez and George argue, because treatment for diabetes is often described as a project of individual care that contravenes the communal nature of meals for many

Polynesians and because of the sense of genetic "inevitability," many Polynesians do die from diabetes.

Nonetheless, genomics continues to be promoted to Polynesian communities as holding potential answers to diabetes and other diseases. Below, I focus on the proposed Hawaiian Genome Project (HGP) and the negative response it elicited from Native Hawaiians. Yet it is important to point out from the outset that there is no singular response from the Native Hawaiian community toward genomic projects targeting Native Hawaiians. Some Native Hawaiians are in favor of such projects, as long as they conform to certain guidelines that ensure Native Hawaiians are provided free, prior, informed consent and some form of governance and continued information about the ways their genetic samples are used. A study by Maile Tauali'i and colleagues, for example, showed that among ninety-two participants in focus groups throughout Hawai'i, all of them theoretically supported biobanking because of the potential "benefits of medical research and how it led to advancements in preventing, diagnosing, and treating disease."[71] Further, the study showed that many of the participants "noted that participating in research operationalized the Native Hawaiian value of helping others and contributing to the common good."[72]

Tauali'i and colleagues, along with many other scholars, including TallBear and Reardon, have written productive critiques which suggest a variety of ways to ethically engage Indigenous communities in genomic research—from rigorous standards of free, prior, informed consent (and re-consent) and approvals by both university and Indigenous nations' institutional review boards to innovating new methodologies to incorporate cultural protocols, or understanding Indigenous DNA samples as "on loan" and to be returned to the Indigenous community along with the results of the study after its completion.[73] Such critical work is undeniably essential to protecting Indigenous peoples' rights. Though indebted to such productive scholarship, my analysis is interested in how Native Hawaiians, and other Polynesian and Indigenous peoples, might effectively refuse not (just) genomic studies per se but the broader rhetoric of "helping others" and contributing to the "common good," because of the deeply exploitative, settler colonial underpinnings of such rhetoric that works to incorporate Indigenous peoples into a Western ideal of Man (with often dire consequences for Indigenous peoples). In other words, I am interested in Indigenous peoples having the sovereignty to say no to scientific research, and being able to enforce that without any questions or lingering coercion/shame. As TallBear and Reardon brilliantly point out, the rhetoric of genomic studies of Native peoples is a barely updated version of nineteenth-century American anthropological claims that studying Native American resources would contribute to the study of all humankind, making white scientists forever entitled to claiming Native American resources for themselves.

Saying no to scientific research may require repositioning all people within Indigenous conceptions of the human, and liberating us all from the Western ideal of Man as the individual, transcendent subject. Indeed, in response to the Hawaiian Genome Project, some Native Hawaiians repositioned themselves within a Native Hawaiian understanding of humanity, rather than a European one. I believe this example hints at what Indigenous peoples and their allies might do to effectively decolonize the relationships between science and settler colonialism, beyond simply making science more culturally competent or including better consent (though these should indeed be necessary requisites to any scientific project). Below, I offer first the context of the HGP before discussing some Native Hawaiian responses.

Charles Boyd, a professor at the Pacific Biomedical Research Center at the University of Hawai'i at Mānoa, proposed the Hawaiian Genome Project in 2003 as a type of genebank, which can be defined as "a stored collection of genetic samples in the form of blood or tissue, that can be linked with medical and genealogical or lifestyle information from a specific population, gathered using a process of generalized consent."[74] The most famous genebank is the deCODE project, run by a U.S.-based company but located in Iceland. deCODE was authorized by the Icelandic Parliament in 1998 and heralded the potential to map the genome of the Icelandic people, in the interest of discovering possible genetic causes of (and remedies for) diseases.[75] This was conducted through analysis of the health records of all Icelandic people, which Iceland's government licensed to deCODE, along with blood samples volunteered from about half of the country's citizens from whom DNA information was extracted. deCODE was interested in the Icelandic population because it was relatively homogeneous, given its isolated island location as well as having experienced several historic catastrophes (the Bubonic Plague in the 1440s, and smallpox as well as a devastating volcanic eruption in the 1700s). These catastrophes resulted in "genetic bottlenecks"; in other words, the deaths of large percentages of the population reduced the population's available genetic material. Those who survived these catastrophes in isolated locations become a relatively small group of "founders" for the following generations, resulting in a significant narrowing of the population's genetic diversity.

The genetic homogeneity of Iceland and the overall importance of genetic studies focused on populations shaped by "founder effects" are both contested.[76] Yet the common reasoning given for why genetic homogeneity is important is that genomics studies on disease depend on uncovering genetic causes (different genetic mutations) in a population with a certain disease by comparing that population's genetic data to a "healthy" population. A genetically heterogeneous population presents a less reliable data set for this purpose because greater genetic diversity overall makes the differences between healthy and unhealthy populations less apparent. Somewhat ironically given Hawai'i's constant praise today as a melting pot, it was precisely the Native Hawaiian population's perceived genetic homogeneity that interested Boyd and colleagues in sequencing a "Hawaiian genome." As Lindsey Singeo describes it, "Already an isolated society, the Hawaiian population became even more homogenous as a result of massive epidemics and population reduction during the mid-1880s. During this time, foreigners introduced previously unknown diseases to Native Hawaiians, including measles, whooping cough, mumps, and smallpox. Unlike the foreigners, Native Hawaiians lacked the immune system resistance and suffered significantly high mortality rates."[77] Thus, in a strange (or perhaps only fitting) way, it was precisely the effects of colonialism—depoliticized in the rhetoric of the project's proposers as the natural if tragic impact of measles, whooping cough, mumps, and smallpox—that made the Native Hawaiian population genetically homogeneous and particularly attractive to genomics researchers. Yet the project obliquely proposed to compensate for the contemporary legacies of colonialism—namely, health disparities faced by the Native Hawaiian community—by potentially providing genetic information to explain Native Hawaiians' higher risk for diseases including diabetes, hypertension, and renal disease.[78]

If the "Hawaiian genome" proved fruitful, it could be licensed to the University of Hawai'i researchers by the Native Hawaiian community (after the Icelandic model), for a certain monetary amount. A magazine article accordingly announced the project by advertising its potential for providing medical and financial benefits to the Native Hawaiian community, claiming, "It's a potentially lucrative market—Roche pharmaceutical company paid $200 million outright for rights to the Icelandic genome, which underwent a similar bottleneck."[79] In any case, how much commercialization the Hawaiian Genome Project might involve was unclear at the time the article was published. Other models that the HGP could have drawn from would not have any corporate involvement or would limit such involvement instead of granting companies exclusive rights.[80] Yet there had also recently been a genebank project proposed in Tonga in 2000 by Autogen, an Australian biotechnology company, which did closely follow the Icelandic model. The Tongan project was never carried out, due to local opposition, especially from church groups who, as Austin and colleagues report, opposed the "conversion of God-created life-forms, their molecules or parts into corporate property through patent monopolies."[81]

The Native Hawaiian community also strongly objected to the proposed

HGP. As with the Tongan project, licensing a "Hawaiian genome" to the university violated a number of cultural and religious beliefs. Further, the HGP seemed to many Native Hawaiians to be both an obvious extension of historic and ongoing colonial expropriation of Native Hawaiian lands and resources, and a potential replication of other seemingly exploitative genetic studies such as the patenting of a cell line of an Indigenous Hagahai man from Papua New Guinea by the U.S. National Institutes of Health.[82] In November 2003 the Association of Hawaiian Civic Clubs issued a resolution, "Urging the University of Hawai'i to Cease Development of the Hawaiian Genome Project or Other Patenting or Licensing of Native Hawaiian Genetic Material until Such Time as the Native Hawaiian People Have Been Consulted and Given Their Full, Prior and Informed Consent to Such Project."[83] This resolution made explicit reference to the modeling of the HGP after the Icelandic deCODE project, and asserted that such licensing of Native Hawaiian genetic material and the mapping of a Hawaiian genome would require the prior, informed consent of all Native Hawaiian people, since "the Hawaiian genome represents the genetic heritage of our ancestors and is the collective property of the Native Hawaiian people."[84] The resolution further drew comparisons to the activism of other global Indigenous people, arguing that "other Indigenous peoples globally and regionally have declared a moratorium on any further commercialization of Indigenous human genetic materials until Indigenous communities have developed appropriate protection mechanisms."[85] Another declaration was also issued after a Native Hawaiian Intellectual Property Rights Conference in October 2003 further condemned as acts of "biocolonialism" the theft of "the biogenetic materials of our peoples, taken for medical research for breast cancer and other diseases attributable to western impact."[86]

In the end, these protests led to the HGP being discontinued. The strong response from the community surprised the project's founders, who seem to have genuinely believed that the "self-evident" medical and financial benefits to Native Hawaiians would accord them a willing participatory population. This response was thus very similar to a more famous example of genomic researchers' surprise: namely, in regard to the case protesters brought against the Human Genome Diversity Project (HGDP) shortly after its proposal in 1994.[87] Given the HGDP's sincere efforts to respond to the critiques ethically, scholar Jenny Reardon argues:

> These were not self-seeking researchers who sought to extract the blood of indigenous peoples for the sake of financial and political gain. They were scientists who sincerely hoped to create a project that would deepen the stores of human knowledge while fighting racism and countering Eurocentrism. It would be historically inaccurate, and morally insensitive, to understand the Diversity Project as an extension of older racist practices by labeling the initiative

the product of white scientists wielding the power of science to objectify and exploit marginalized groups. The story of the Project is more complicated. It raises questions that cannot be resolved so easily.[88]

I doubt neither the sincerity of Cavalli-Sforza's desire to conduct antiracist work, nor the functional difference Reardon is pointing out between "research for research's sake" (or, "research for humanity's good") and research to fuel a business's profits. Certainly both types of research exist within the genomics field—from rather questionable DNA ancestry tests offered by biogenetic companies on one end of the spectrum, to federally funded top-tier genomics research on the other.[89] The wide variety of genomic scientists and entrepreneurs cannot all be branded the same. Yet the problems attending the projects of those scientists who are surprised at the apparent failure of their "do-gooder" intentions seem to me the most urgently needed. For it is precisely this liberal universalism, and incorporation of Polynesians into whiteness, that was so formative of the Polynesian Problem literature of the late nineteenth and early twentieth centuries. Decolonizing Hawai'i and Polynesia more broadly will continue to require wrestling with not only problems of what Reardon terms "older racist practices" but also the more fundamental colonial practices that are compatible with and constitutive of contemporary liberalism and capitalism.

To begin with, the very invention of something that can be recognized as "the" Hawaiian genome, much less that thing's total sequencing and potential licensing/ownership, deserves more reflection. For in the manifestation of a genome, concerns of possession and property reveal themselves in particularly complicated ways. A genome denotes an organism's complete set of genes, and thus genomics denotes the study of the interactions between those sets of genes, whereas genetics more specifically refers to the study of singular genes, in relative isolation. A genome is at once a living part of a human being, and an abstraction based on relative genetic similarities in a defined population—in this case, the population being "Native Hawaiians." Thus a genome is a kind of organic "thing" that nonetheless can only be materialized and studied in the "captivity" of a laboratory. In the particular genebank model that the Hawaiian Genome Project proposed, the DNA samples collected from Native Hawaiians likely would have been subject to "immortalization" in lymphoblastoid cell lines, as the samples collected in the Human Genome Diversity Project were.[90] This immortalization allows the DNA sequences to be preserved and replicated, shared and sold, among scientists according to the specific types of consent and ethical protocols under which the samples were collected.

As pitched to Native Hawaiians, we can understand the HGP as having offered Native Hawaiians a share in the ownership of a "Hawaiian genome."

This genome was a newly conceptualized kind of private property potentially to be held in common by Native Hawaiians as a group. The subtle, motivating logic of the HGP in exhorting Native Hawaiians' participation was classically liberal: since, theoretically, all Native Hawaiians would have access in their own bodies to the materials necessary to creating this genome, they had a moral, national, and civilizational duty to exploit those resources for their own and the common good. By refusing to license or lend their genome to the university, or even to acknowledge that such an entity exists that is perfectly described by Western science, Native Hawaiians risked seeming not only "stingy"—denying the common good of science—but also self-destructive, refusing a desperately needed opportunity that would potentially offer medical answers and treatments, as well as money.

Such subtly implied self-destruction uncannily recalls turn-of-the-century discourse on the reasons for the degeneration of the Polynesian race. For Native Hawaiians, degeneration was an especially influential discourse at the time of Hawaiʻi's annexation to the United States in 1898. Alexander Twombly, author of *The Native Hawaiian of Yesterday and To-day*, published in 1901, put it this way:

> There is no recuperative power in the native such as most white races possess. Advance in civilization enables the Anglo-Saxon to overcome even hereditary tendency to disease. Hawaiians die when the white man lives. The latter exercises a measure of self-control for selfish ends. The former shows little or no self-control for any ends.
>
> To sum up, the native Hawaiian of to-day is an anomaly in civilization. He cannot understand its significance or adjust himself to its requirements. Citizenship is only a condition to him, not an inspiration. The half-caste has not the same obstacles to contend with, and assimilates in greater degree with modern progress.[91]

Twombly demonstrates here his belief in the "half-caste" as the only possible future of the Hawaiian race because it is necessary to physically infuse the Hawaiian race with "a measure of self-control for selfish ends"—a critically apt description of the requirements of U.S. citizenship, for Twombly particularly glimpsed Hawaiians' degeneration in their failure to grasp the importance of owning land. He wryly noted, "It is a sign of the tendency to degenerate when men care little for the possession of land."[92] The apparently extreme depths of this degeneration, though described as moral, behavioral, or cultural failings, were ultimately blamed on the biological. Twombly, like many others, believed that nothing could be done for Native Hawaiians until they had received a substantial racial infusion of whiteness. Ultimately the Hawaiian race would disappear, but be replaced by the growing numbers of "half-castes" more biologically disposed to become part of the white settler society.

In the context of genomics, Native Hawaiians' refusal to participate in the development of biotechnology which might produce innovative new medical treatments for diseases to which they are susceptible to can still be read as a failure to exercise "a measure of self-control for selfish ends," and thus to give into degeneration even when it is not environmentally inevitable. This situation also illustrates the point that whiteness is understood as a kind of property that one must carefully manage, protect, and control—because as Cheryl Harris reminds us, controlling one's whiteness is a mode of controlling one's expectations for the future, and one's very personhood depends on the realization of these expectations.[93] Seen this way, controlling, decoding, objectifying, and commercializing one's genome has developed as a new form of whiteness as property that one must carefully manage and protect.

Science studies scholars have offered relevant analyses of this situation, though often without substantial concern for the particulars of Indigenous cultures and politics.[94] Melinda Cooper, for example, in *Life as Surplus*, makes an important connection between the nineteenth-century revolution in biological science and accompanying revolutions in economics.[95] Drawing on Foucault's formulation of biopower, she argues that after Darwin there was a "relocation of wealth" from the "fruits of the land" (as in the philosophy of Adam Smith) to "the creative forces of human biological life."[96] Cooper quotes Foucault in describing this change as one in which the "organic becomes the living and the living is that which *produces, grows and reproduces*; the inorganic is the non-living, that which neither develops nor reproduces; it lies at the frontiers of life, the inert, the unfruitful—death."[97] Neither Cooper nor Foucault extend this analysis to the structure of settler colonialism, yet Foucault's use of the phrase "frontiers of life" is particularly evocative here: white settlers in the United States having long understood manifest destiny throughout the U.S. West and even to Hawai'i as spreading the inherent and common good of civilization and capitalism.[98] In my analysis, Foucault's description aptly explains the difference that settler colonialism institutes between settlers and Indigenous peoples. The settler "*produces, grows and reproduces*," while the native "lies at the frontiers of life," vanishing and destined only to die out.

Thus the push for studying, decoding, and in fact producing something called a "Hawaiian genome" is deeply shaped by this Western scientific/economic epistemology of organic life: that which produces, grows, and reproduces. While the "Hawaiian genome" will be realized and produced largely by Western scientists, with the donation of genetic material from Native Hawaiians, liberal, antiracist scientists imagine that they are also helping to produce, grow, and reproduce Native Hawaiianness or Native Hawaiian personhood itself. Choosing to opt out of the HGP seems almost nonsensical to

Western scientists because that would mean Native Hawaiians are choosing to align themselves with the inorganic—"that which neither develops nor reproduces . . . the inert, the unfruitful—death." Native Hawaiians refusing the "organic" process implied in the HGP registers within this settler colonial framework as a refusal of development, reproduction, and life itself—a choice that scientists find difficult to parse, especially after they prove themselves eager to combat the valid problems of racism and colonialism. An analogous situation also arose between the Native Hawaiian community and the University of Hawai'i when researchers there proposed to genetically modify *kalo*, the Hawaiian name for the taro plant, a traditional staple starch in the Hawaiian diet. As Noelani Goodyear-Ka'opua notes in her analysis of protests against GMO taro that took place beginning in 2006, "Community organizers and farmers . . . saw in any move to commodify kalo connections to the encroaching forms of commercial agriculture practices by large biotechnology corporations [such as Monsanto], including genetic modification and field testing in Hawai'i."[99]

Native Hawaiian leaders including Walter Ritte spoke out against genetic modification of *kalo*, noting that "genetic engineering" was a kind of "mana mahele, which means owning and selling our mana or life force."[100] While Kanaka Maoli argued that *kalo* was sacred and inextricable from Kanaka Maoli lives, and thus that it would be reprehensible to genetically modify it, researchers promoted the genetic modification as a biotechnological improvement that was "necessary to increase crop yields, improve pest and disease resistance and advance scientific research."[101] Though a provisional five-year moratorium on genetically modifying taro was passed in the state legislature in 2008, the Native Hawaiian case was often represented as simply a "cultural" one, whereas biotechnology proponents represented "progress"—delayed for now, but destined to win out, through more "culturally competent" means if necessary.[102]

Yet, upon closer scrutiny, the Native Hawaiian protests against the HGP and the genetic modification of *kalo* were significantly more complicated than their gloss as "cultural difference" implies. This becomes clear by examining the two statements issued in response to the HGP in 2003 by the association of Hawaiian Civic Clubs and the Native Hawaiian Intellectual Property Rights Conference. For the Hawaiian Civic Clubs, there is not a strict critique of capitalism or the notion of isolating a Hawaiian genome. In fact, their resolution takes as a given both the existence of a Hawaiian genome, and the classification of this genome as property, stating, "The Hawaiian genome represents the genetic heritage of our ancestors and is the collective property of the Native Hawaiian people."[103] Thus the Civic Clubs object less to the science of the HGP than to the assumption that a genebank could commercialize "the Hawaiian genome." In their account, the HGP is not viable until there are better protections in place for Native Hawaiians to properly be informed and benefit or "equitably share" the results from such a project.[104]

The Paoakalani Declaration issued by the Native Hawaiian Intellectual Property Rights Conference (NHIPRC) goes further in its critique, which it does not limit to the HGP. Nor does the declaration refer to anything called a "Hawaiian genome." Rather, it forcefully problematizes "bioprospecting and biotechnology institutions and industries" which are "imposing western intellectual property rights over our traditional, cultural land-based resources. This activity converts our collective cultural property into individualized property for purchase, sale, and development."[105] Further, the NHIPRC group insists on a complete moratorium on any kind of genebank project: "Kanaka Maoli human genetic material is sacred and inalienable. Therefore, we support a moratorium on patenting, licensing, sale or transfer of our human genetic material."[106] For the Paoakalani Declaration, it is not only the University of Hawai'i that is the subject of critique but also "the pharmaceutical, agricultural and chemical industries, the United States military, academic institutions and associated research corporations," all of which are implicated in biocolonialism in Hawai'i.[107]

While this Declaration draws on the notion of human rights and references other resolutions supporting Indigenous rights, as the Civic Clubs resolution also does, it also calls for a more fundamental unsettling of what constitutes humanity. The NHIPRC authors reformulate the place of humanity within Hawaiian epistemology rather than accepting wholeheartedly the purportedly "universal" Western notion of humanity:

> According to the Kumulipo, a genealogical chant of creation, Po gave birth to the world. From this female potency was born Kumulipo and Po'ele. And from these two, the rest of the world unfolded in genealogical order. That genealogy teaches us the land is the elder sibling and the people are the younger sibling meant to care for each other in a reciprocal, interdependent relationship. Humanity is reminded of his place with the order of genealogical descent. The foundational principle of the Kumulipo is that all facets of the world are related by birth. And thus, the Hawaiian concept of the world descends from one ancestral genealogy.[108]

Thus, this Declaration repositions humanity as the apex of all organic life, putting humans as the "younger siblings" of the "elder sibling," land. In Hawaiian epistemology, then, land is not property but a form of genealogy and knowledge. This knowledge is actively formed and participated in, rather than simply accessed, shaped by a "reciprocal, interdependent relationship" among family members, humans, and the land. This unsettles completely the Western scientific and economic differentiation between the "organic" and "inorganic," as discussed by Cooper and Foucault. Rather than valuing "the creative forces of human biological life" over the simple "fruits of nature," the declaration reminds its readers that human life is interdependent with the life of the land; and land is indeed a living, knowing thing to which all humans look up to as to a wiser elder sibling. The ways that this epistemology subverts popular heteropatriarchal notions of land as "virgin" or "mother" is also significant. The creator of the world was a "female potency," not necessarily a maternal figure. Land is not "Mother Earth," nor a sexualized thing to conquer and make reproduce, but humanity's sibling, someone with whom humans might have a complex, mutually sharing relationship.

Overall, what the Paoakalani Declaration envisions is a form of Native Hawaiian Indigeneity that is not property, as whiteness is; something that is not possess-able by whiteness at all, since it is premised on entirely different conceptualizations of land and the human. Compared to the Hawaiian Civic Clubs resolution, the Paoakalani Declaration intends to have a broader impact. For the declaration recognizes, similarly to the Hawaiian Civic Clubs resolution, that Native Hawaiians need protections within laws that privilege the Western concept of Man, but refuses that they should *only* understand themselves, their "genetic material," and other "collective cultural property" within such colonial frameworks. Both approaches of the Hawaiian Civic Clubs and the NHIPRC are regenerative, in my analysis—both seek to avert new forms of colonialism and thus promote a different kind of future for Native Hawaiians. But where the Hawaiian Civic Clubs responded within the existing Western frameworks of institutional review boards and principles such as "reciprocity" and "equitable sharing," the NHIPRC challenged the very foundations of such principles. Thus NHIPRC points out how making genomic science more culturally competent and alert to Indigenous peoples' rights to free, prior, informed consent will not necessarily overturn the colonial basis of such science.

In conclusion, this essay has argued for the importance of understanding the logic of possession through whiteness, first produced in the Polynesian Problem social scientific literature of the late nineteenth and early twentieth centuries, as continuing to inform and naturalize the process of settler colonialism in Hawai'i. While contemporary science insists that biological racism has long been debunked and imagines genomic population histories as a method of permanently eradicating racism and even the boundaries of ethnicity, I have argued that such eagerness to move beyond "race," and the "surprise" of liberal scientists who find their "savior" efforts rebuffed by Indigenous protests, really demonstrates the many ways that contemporary science remains rooted to Western, colonial, and racist definitions of Man. Despite these colonial echoes in genomic science, Native Hawaiians are among global Indigenous peoples leading efforts to effectively decolonize science and Western notions of humanity altogether, particularly through pointing out the false distinctions between organic and inorganic, or Man and nature.

MAILE ARVIN (Native Hawaiian) is assistant professor of ethnic studies at the University of California, Riverside.

Notes

1. Qtd. in Victor Bascara, *Model-Minority Imperialism* (Minneapolis: University of Minnesota Press, 2006), xxiii–xxiv.

2. This characterization of Polynesians as "almost white" has a long history, dating from the descriptions of Polynesians by the earliest European encounters in the Pacific (such as Louis Bougainville's descriptions of Tahitian women as classically Venus-like). Such ideas continued to percolate in Western travelogues, fiction (notably Herman Melville's *Typee*), film, and scientific studies (including ethnology, archaeology, anthropology, and sociology) through at least the early to mid-twentieth century. See, for example Nicholas Thomas, "The Force of Ethnology: Origins and Significance of the Melanesia/Polynesia Division," *Current Anthropology* 30, no. 1 (1989): 27–41; Nicholas Thomas, *In Oceania: Visions, Artifacts, Histories* (Durham, N.C.: Duke University Press, 1997); Jocelyn Linnekin, "Contending Approaches," in *The Cambridge History of the Pacific Islanders*, ed. Donald Denoon et al. (Cambridge, U.K.: Cambridge University Press, 1997), 3–31; Jeffrey Geiger, *Facing the Pacific: Polynesia and the American Imperial Imagination* (Honolulu: University of Hawai'i Press, 2007).

3. Charles de Brosses, *Histoire des navigations aux terres australes* (Paris: Durand, 1756). See also Bronwen Douglas, "Comments," in John Edward Terrell, Kevin M. Kelly, and Paul Rainbird, "Foregone Conclusions? In Search of 'Papuans' and 'Austronesians,'" *Current Anthropology* 42, no. 1 (2001): 112.

4. S. J. Whitmee, "The Ethnology of Polynesia," *Journal of the Anthropological Institute of Great Britain and Ireland* 8 (January 1879): 261–75.

5. Douglas, "Comments," in Terrell, Kelly, and Rainbird, "Foregone Conclusions?" 112.

6. Many people continue to identify as Polynesian, and it is often used to mark connections between different Indigenous peoples in the area designated as Polynesia, but it does not always follow the meaning derived from the original ethnological and racial divisions. I am not arguing against the use of Polynesian by Polynesian peoples, but against the Western construction of Polynesians as almost white, and the ways that such a construction has at times created tensions and racism between Polynesian, Micronesian, and Melanesian peoples. For further discussions on the connections and disjunctures between Oceanic peoples, see, for example, Epeli Hau'ofa, *We Are the Ocean: Selected Works* (Honolulu: University of Hawai'i Press, 2008); Alice Te Punga Somerville, *Once Were Pacific: Māori Connections to Oceania* (Minneapolis: University of Minnesota Press, 2012).

7. "About the Polynesian Society," University of Auckland, n.d., Arts.Auckland.ac.nz.

8. Denise Ferreira da Silva, *Toward a Global Idea of Race* (Minneapolis: University of Minnesota Press, 2007); Sylvia Wynter, "Unsettling the Coloniality of Being/Power/Truth/Freedom: Towards the Human, after Man, Its Overrepresentation—An Argument," *CR: The New Centennial Review* 3, no. 3 (2003): 257–337.

9. While many scholars in anthropology (largely non-Indigenous and located in British institutions) have noted the construction of Polynesians as almost white (see note 2, above), few have engaged in the study of race and Indigeneity as engaged with settler colonialism in the Pacific. Notable exceptions include Damon Ieremia Salesa, *Racial Crossings: Race, Intermarriage, and the Victorian British Empire* (New York: Oxford University Press, 2011); Hokulani K. Aikau, *A Chosen People, a Promised Land: Mormonism and Race in Hawai'i* (Minneapolis: University of Minnesota Press, 2012). Similarly, few have considered what the historical construction of Polynesians as nearly white (and Melanesians as black) has had on contemporary constructions of race and Indigeneity in the Pacific today.

10. See also Noelani Goodyear-Ka'ōpua, *The Seeds We Planted: Portraits of a Native Hawaiian Charter School* (Minneapolis: University of Minnesota Press, 2013); ku'ualoha ho'omanawanui, *Voices of Fire: Reweaving the Literary Lei of Pele and Hi'iaka* (Minneapolis: University of Minnesota Press, 2014).

11. J. Kēhaulani Kauanui, *Hawaiian Blood: Colonialism and the Politics of Sovereignty and Indigeneity* (Durham, N.C.: Duke University Press, 2008); Judy Rohrer, "'Got Race?' The Production of Haole and the Distortion of Indigeneity in the Rice Decision," *The Contemporary Pacific* 18, no. 1 (2005): 1.

12. Geiger, *Facing the Pacific*; James Cook, *The Voyages of Captain Cook* (Ware, U.K.: Wordsworth Editions, 1999).

13. Patty O'Brien, *The Pacific Muse: Exotic Femininity and the Colonial Pacific* (Seattle: University of Washington Press, 2006); Pamela Cheek, *Sexual Antipodes: Enlightenment, Globalization, and the Placing of Sex* (Stanford, Calif.: Stanford University Press, 2003).

14. Geiger, *Facing the Pacific*, 29.

15. Ibid.

16. John Dunmore Lang, *View of the Origin and Migrations of the Polynesian Nation; Demonstrating Their Ancient Discovery and Progressive Settlement of the Continent of America* (London: Cochrane and M'Crone, 1834); Edward Tregear, "Polynesian Origins (Continued)," *Journal of the Polynesian Society* 13, no. 3 (1904): 133–52; W. D. Alexander, "The Origin of the Polynesian Race," *Journal of Race Development* 1, no. 2 (1910): 221–30; William Churchill, *The Polynesian Wanderings: Tracks of the Migration Deduced from an Examination of the Proto-Samoan Content of Efaté and Other Languages of Melanesia* (Washington, D.C.: Carnegie Institution of Washington, 1911).

17. Herman Melville, *Typee: A Peep at Polynesian Life, during a Four Months' Residence in the Valley of the Marquesas* (London: G. Routledge, 1850); Jack London, *South Sea Tales* (New York: Regent Press, 1911).

18. Abraham Fornander, *An Account of the Polynesian Race, Its Origin and Migrations and the Ancient History of the Hawaiian People to the Times of Kamehameha I*, 3 vols., English and Foreign Philosophical Library Extra Series (London: Trübner, 1878–1885), vol. 2.

19. Ibid., xviii.

20. Ibid., vi.

21. ho'omanawanui, *Voices of Fire*, 45.

22. Ibid.; Denise Noelani Arista, "Histories of Unequal Measure: Euro-American Encounters with Hawaiian Governance and Law, 1793–1827" (PhD diss., Brandeis University, 2010); Noenoe K. Silva, *Aloha Betrayed: Native Hawaiian Resistance to American Colonialism* (Durham, N.C.: Duke University Press, 2004).

23. William Jones, Anna Maria Jones, and John Shore Teignmouth, *The Works of Sir William Jones: In Six Volumes* (London: G. G. and J. Robinson and R. H. Evans, 1799). From Jones's linguistic work, the "Aryan concept" would become influential across many fields of European thought. John Dunmore Lang, for example, acknowledged Jones's scholarship but disagreed with Jones that the Polynesian language and "Polynesian nation" had Sanskrit origins. Where Jones understood Sanskrit as the "common parent" of both "Malay" and "Polynesian" languages, Lang argued that these two languages had originated in "Chinese Tartary" (an outdated term for the area around present-day Mongolia). By the time of Fornander's writing, the publication of the work of Max Müller had further developed the discourse of Aryanism into a popular subject in Europe, and Fornander would draw heavily from Müller's work.

24. Tony Ballantyne, *Orientalism and Race: Aryanism in the British Empire* (New York: Palgrave, 2002), 5.

25. Ibid., 19.

26. Gregory Moore, "Nietzsche, Degeneration, and the Critique of Christianity," *Journal of Nietzsche Studies* 19 (April 2000): 1.

27. Ibid.

28. Cathy Gere, *Knossos and the Prophets of Modernism* (Chicago: University of Chicago Press, 2009), 7. See also Lewis Henry Morgan, *Ancient Society; or, Researches in the Lines of Human Progress from Savagery, through Barbarism to Civilization* (New York: H. Holt and Company, 1877), vii. This text opens with a dramatic announcement of the radical potential of new scientific proof of humankind's underlying unity. He goes on to praise the study of the American Indian because, "forming a part of the human record, their institutions, arts, inventions and practical experience possess a high and special value reaching far beyond the Indian race."

29. Gere, *Knossos and the Prophets of Modernism*, 11.

30. Ibid., 8.

31. Ibid.

32. Ibid.

33. Friedrich Max Müller, *India: What Can It Teach Us? A Course of Lectures Delivered before the University of Cambridge* (New York: Funk & Wagnalls, 1883), 47–48.

34. Ibid., 32–33.
35. Silva, *Toward a Global Idea of Race*.
36. Gere, *Knossos and the Prophets of Modernism*.
37. Fornander, *An Account of the Polynesian Race*, vol. 2, vii.
38. Ibid.
39. Ibid., vol. 1, 59.
40. Ibid., 71, 98.
41. Ibid.
42. Ben-zvi Yael, "Where Did Red Go? Lewis Henry Morgan's Evolutionary Inheritance and U.S. Racial Imagination," *CR: The New Centennial Review* 7, no. 2 (2007): 201–29; Jenny Reardon and Kim TallBear, "'Your DNA Is Our History': Genomics, Anthropology, and the Construction of Whiteness as Property," *Current Anthropology* 53, no. S5 (2012): S233–45.
43. Reardon and TallBear, "Your DNA Is Our History," S236.
44. Jodi A. Byrd, *The Transit of Empire: Indigenous Critiques of Colonialism* (Minneapolis: University of Minnesota Press, 2011).
45. Native Americans were also at times characterized as almost white in Western social scientific accounts, and as having migrated from Asia via the Bering Strait. Jodi Byrd examines the narrative the Bering Strait theory enables about Native Americans as the original "Yellow Peril." Ibid., 200–201.
46. Ballantyne, *Orientalism and Race*, 76.
47. Ibid.
48. Silva, *Aloha Betrayed*, 71–72; Geiger, *Facing the Pacific*, 64.
49. Silva, *Aloha Betrayed*, 97.
50. Ballantyne, *Orientalism and Race*, 76–77.
51. Damon Ieremia Salesa, *Racial Crossings: Race, Intermarriage, and the Victorian British Empire* (New York: Oxford University Press, 2011).
52. Tangata Whenu is the Māori-language term Salesa prefers to use in reference to the Indigenous peoples of New Zealand.
53. Salesa, *Racial Crossings*, 205.
54. Lorenzo Veracini, "Introducing Settler Colonial Studies," *Settler Colonial Studies* 1, no. 1 (2011): 1–12.
55. Morgensen, "The Biopolitics of Settler Colonialism: Right Here, Right Now," *Settler Colonial Studies* 1, no. 1 (2011): 52–76.
56. Maile Arvin, Eve Tuck, and Angie Morrill, "Decolonizing Feminism: Challenging Connections between Settler Colonialism and Heteropatriarchy," *Feminist Formations* 25, no. 1 (2013): 8–34; Qwo-Li Driskill, Chris Finley, and Brian Joseph Gilley, *Queer Indigenous Studies: Critical Interventions in Theory, Politics, and Literature* (Tucson: University of Arizona Press, 2011).
57. However, the attribution of settler colonialism to other contexts including Tibet, Hokkaido, Okinawa, and Palestine, for example, may push all of our theories of settler colonialism and/or colonialism in new directions—if we pay particular attention to the ways race, gender, and sexuality are deployed in each context.
58. I have occasionally been questioned about why I talk about "Polynesian things" in Native American/Indigenous studies contexts, which signals to me

a troubling misunderstanding of who Native Hawaiians are and a lack of recognition of Native Hawaiians as Polynesians and Pacific Islanders due to the occupation of their lands by the United States. It seems especially important as Native Hawaiians are targeted for deeper incorporation into the federal government's recognition apparatus designed for Native American tribes, that Native American/Indigenous studies recognize that Native Hawaiians and other Pacific Islanders have been racialized differently from Native Americans. I believe that attending to such differences helps sharpen the basis of our alliances, our analyses of settler colonialism, and our theories and practices of decolonization for all.

59. Cheryl Harris, "Whiteness as Property," *Harvard Law Review* 106, no. 8 (1993): 1707–91; Warwick Anderson, *The Cultivation of Whiteness: Science, Health, and Racial Destiny in Australia* (Durham, N.C.: Duke University Press, 2006); Steve Garner, *Whiteness: An Introduction* (New York: Routledge, 2007); Matthew Frye Jacobson, *Whiteness of a Different Color: European Immigrants and the Alchemy of Race* (Cambridge, Mass.: Harvard University Press, 1999); Ian Haney López, *White by Law: The Legal Construction of Race* (New York: NYU Press, 2006); Noel Ignatiev, *How the Irish Became White* (New York: Routledge, 2012); Aileen Moreton-Robinson, *Talkin' Up to the White Woman: Aboriginal Women and Feminism* (Brisbane: University of Queensland Press, 2000).

60. Harris, "Whiteness as Property."

61. Rey Chow, *The Protestant Ethnic and the Spirit of Capitalism* (New York: Columbia University Press, 2002).

62. Geiger, *Facing the Pacific*, 59.

63. For example, Matthew Frye Jacobson has written about the public fears of adding Native Hawaiians, a "dark" race, to the American population around the time of Hawai'i's annexation in 1898. See *Barbarian Virtues: The United States Encounters Foreign Peoples at Home and Abroad, 1876–1917* (New York: Hill and Wang, 2000). Later, sociologist Romanzo Adams would testify to the absence of race problems in hearings leading up to Hawai'i's statehood. See Christine Manganaro, "Assimilating Hawai'i: Racial Science in a Colonial 'Laboratory,' 1919–1939" (PhD diss., University of Minnesota, 2012).

64. Jacobson, *Barbarian Virtues*.

65. Patrick Wolfe, *Settler Colonialism and the Transformation of Anthropology: The Politics and Poetics of an Ethnographic Event*, Writing Past Colonialism Series (New York: Cassell, 1999), 5.

66. Reardon and TallBear, "Your DNA Is Our History," S235.

67. Kim TallBear, *Native American DNA: Tribal Belonging and the False Promise of Genetic Science* (Minneapolis: University of Minnesota Press, 2013), 71.

68. Jon Stokes, "Maori 'Warrior Gene' Claims Appalling, Says Geneticist," *New Zealand Herald*, August 10, 2006; "Once Were Warriors: Gene Linked to Maori Violence," *Sydney Morning Herald*, August 9, 2006; Julian Sonny, "Why Polynesians Are Genetically Engineered to Be the Best Football Players in the World," *Elite Daily*, EliteDaily.com, September 30, 2014.

69. Lena Rodriguez and James Rimumutu George, "Is Genetic Labeling of

'Risk' Related to Obesity Contributing to Resistance and Fatalism in Polynesian Communities?" *The Contemporary Pacific* 26, no. 1 (2014): 81.

70. Ibid.

71. Maile Tauali'i et al., "Native Hawaiian Views on Biobanking," *Journal of Cancer Education* 29, no. 3 (2014): 572.

72. Ibid.

73. Health and Social Services Committee of the Navajo Nation Council, Approving a Moratorium on Genetic Research Studies Conducted within the Jurisdiction of the Navajo Nation until Such Time That a Navajo Nation Human Research Code Has Been Amended by the Navajo Nation Council (Montezuma Creek, Navajo Nation [Utah], April 2, 2002); John Bohannon, "A Home for Maori Science," *Science* 318 (November 2007): 907; Laura Arbour and Doris Cook, "DNA on Loan: Issues to Consider When Carrying Out Genetic Research with Aboriginal Families and Communities," *Community Genetics* 9, no. 3 (2006): 153–60.

74. Melissa A. Austin, Sarah Harding, and Courtney McElroy, "Genebanks: A Comparison of Eight Proposed International Genetic Databases," *Community Genetics* 6, no. 1 (2003): 37.

75. Gísli Pálsson and Paul Rabinow, "Iceland: The Case of a National Human Genome Project." *Anthropology Today* 15, no. 5 (1999): 14–18; Austin, Harding, and McElroy, "Genebanks."

76. Austin, Harding, and McElroy, "Genebanks," 42.

77. Lindsey Singeo, "The Patentability of the Native Hawaiian Genome," *American Journal of Law and Medicine* 33, no. 1 (2007): 121.

78. Ibid.

79. "Licensing Hawaiian Genes for Medical Research," *Mālamalama, the Magazine of the University of Hawai'i System*, July 2003, 16.

80. See examples from note 73 above.

81. Qtd. in Austin, Harding, and McElroy, "Genebanks," 42.

82. Debra Harry, "Indigenous Peoples and Gene Disputes," *Chicago-Kent Law Review* 84, no. 1 (2009): 180.

83. Association of Hawaiian Civic Clubs, "A Resolution Urging the University of Hawai'i to Cease Development of the Hawaiian Genome Project or Other Patenting or Licensing of Native Hawaiian People Have Been Consulted and Given Their Full, Prior and Informed Consent to Such Project" (Nukoli'i, Kaua'i: Association of Hawaiian Civic Clubs, November 15, 2003).

84. Ibid.

85. Ibid.

86. *Paoakalani Declaration* (Ka 'Aha Pono Native Hawaiian Intellectual Property Rights Conference, 2003), KaAhaPono.com.

87. The HGDP responded to such critiques by implementing a feasibility and ethics study led by a committee from the U.S. National Research Council of the National Academy of Sciences from 1994 to 1997. The project proceeded in 1997 with strict ethical research guidelines established. See Luca Cavalli-Sforza, "The Human Genome Diversity Project: Past, Present, and Future," *Nature Reviews: Genetics* 6, no. 4 (2005): 333–40.

88. Jenny Reardon, *Race to the Finish: Identity and Governance in the Age of Genomics* (Princeton, N.J.: Princeton University Press, 2005), 2.

89. Kim TallBear's *Native American DNA* is a rich resource for understanding some of the different commercial genomics products offered to consumers, including tests that promise to tell the customer what genetic percentage Native American they are.

90. Cavalli-Sforza, "Human Genome Diversity Project."

91. Alexander Twombly, *The Native Hawaiian of Yesterday and To-day* (n.p., 1901, accessed in Ayers Special Collection, Newberry Library, Chicago), 10.

92. Ibid., 8.

93. Harris, "Whiteness as Property," 1730.

94. As mentioned above, TallBear's *Native American DNA* is a notable exception.

95. Melinda Cooper, *Life as Surplus: Biotechnology and Capitalism in the Neoliberal Era* (Seattle: University of Washington Press, 2008).

96. Ibid., 6.

97. Ibid., 6–7.

98. Reginald Horsman, *Race and Manifest Destiny: The Origins of American Racial Anglo-Saxonism* (Cambridge, Mass.: Harvard University Press, 1981); Henry Nash Smith, *Virgin Land: The American West as Symbol and Myth* (Cambridge, Mass.: Harvard University Press, 1970).

99. Goodyear-Kaʻōpua, *Seeds We Planted*, 229–30.

100. Qtd. in ibid., 230.

101. Mark Niesse, "Hawaii Targets Taro Genetic Modification," *USA Today*, April 7, 2008.

102. Ibid. On Kanaka Maoli's genealogical relationship to *kalo*, see Silva, *Aloha Betrayed*, 101–2; Goodyear-Kaʻōpua, *Seeds We Planted*.

103. Association of Hawaiian Civic Clubs, "A Resolution."

104. Ibid.

105. *Paoakalani Declaration*, 2.

106. Ibid., 6.

107. Ibid.

108. Ibid., 3.

ANGELA PARKER

Photographing the Places of Citizenship: The 1922 Crow Industrial Survey

CROW TRIBAL MEMBERS Hazel Red Wolf and her husband, Three Foretops, received a visitor on July 12, 1922 at their log house in the Little Horn Valley, a mile above the town of Lodge Grass, Montana. Crow Agency Superintendent Calvin Asbury came to visit them, their three children, and one grandchild—equipped with a camera and a survey to complete. Asbury intended to photograph their house as a supplement to a narrative survey form requested by the Office of Indian Affairs (OIA), as part of their massive Industrial Survey project (1922–29).

The OIA initiated the Industrial Survey—an attempt to photograph and narrate every household on every federally recognized Indian reservation across the country—two years before the 1924 Indian Citizenship Act, "to ascertain their condition, needs, and resources, with the view to organizing the work of the reservation service so that each family will make the best use of its resources."[1] Asbury's survey sought information ranging from demographics to qualitative data on the "industry" and "health" of tribal members, and their household's "general condition." The photographs he took, however, made the 1922 Crow Industrial Survey unique within the context of the dozens of surveys commissioned by the OIA of the reservation era (1880s–1934). For this represented the OIA's first and last unified, national attempt to connect its data to a vast visual archive of Indian households under government "guardianship"—which during this time period included even "citizen Indians" nominally, but not actually, free of government supervision.

We do not know what Three Foretops and his wife thought when Asbury arrived at their home. Asbury's impressions, however, constitute the remaining archival record of the visit. Asbury wrote of the family's home, "Fair house, fairly kept."[2] His overall assessment reads, "The conditions are only fair. They live at home most of the time and have this year some very good crop. . . . [Three Foretops] says that he is getting too old for work and has to go slow, but he does considerable farming." Supplementing Asbury's assessment was this photograph.

Three Foretops's log cabin dominates the center of the image; the sky above the house is clear, and in the distance rambles a low line of trees to the

FIGURE 1. Three Foretops and Hazel Red Wolf home, Crow Industrial Survey. Photograph by Charles Asbury; courtesy of the National Archives and Records Administration, Washington, D.C.

left and foothills to the right. Three Foretops and Hazel Red Wolf, two tiny figures in front of their log cabin, remain mysterious. We cannot see their faces, even though the photograph exposes their bodies, their house, and a portion of their lands to Asbury, to the impersonal and assessing gazes of the OIA bureaucracy members who received and filed the survey documents, and to our own gaze.[3]

This photograph—along with the blizzard of similar images produced as part of the Crow Industrial Survey and the larger Industrial Survey project completed across the country—represents a valuable source base for historians of Native America. The survey and its photographs provide a literal and discursive snapshot of Native American life in the late reservation era, on the eve of the Indian Reorganization Act. And although the national Indian Affairs bureaucracy planned the survey, local Indian agents and their agency employees—"boss farmers," clerks, and the like—saturate the narratives and photographs with their own voice and framings. Thus, interrogating the Crow Survey—a survey of a "small place," distinctive and specific—reveals not only Native lives, but also the lives of reservation Indian Agency bureaucracies and the priorities and intentions of the national Indian Affairs bureaucracy itself. The Crow Survey lends itself to this analysis not only due to its manageable size (photographs and narratives of approximately 250 households), but also because of the well-developed historical work on the reservation-era Crow.

This essay explores the sources that make the OIA's Industrial Survey truly unique: its photographs. To do so, I read the images using the context of their accompanying narratives, photographic genres that influenced their visual syntax, other photographs of Crow lives and places taken in the late reservation era, and their historical context. I do not care to assess the photographs or their accompanying narrative as true or false, hateful or fair. But I do assume that the process of surveying and its eventual photographic and written contents contributed to a powerful epistemology with concrete consequences in the lives of Indigenous people.[4] The following section provides a historical context for place, citizenship, and the Industrial Survey itself during the reservation era. The final three sections explore land, homes, and bodies as three categories of place that frame the contestation over control between the Indian Affairs bureaucracy (both local and national) and the tribal community on the Crow Indian Reservation in southeastern Montana. These explorations expose a key realization: that the key *places*[5] of Indian life—the intimate, lived physicality of Native bodies, homes, and lands—served as crucial sites of citizenship.

Place and Citizenship in the Reservation Era

In early 1922 the OIA issued Circular 1774 to each of its Indian agents and superintendents: an order to compile and produce Industrial Survey Reports for every federally recognized Indian reservation in the United States. The OIA's directive included a sample of how each survey form and photograph should look. Labeled "John Doe," the sample survey photograph shows the front view of a house that dominates its frame. A broad, flat plain with small trees constitutes the background, and two small human figures sit in the graphic center of the house.

The sample survey narrative identifies John and Mary Doe—and their children Susan, Will, and Sam—not only by name, age, and schooling, but also by whether they hold land allotments, and if allotted, how much land and how it is being used. This information is not innocent. The aggregation of biopolitical data served as a step in working to undermine Native family structure and the tribal unit itself. How else would the partitioning, enclosing, identifying, locating, supervising, judging, and calculating[6] take place? Surveys of husbands

John Doe

Allottee No.	Degree	Status	Family
1625	Full	Ward	Wife and three children.

Picture shows John Doe and wife at their home.

John Doe 45 years old. He attended the reservation school through the 6th grade and had 2 years at Haskell. He is handy with tools and can make repairs about the place. Of his allotment of 160 acres, 40 acres are in timber and the remainder under cultivation. He takes great interest in the Rock Creek Chapter of the Reservation farmers organization, holding the position of Secretary.

Mary Doe, wife, 35 years old. Attended reservation school through 5th grade and mission school 2 years. Understands how to can vegetables and fruit, sews quite well, and is a good housekeeper. Her allotment of 160 acres is leased for $50 a year.

Susan Doe, daughter, 15 years old; is in the 5th grade in the reservation school. Her allotment of 80 acres is not leased at present.

Will Doe, son, 12 years old, is in the 3rd grade in the reservation school. Not allotted.

Sam Doe, son, 10 years old, is in the 1st grade in the reservation school. Not allotted.

This family is living about two miles from the agency, on John's allotment. They have a four-room frame house, shingle roof. It is plainly furnished and fairly well kept. He is planning to paint it as soon as possible. The family takes pride in having the surroundings neat and in having flowers. There is a smoke house, barn, granary, cowshed, chicken house, cave, orchard and a good well on the place.

FIGURE 2. Survey sample page 1, included with Circular 1774, an order to complete the OIA's Industrial Survey. Produced by the Office of Indian Affairs; courtesy of the National Archives and Records Administration, Washington, D.C.

and wives, their children, their allotments, their educational levels, and incomes did real work in this contest over Native futures.[7]

The OIA birthed its Industrial Survey from a half century of attempted control over Native lands, homes, and bodies. The major federal policies of its era—allotment, boarding schools, and Indian Office surveillance and discipline—all labored to supervise the places of Indian life. By the time of the OIA's Industrial Surveys, the Dawes Allotment Act had worked for nearly four decades to assimilate Native people and lands into the U.S. body politic by shattering communal land holdings. Meanwhile, Indian boarding schools disciplined tribal communities through the violent control of their children's bodies and consciousness. Indian Office bans on and prosecution of Indigenous cultural expression, or through its "boss farmers" and field matrons, also targeted Native bodies, homes, and allotted lands.[8] The Indian Affairs bureaucracy, swollen like a tick after burrowing deep into the Native land base, struggled with tribal communities over the definition of and control over their places throughout the entire reservation era.

The OIA sought to measure, define, and control these places because they represent, hold, and communicate awareness and culture.[9] Our bodies shape our awareness, build and curate homes that house our kin, and move within our landscapes to produce culture.[10] Foucault's revelation that disciplinary power targets the body[11]—to monitor and punish, to train and work, to rank and observe in order to create docility in individuals and a population—means that the state must also exert its discipline on our homes and landscapes. In its Industrial Survey—as in all survey projects—the Indian Affairs bureaucracy transformed the living flesh and physicality of Native bodies, homes, and lands into numbers, aggregates, images, icons, and photographs.

The photographs of the OIA Industrial Survey worked with the survey narrative to create an archive that intended to narrate and thus control the meanings associated with Indian homes and family life. This project asserted power: the power to define Native people and communities as deviant or respectable using middle-class Euro-American norms. Many bureaucratic institutions invested in photography both as a technology and as an explanation[12] based on photography's supposed replication of physical reality. Photographs, however, can be read multiple ways. To counter the potential multiplicity of meanings, the OIA's project created a "blizzard of photographs"[13]— achieved through the accumulation of a photographic archive—that erased the images' original, contextual meanings. The need to bring order to a chaotic visual archive "required" a subjective survey narrative to accompany the collected "objective" photographs.[14] And through the Industrial Survey, the OIA worked to create a vast "territory of images"[15] of the places of Native life, in order for their bureaucracy to define and measure ever-shrinking Indian territories. Such representations worked not only to measure an assimilationist project, but also to fix[16] or define Native identities into "knowable" foils[17] of the larger society. Alternately pure or degenerate, noble or servile, the eternal other that could also be possessed,[18] such images of Native existence during the reservation era worked to define not only the possibilities and limits of Native citizenship, but also to consolidate the normativity of white America.[19]

The OIA intended the photographs and text of the Industrial Survey to measure Native progress toward assimilation. By requiring descriptions of education levels, health status, and assets, the surveys gave the local Indian agent conducting them both a cognitive map of the reservation as well as a benchmark of how tribal members used and worked on their land. These benchmarks could then measure the success of—or need for—their assimilationist work. Charles Burke, Commissioner of Indian Affairs, wrote to his superintendents in 1923, "It is important for Indians to do better every year. They can not stand still. If they do not move forward they go backward. All Indians who do not respond will ultimately be left behind in the march of progress. Impress this thought upon each individual Indian. . . . We want every Indian to take account of his situation. If now farming, induce him to farm more and better; if not farming or engaged in some other occupation, get them busy at something that will add to their comfort and welfare."[20] The proof of progress Burke sought intended to silence the critiques of aggressive reformers. But it also confirmed OIA accounts of Indian backwardness—a narrative that justified their position as service providers.

Indian backwardness, lack of progress, and need for further assimilation linked directly to U.S. citizenship status. The narrative of Indian incompetence and assimilation as progress circulated within the legislation, writings, and decisions produced by the OIA, Congress, the courts, and even Indigenous intellectuals such as those who debated the terms of U.S. citizenship in the Society of American Indians.[21] The fallout from the Dawes Allotment Act fueled much of this discourse. Allotment intended to tie private land ownership to a citizen status but instead produced a maze of assessments—the OIA classified Native individuals as "competent" or "incompetent" depending on a constellation of race- and culture-based evaluations. Supposedly, Indians "competent" to manage their own affairs could provide a living for themselves from their allotment, and dressed and spoke as closely to white Americans as possible. Once deemed "competent," the OIA transferred ownership of their allotment in fee simple, their lands then subject to taxation. The U.S. government viewed "incompetent" Indians as dependent, in need of guardianship until able to assume the full rights and responsibilities of citizenship. The paths open to Native people interested in becoming U.S. citizens included service in the armed forces; renouncing tribal membership or leaving the tribal land base and adopting "the habits of civilized life"; accepting an allotment; or after amendments modified the Dawes Act, being deemed "competent" to manage one's own affairs.[22]

Tribal norms and concerns, however, controlled Indigenous political identity just as much as such discourses over U.S. citizenship did. Two years after the initiation of the Industrial Survey, the Indian Citizenship Act (ICA) of 1924 would blanket Indian Country with the formal designation of U.S. citizenship for every individual Indian. Some tribes rejected U.S. citizenship outright. Even in more amenable communities, Native people constructed political identity not only in relation to U.S. citizenship but also in relation to their community—distinguishing membership through kinship, clan, and cultural life. These aspects of community life, while not necessarily political or formally framed through concepts such as "citizenship" or "sovereignty," shaped the everyday lives and behaviors of tribal members—including in the political realm. Before and after the ICA passed, however, Native communities used existing community structures and employed activist tactics that demanded the right to survive and build a future.[23] Whether accepting or rejecting U.S. citizenship, Native communities built their political identities—as tribal members and in relation to U.S. citizenship—from below just as powerfully as various arms of the U.S. government, or debates among Indian intellectuals, imposed an identity from above.

Developments in Native political identity were structured not only by conceptions of U.S. citizenship, or preexisting community norms, but also by the contestation of control in the places they lived. Native communities recalibrated the places of their lives[24]—villages, settlements, hunting territories, sacred areas—in order to adjust to and at times contest[25] the spatial and political order imposed by the OIA. At Crow, despite experiencing a demographic nadir that did not begin to rebound until the 1920s, Crow family structures and a "locally generated political agenda" continued to structure and sustain political and social life. Although Crow leadership transitioned during the first decades of the twentieth century from pre-reservation leaders to a new guard of boarding school–educated Crow men, these leaders continued to focus on the defense and maintenance of tribal territories. For example, the tribal government shaped the 1920 Crow Act. Although the legislation further allotted reservation lands, Crow leadership set its terms in the face of more than a decade of non-Native agitation for allotment; the Crow version of allotment included the retention of tribal mineral rights and a tribally directed opening of tribal lands to non-Native homesteaders.[26] Although Crow tribal members may not have self-identified as either a Crow "citizen" or a U.S. citizen during this period, their politically independent and self-asserting actions speak louder than words.

By the time Superintendent Asbury received Circular 1774 with its directive to gather visual and narrative data on every Crow household, Crow notions of place on the reservation held daily power. The five major communities dividing the reservation evolved from the settlements of key, pre-reservation Crow leaders.[27] Crow leadership blunted the final land grab on Crow by using community-generated priorities to set the terms of the 1920 Crow Act. Asbury held significant financial and political control, but it was far from complete. When he bemoaned the need at Crow for "more staying at home, . . . less Indian dances, better homes, more barns, root cellars, wells, more industry and pride,"[28] his list testifies to the primacy of Crow social organization that took them away from their allotted lands to engage in tribal social, religious, and political life. The places of Crow reservation life in the 1920s—Crow lands, homes, and bodies—conformed not to the OIA version of Native industry, but to a "multivalent space"[29] of which Crow social norms formed the backbone. As Asbury worked to respond to the directives of Circular 1774 and to fit Crow households into the neat narrative and visual confines of the circular's survey sample, Crow tribal members made that task impossible.

The dynamics introduced in this section—the importance of place as a site of control, the OIA's imposition of their conception of U.S. citizenship tied to assimilative progress, the centrality of Crow norms and concerns, and how the contestation between these two visions in the smallest places of Crow life structured a novel version of political life and citizenship—saturate the following sections. By exploring the photographic narratives of Crow Industrial Survey through the lens of land, homes, and the body, the following sections reveal the enmeshment of place and citizenship in the late reservation era.

Lands

During the lifetime of tribal members like Three Foretops and Hazel Red Wolf, Crow land ownership underwent chaotic change. Between 1880 and 1904, the United States took large chunks of the reservation for the Northern Pacific Railroad, to "open" lands to homesteaders, and for an allotment bill driven by non-Native citizens and politicians. By 1915, of the over 400,000 acres allotted, Crow tribal members farmed only 6,200 acres. Historian Frederick Hoxie notes that by 1920, a few years before the Industrial Survey, less than two million acres remained in collective ownership, and non-Native stockmen leased almost all of them. During the early twentieth century, he asserts, "reservation lands were gradually being turned into cash."[30] The

FIGURE 3. Aimsback, Blackfeet Industrial Survey, 1921. Courtesy of the National Archives at Denver, Record Group 75, Bureau of Indian Affairs, Blackfeet Agency, Entry 64, Blackfeet Industrial Survey, 1921, Box 1, p. 15.

FIGURE 4. Guy Black Hawk home, Fort Berthold Industrial Survey, circa 1922–29. Courtesy of the National Archives and Records Administration, Kansas City, Missouri.

federal government tied allotment and private land ownership to citizenship,[31] initially conferring it via individual land ownership, later through its crude assessment of individual Indians as "competent" or "incompetent" to assume the roles and responsibilities of citizenship.[32]

Both the photography and the narrative of the Industrial Survey referenced and defined tribal members' allotted lands. The survey narrative duplicated the processes of tying citizenship to allotment each time it sought to assess the success of allotment. The assessment of "competency" and "industry" intertwined not only with land ownership and assimilation, but also with the relative readiness for the rights of citizenship. The framing of the Crow Industrial Survey photographs, which correspond with the OIA circular, suggest a photographer concerned not only with defining the Crow home, but also with the allotted lands on which it sat. Lest this interpretation seem a stretch—because the photographs follow the example set by Circular 1774—images from other northern Plains reservations show how the photography for the same survey project differed depending on the photographer.

Powerful U.S. mythologies regarding land, work, and ownership saturate survey photographs. At times, the photographs of the Crow Industrial Survey evoke older representations of homesteaders: immigrant families eking out a living on their prairie homesteads, sometimes with possessions spread in

FIGURE 5. Bearsheart (Old Time Dancer) homestead, Standing Rock Industrial Survey, circa 1922–29. Courtesy of the National Archives and Records Administration, Kansas City, Missouri.

front of their sod houses, claiming and working parcels of "free land"—160 or 320 acres—as the right of or progress toward U.S. citizenship. The land became theirs through *work*,[33] a labor that sought to extract agricultural wealth from the soil for a larger market. Homesteader photographs themselves represented a visual marking of the progress of European immigration across the North American continent, and reflected a visual rhetoric that, like late nineteenth-century landscape photography in the U.S. West, "took for granted the right of European-Americans to expropriate the land of nonwhites and develop it to support exclusively European-American cultural values."[34]

This homesteader trope echoes in the Crow Industrial Survey photographs. Consider Bear Ground's photograph. His house, a Euro-American-style frame house or log cabin, works as a symbol of Indian assimilation to white norms. The house, the family arrayed in front, the narrative accounting of their worldly possessions, and the photograph itself—all together, suggest the larger goals of the project: land reform, a new way of marking space

FIGURE 6. John and Marget Bakken sod house, Milton, North Dakota, circa 1895. Photograph by Fred Hultstrund; courtesy of the Fred Hultstrund History in Pictures Collection, North Dakota Institute for Regional Studies—North Dakota State University.

FIGURE 7. David Hilton family near Weissert, Nebraska, circa 1887. Photograph by Solomon D. Butcher; courtesy of Library of Congress, Washington, D.C.

based on the Dawes Allotment Act (itself modeled on the Homestead Act), and an attempt to conform to a homesteader citizenship through work and assimilation.

Yet Crow tribal members did not conform to the OIA's vision of Native yeoman farmers who stayed on their allotments taking care of their farms and producing agricultural goods for consumption. In the survey narrative, Crow tribal members ride their automobiles around the country. They take off to Crow Fair, to Fourth of July powwows, and to visit their relatives.[35] Asbury's survey photographs, exemplified by Figure 8, present a nuclear Crow family contained within a frame house, the house itself contained within a photograph and within the boundaries of an allotment, the allotments contained on a reservation. His survey narrative, however, reveals irritation at the community's refusal of containment. Asbury often wrote dismissively and sarcastically of tribal members who possessed a relatively new technology of mobility: the automobile. Of one family he observed, "They have an automobile, which requires a good deal of money that should be used for providing a better home. Their house is poor and rather poorly kept, but they are not able to sacrifice the use of an automobile for such common things as paint and paper or better shelter for their horses."[36] His displeasure signals that while he wished Crow to assimilate to white norms, he did not want them to claim the equal privileges of automotive mobility.[37] The mobility of Crow tribal members and the foundational role of Crow cultural norms may have spurred a photographic representation that reflected the deepest wishes of the OIA: static tribal members contained within Euro-American housing built on their allotments—all within reservation boundaries. OIA bureaucrats seemed to believe that containment would engender "industry," which connoted progress and assimilation, all of which would produce worthy citizens.

Despite participatory democracy being a cornerstone of U.S. citizenship, in the survey narrative Asbury portrayed Crow tribal members who spoke up and had an opinion (and probably made waves in the local agency) as deficient, in need of assimilative efforts, and decidedly not industrious. He found it distasteful when Crow tribal members had opinions and shared them. Asbury wrote dismissively of Ben Spotted Horse: "He is usually too busy with tribal matters and telling the Indians how the Government should be run to spare time for an ordinary thing like farming." Of another tribal member he wrote, "Arnold Costa is of the smart variety. He knows more about how the government should be run than the President or Secretary." Asbury characterized

FIGURE 8. Bear Ground home, Crow Industrial Survey. Photograph by Charles Asbury; courtesy of the National Archives and Records Administration, Washington, D.C.

another man as "another one of the very smart advisors and counselors, and if fluent talk in council or in private, would produce potatoes, he would never go hungry." Of another man he first characterized as one of the "champion beggars" for his relatives' food, he stated, "He should have been a Senator or Congressman or Judge, rather than a farmer, because they are both strong on talk, but do not like the odor of their own perspiration."[38]

Yet these men (and likely women) with opinions were building Crow political life and citizenship. The massive land thefts of the late nineteenth and early twentieth centuries shaped a Crow politics that centered on the defense of cultural values,[39] land use, and land rights. Crow leadership, forged while shaping the Crow Act, also curbed overgrazing by non-Native lessors, and opposed "dubious oil leases" approved by Asbury.[40] In this context, Asbury's dismissal of Crow men with political opinions not only conveys his opinion of Crow leadership but implies his notions about the land base, how it should be used and owned, who should profit from it—as well as his resentment toward a Crow body politic and leadership structure that successfully challenged his ideas about their landscape.

The visual and written narratives produced through the OIA's Industrial Survey drew from and mirrored powerful U.S. assumptions about land, work, ownership, and control. These assumptions required that Crow tribal members be characterized as deficient stewards, inconvenient within their own landscape. The same survey, however, shows that Crow tribal members refused to be contained by these ideas—much as they refused to be contained by allotment or reservation boundaries. Crow social and political life, centered on defending their lands, served as the meat and sustenance for their assertion of a Crow political consciousness and citizenship.

Homes

The Industrial Survey's photographic meat, and ultimate symbol of assimilative progress, was the Indian home. The Crow Industrial Survey—as in previous and subsequent surveys—counted Crow houses and their families, noted how many of the households lived in tents, had toilet facilities, or water sources.[41] In the OIA's hierarchy of homes, frame houses symbolized the pinnacle of assimilation and personal industry. Log homes were less acceptable, and tents or tipis unacceptable. A nuclear family living in a permanent house structure such as a frame or log house was ideal, but the OIA found it objectionable when extended or multiple families lived in the same house or even on the same allotment. The OIA saw these assessments and accountings as necessary not only to measure progress, but also to account for the population as a whole. As Asbury noted in 1927, birth figures on Crow were difficult to obtain because "Indians move around so much in the summer and other times [it is] hard to get an accurate count."[42]

The two photographic entries for Crow tribal member Plenty Buffalo illustrate the use of the Industrial Survey to measure assimilation via housing. These photographs show two different houses that served as Plenty Buffalo's homes. Asbury sent the bottom picture, the first home of Plenty Buffalo, with the original Crow Industrial Survey. Asbury sent the top photograph, Plenty Buffalo's second home, as a supplement a few years later. He noted in his letter accompanying the top photograph what the exact improvements entailed, closing with the statement, "While Plenty Buffalo has an improved house, he has not shown much improvement in his agricultural industry."[43] These two photographs, specifically the houses pictured, were intended to illustrate progress.

Improvement to the physical house referenced a hoped-for improvement in industry and assimilation. Assistant Commissioner of Indian Affairs E. B. Merritt replied to Asbury, "Now that he has a comfortable home and a good well on the place this man will surely take interest in cultivating the land and raising sufficient crops to fill his barn and insure a good living throughout the year."[44] The bureaucracy that eventually hoped to end its guardianship of (and fiscal responsibility for) what they deemed their Indian "wards" hungered for the progress implied in the photographs of Plenty Buffalo's two houses: Crow progress not only toward assimilation, but also toward a Progressive Era conception of American citizenship.

States often consider the home a site of reform. After all, we return to these places every night, to eat and sleep, and they represent a location of both sustenance and vulnerability. Homes are "an extra skin, carapace or second layer of clothes," serving to "reveal and display as much as it does to hide and protect." We make meaning of those home places, imbuing them with and using them to define notions of kinship, acceptable behavior, love, pleasure, and of course identity.[45] Homes are also associated with notions of domesticity, of women's work, and of judgments of deviance or respectability,[46] and serve as sites of memory, personal history, and political consciousness.[47] This constellation of ideas overlaps with components of citizenship and the idea of the nation[48]—in particular, family, blood, land, work, appropriate behavior, history, and identity. The family itself has often been considered the smallest unit of the nation, a symbol of societal health or endangerment. It thus follows that reformers, muckrakers, social critics,[49] and even the OIA would use the house—the physical structure embodying the home and housing the family—to measure social deviance or conformity.

The Crow Industrial Survey documented the exterior of the Crow house using bureaucratic technologies developed and implemented in the urban

FIGURE 9. Two homes of Plenty Buffalo, Crow Industrial Survey. Photograph by Charles Asbury; courtesy of the National Archives and Records Administration, Washington, D.C.

East. The survey's focus on Indian homes mirrored in some ways the 1909 Pittsburgh Survey, undertaken to mark and measure the "social conditions" of that city's class structure.[50] The Pittsburgh Survey's same bureaucratic management and social science methods underlay the bureaucratic aims of the OIA's Industrial Survey. But whereas the Pittsburgh Survey created synecdochic images representing the houses of various classes, the OIA's Industrial Survey concerned itself with particularity.[51] The OIA sought not to find and exhibit a *representative* set of Indian homes; rather, they sought to accrue an archive of *every* Indian home.

In this respect, the Industrial Survey photographs hold more in common with the older technology of the mug shot in which, as John Tagg describes, "the bodies—workers, vagrants, criminals, patients, the insane, the poor, the colonized races—are taken one by one: isolated in a shallow, contained space; turned full face and subjected to an unreturnable gaze; illuminated, focused, measured, numbered, and named; forced to yield to the minutest scrutiny of gestures and features."[52] The standard focal length Asbury followed faithfully was not new or unusual. This decision, however, coming as it did well after Bertillon's systematic focal length, lighting, and fixed distance between the camera and a criminalized sitter, resonates with the criminality suggested by such standardized treatment. Because our viewing culture is accustomed to full frontal photographs of places—buildings in particular—the effect of the OIA's photographic directive may seem innocent. Yet as Susan Sontag asserted, "To photograph is to frame, and to frame is to exclude."[53] The photograph the OIA attached to Circular 1774 focused just such a gaze on the house as the site of the family—a visual framing faithfully reproduced within the Crow Industrial Survey. The "documentary rhetoric" inherent in the frontality of the photographs of Indian homes should be seen as one decision among many that "sets the stage for either critique or celebration, but in either case evaluation."[54]

While the Industrial Survey narrative comments on the quality and type of housekeeping and furnishings in each household, it never introduces photographs of a household interior. Rather than a romantic elegy to the joys of the domestic sphere, the Crow Industrial Survey presented photographs of Crow homes as individual examples of a larger, universal archive that could allow any individual household to be measured as deviant or industrious— not only by comparing them to one another, but by laying them bare for comparison to an idealized version of white domesticity and industry.[55] The OIA and Asbury did not draw a curtain of privacy by excluding the house interior. After all, the OIA's investment in their field matron program and the work done to build the skills of white middle-class domesticity in boarding schools show a deep investment in regulating the interior spaces of Indian homes.[56] Rather, the exterior focus disregards Crow women's work.

Compare survey photographs with Richard Throssel's 1910 "Interior of the Best Indian Kitchen on the Crow Reservation." The Crow adopted (and even allotted) Throssel, a Canadian Cree who worked for the Office of Indian Affairs at Crow Agency and was the chief photographer for a 1910 survey on health conditions on Indian reservations. He produced "Best Indian Kitchen" for an OIA project intended to model hygienic practices to prevent trachoma and tuberculosis, communicable diseases rampant throughout Indian Country. His photograph presents an Indian family eating at a dining table in their kitchen. Their surroundings indicate relative wealth for the time and context—wallpaper on the walls, a nice hutch, tablecloth, and elaborate beadwork on their clothing. The family, stiff in their pose, makes the tableau seem over-studied. But the Crow woman pictured in her traditional elk tooth dress sits near the center of the photograph.[57]

In fact, Throssel's photograph illuminates a tableau of women's work. The staging resonates with Euro-American domesticity. But the beadwork and Crow dress details are just as important—and not only because the Crows

FIGURE 10. "Interior of the Best Indian Kitchen on the Crow Reservation." Photograph by Richard Throssel, circa 1910; courtesy of National Anthropological Archives, Washington, D.C.

have a reputation for "distinctive and technically excellent beadwork."[58] The beadwork expressed public and private meanings—care, love, attention, respectability, pride, artistic talent, and industry. The elk tooth dress might have been a gift from the husband to wife, or made in the woman's few spare hours in a busy household.[59] The creator intended that all the adorned clothing be "touched, worn, smelled," and kept close to the bodies of beloved family members.[60] So while the picture signals respectability and reenacts tropes of Euro-American domesticity, Crow women's work literally clothes, sustains, and beautifies the family and the physical structure of the home. Throssel's photograph depicts the centrality of the work Crow women undertook to organize the Crow family, homes, kinship networks, and, by extension, the structures of Crow social and political life. His interior of a Crow home throws the visual rhetoric of the Crow Industrial Survey into relief—a photographic project whose exterior focus chronicled Crow women only in the visual and narrative margins.

Another Throssel photograph, of Crow tribal member Bear Ground, exposes the photographic framing of the Crow Industrial Survey that rendered an emotional distance between Crow men and their families. In Bear Ground's survey photo (Figure 8)—posed like many other Crow men in survey photographs—he stands in front of his house, hands in pockets, noticeably separate from his children.[61] Taken and developed indifferently, the photograph in the Bureau of Indian Affairs archives is washed out, in some places barely legible. Produced twelve years earlier, Throssel's composition focuses on Bear Ground, and the sight lines of all the other people in the picture run toward him. Throssel's photograph shows Bear Ground and his family in front of a tipi, likely camped by a river for the summer, as many Crow still did well into the 1920s and 1930s. The photograph feels intimate as he carefully holds his child, and the image framing pulls the viewer's eyes toward the tipi in the center—and thus toward the figure of Bear Ground, who stands near the center of the tipi. In Throssel's photograph, Bear Ground does not just have a family; he loves his family.

The erasure of Crow women's work and of men's familial ties is especially notable in "a community rich with intimate relatives," in which kinship organized not only community membership but also political structure. Hoxie states, "Households made up of grandparents, parents, children and other relatives formed the basis for Crow family life in the reservation era."[62] Crow family structure went far beyond the nuclear family. The sisters of one's mother were also considered mothers, and the father's brothers were considered fathers. This pulled an extended kin group into tightly woven relationship ties. The matrilineal Crow clan system further multiplied kinship ties, since a person was a member of their mother's clan and treated their

FIGURE 11. "Bear Ground (Man) Holding Child outside Tipi; and Open Eye Old Lady; Child." Photograph by Richard Throssel, circa 1910; National Anthropological Archives, Washington, D.C.

fellow clan members as "brother" and "sister." Additionally, one's father's clanmembers would treat that individual as one of their own children.[63] Women and men were admired for their ability to fulfill and honor the multiple obligations of this family structure. Asbury, in his Crow Survey narratives, showed deep antipathy toward the Crow family structure and the extensive associations necessary to fuel and maintain it. His survey prose reached a nadir when he wrote that the near-total deafness of one man "may be . . . a good thing. Possibly it detracts from the pleasure of social groups and thus results in his staying at home more. If that is the case, it might be advisable to promote deafness."[64]

The deviance of Crow domesticity—a domesticity founded on the intimacy of Crow family and clan relations, supported by the work of Crow women, and based largely or perhaps even entirely in Crow social norms—constituted the foundation of Crow citizenship even as it produced anxiety for the local OIA bureaucracy. On the eve of the Indian Citizenship Act, the stasis and measurability implied by the Industrial Survey may have comforted the OIA even as the nature and practice of Crow citizenship—and Indian citizenship across the country—remained unresolved in a maze of allotment-generated confusion. But though the visual rhetoric of the Crow Industrial Survey disregarded both Crow women's social labor and Crow men's family intimacy, Crow tribal members insisted on living full lives steeped in Crow social and cultural concerns. Home places helped structure Crow identity and citizenship.

Bodies

The photograph that began this essay, of Hazel Red Wolf and her husband, Three Foretops, illustrates the centrality of strategies of the body in constructing Native citizenship identity. Although the photograph replicates the visual syntax of the Industrial Survey, Hazel Red Wolf disrupted the process. Asbury wrote, "When I suggested to them that they get in the picture, that I was taking, there was some delay while she [Hazel Red Wolf] went to put on her Indian elk tooth dress, which was rather a waste of energy since the photograph does not give her the benefit of that attention."[65] Asbury was correct to assert that the details of the elk tooth dress were lost within the photograph—had the narrative not presented the fact, it would be difficult to know what the woman in the image is wearing.

Regardless, Red Wolf's attempt to turn an instrument of measurement and classification into a portrait reveals the corporeal foundations of citizenship identity. Hazel Red Wolf's determination to wear her elk tooth dress suggests a claim of respectability, or perhaps the fondness she felt for her marriage bonds. It may have been an assertion of wealth or status.[66] It may have simply been her favorite dress—the one in which she felt most beautiful or accomplished. Many families use portraits—of themselves and their families—not only to display in their homes for enjoyment or to mark status, but potentially also to "construct identity, to mark an occasion for posterity, and to stabilize family relationships in the face of complexity and change."[67] And just as Lakota leader Red Cloud claimed the position of photographic subject, seeking control over his image in a "larger struggle for cultural survival,"[68] Hazel Red Wolf also claimed a subject position.

Assimilation begins with the body, the same place a subject position begins. Assimilationist policy permeated the United States during the early twentieth century. Legislators and judges pondered, debated, and created policy on how to define the subjects of U.S. imperialist territorial claims in Puerto Rico and the Pacific. Corporations, philanthropists, tenement workers, and maternalist thinkers attempted to treat the immigrant, the impoverished body, by targeting what they perceived as the illness: cultural difference.[69] Native bodies, however, represented a source of cultural difference that could not be legislated away or contained through immigration quotas.

Thus Native bodies and their clothes assumed a citizenship valence.[70] For example, the OIA's Last Arrow ceremonies, practiced until 1924, required that tribal members receiving citizenship and fee-simple title to their allotment lands perform a corporeal assimilation in order to claim the rights and status of citizenship. Men, dressed in traditional clothing, shot their "last arrow"[71] before an assembled crowd of tribal members, after which they entered a dwelling and changed into Euro-American-style clothes—their "citizen clothes." After the new "citizen Indian" emerged, the local Indian agent placed their hands on the handle of a plow, explaining that "this act means that you have chosen to live the life of a white man—and the white man lives by work. . . . Only by work do we gain a right to the land or to the enjoyment of life."[72] Women underwent a similar ceremony, minus the shooting of the last arrow, and the Indian agent instead gave her a workbag and purse, stating, "The white woman loves her home. The family and the home are the foundation of our civilization. Upon the character and industry of the mother and homemaker largely depends the future of our Nation." A 1917 newspaper describing the ceremony stated, "The general effect of the ceremonial has proved most happy, and the honor of participating in it has served as a stimulus to many of the Indians to work harder for the privileges of citizenship."[73]

In this context, Hazel Red Wolf's elk tooth dress signifies more than beauty or accomplishment. It signifies identity, even a citizenship identity. Red Wolf's elk tooth dress not only indicated the nexus of the work Crow women's and men's bodies performed—elk teeth, gained two at a time per each elk hunted by men, elaborately ornamented the distinctively Crow-style woman's dress hand sewn, beaded, and decorated by women. It also marked a distinctively Crow body. In a time period in which women's bodies and clothing—and their appropriation or rejection—could become an index of state or even national identity,[74] to insist on wearing the dress for this survey of Crow households hints at an assertion of self-preservation and self-determination.[75] In Hazel Red Wolf's world, and in the portrait she attempted to curate—a Crow woman wearing a beautiful elk tooth dress, her husband at her side, in front of their well-kept log cabin—"Indians aren't weird, heartbroken exiles, or zoo animals for the exposition, endangered species preserved forever in photographic gelatin. . . . They are changed but in control."[76] Just as Sauk women described by Jane Simonsen used images originally produced for white viewers to "unfix and remake them in ways that tell different stories,"[77] Red Wolf did not concern herself with the aims of Superintendent Asbury or the larger OIA bureaucracy. Her concern: to wear her favorite elk tooth dress. If the OIA indeed attempted to measure progress toward citizenship (read: assimilation) through survey photographs, in at least this case their measurement would include an elk tooth dress.[78]

The Crow Survey and many of the other northern Plains Industrial Surveys sidelined women and their bodies, deeming them irrelevant unless found wanting. Asbury's liberties with the structure of the Industrial Survey at Crow erased the substantive importance of women. For example, while the sample survey sent with Circular 1774 detailed the household individual by individual down to the youngest child, the Crow Industrial Survey condenses much of the detailed household information under a general heading "Remarks." This flattens the household information, naming only the male "head of household" and rendering every other family member nameless and ageless. In the survey narrative describing Asbury's interaction with Hazel Red Wolf, Asbury never recorded or alluded to her name. He referred to her only as the "wife" of Three Foretops, and I had to track her name through other sources. The original survey modeled in Circular 1774 imposes a Euro-American family system and gender norms—assuming that only men are heads of households, and assuming that Native families do (or should) conform to the nuclear family model. But the Crow Survey pushes this dynamic further. Women and children, nameless and ageless, are barely counted or noted as individuals.

Although less than half (approximately 40 percent) of survey photographs contain human figures at all—making Crow bodies more an afterthought or accident than an intention—in the narrative Asbury constantly assesses Crow men's bodies. Asbury tied the age, wellness, and abilities of Crow men's bodies to their "industry," or ability and success in providing for themselves and their family through farm or wage labor. For example, "He is poorly, but he could at least stay at home and attend to a garden and some chickens and a cow and contribute something to the support of his family. I regard him as a hopeless case and explained to him that in my opinion he would very soon starve to death and the sooner the better."[79] Asbury also pointedly noted peyote use. The Crow Industrial Survey, and many other Industrial Surveys, associated peyote use not only with addiction but also with a man's lack of industry and inability to support himself and his family. The overweight Indian body evoked disgust, as when Asbury wrote about one man, "This party says himself that he is a good worker, but the condition of his place and his general attitude does not confirm his admission. He appears to weigh somewhere around 300 lbs." Asbury also assessed the heaviness of his wife (unnamed), and concluded, "It seems to be a sort of rendezvous here for those that have a sort of chronic fatigue." Asbury racialized the Indian male body, tying blood quantum to industry and business acumen: "He is practically white and has some education in reservation and non-reservation schools. . . . His tendency, like many of the mixed-bloods, is to want to do things on a big scale and if they can secure the credit, they go in debt too much and are presently broken." Finally, the able-bodied Crow male also came in for his own round of assessment—always through the lens of deficiency and inability to "make a good living" doing farmwork and ranching. Asbury's narrative created a nexus between assessment of the Indian body, productivity, work, and the Crow landscape and allotted lands, as when he wrote, "The land where they live is very good land and should make him a good living, but they do not work. There are not particular tears to be shed in this case. He is an able-bodied young man. His wife is able-bodied. They could make a good living on the land where they live and if they go hungry, it is their own fault."[80] Asbury often used the idea of hunger to comfort himself as he made particularly nasty assessments of Crow tribal members, imagining it as a form of bodily discipline that would teach the deficient Crow agricultural worker the error of idleness. In Asbury's hands, the Crow Industrial Survey assessed Crow bodies largely to dismiss them as wanting.

But Crow tribal members possessed different concerns regarding their bodies, as revealed by Asbury's dismissive comments. Crow bodies—at times infirm, overweight, or racialized—moved. They traversed the Crow, crossing allotment and reservation boundaries to visit relatives, where their family members likely sustained their bodies with delicious food and conversation and laughter. They dressed their bodies as they saw fit, consciously or unconsciously projecting an identity that had little to do with Last Arrow ceremonies and everything to do with their own notions of beauty and accomplishment. In other words, while the OIA might assess Indian bodies as forever deficient regarding the productivity and "industry" necessary to contribute as full citizens, Crow people lived fully in their bodies—the place that houses consciousness and identity—more concerned with Crow norms of community and citizenship than those the OIA attempted to impose. Such commitment to Crow bodily truths surely shaped their political identities as tribal members and, eventually, citizens.

Conclusion

Historians of the late reservation era have developed sophisticated analyses of federal Indian policy, well-known Native writers and cultural brokers, and the complex interaction between nascent culture industries and Native imagery and performances. Through this work, historians now understand the early twentieth century as a time of intense government control, but also one of creative negotiations and advocacy on the part of Native people. Historians of the late reservation era possess an invaluable historical source in the OIA's Industrial Survey, as the survey created literal, statistical, and narrative snapshots of the end of the era through its documentation and accounting of every Indian household on every reservation in the country. The source is rich and compelling, particularly because it weds narrative and statistical data to a vast archive of photographs of the intimate places of Indigenous life.

Examining the valences of the Crow Industrial Survey though the lens of place and citizenship shows, however, that the data and images of the survey must not be taken at face value. Rather, the survey produced visual and written narratives fraught with the anxieties of the OIA's local and national concerns. In reaction to those anxieties, OIA officials attempted to survey, annotate, and define Native bodies, homes, and lands—or what this essay terms the "places" of Indian life. By reading against the grain of the OIA's visual and written narratives—and inserting a tribal historical context—those same flattening and eliding survey photographs and narratives also, perhaps unwillingly, reveal a rich and vibrant community life. Crow political and social values structured this community life, and even the totalizing documents of the OIA's survey cannot hide a Crow body politic that lived and asserted control over their own bodies, homes, and lands in ways that contributed to a Crow-centered citizenship practice.

This analysis—and the contestation it examines between the OIA and tribal members—reminds us that before citizenship is theorized, it is embodied and *placed*. Citizenship happens through the work and performance of our bodies, in the way our bodies curate and develop our homes, and in the way we move through and use our landscapes. Indigenous citizenship—within a tribe or the United States—should contend with the places in which it is forged.

ANGELA PARKER (Mandan, Hidatsa, Cree) received her PhD in U.S. history from the University of Michigan.

Notes

1. Felix Cohen, *Handbook of Federal Indian Law* (Albuquerque: University of New Mexico Press, 1971), 26.

2. Crow Industrial Survey, Crow Agency, 1922, Reports of Industrial Surveys, 1922–1929, Crow-Crow Creek, Records of the Industries Section, Records of the Education Division, Records of the Bureau of Indian Affairs, Record Group 75, National Archives and Records Administration—National Archives Building, Washington, D.C. Hereafter referred to as Crow Industrial Survey, NARA (D.C.).

3. For more on the power dynamics of the photographic gaze, see Margaret Olin, "It Is Not Going to Be Easy to Look into Their Eyes," *Art History* 14, no. 1 (1991): 97.

4. Ann Laura Stoler, *Along the Archival Grain: Epistemic Anxieties and Colonial Common Sense* (Princeton, N.J.: Princeton University Press, 2009), 31.

5. "Place" refers to human practices that create and assign meaning to the landscapes they inhabit. Culture can be seen as produced from the meaning we make at the physical matrix of our sensing/moving bodies and the landscapes we inhabit. Edward Casey, *Getting Back into Place: Toward a Renewed Understanding of the Place-World* (Indianapolis: Indiana University Press, 2009), 346; Keith Basso, *Wisdom Sits in Places: Landscape and Language among the Western Apache* (Albuquerque: University of New Mexico Press, 1996); Edward Casey, "How to Get from Space to Place in a Fairly Short Stretch of Time: Phenomenological Prolegomana," in *Senses of Place*, ed. Steven Feld and Keith Basso (Santa Fe, N.M.: School of American Research Press, 1996), 13–53.

6. Michel Foucault, *Discipline and Punish* (New York: Vintage Books, 1995), 143; Michael Clifford, *Political Genealogy after Foucault: Savage Identities* (New York: Routledge, 2001), 58.

7. For the tie between assimilation efforts and a focus on the future of Native peoples, see Beth Piatote, *Domestic Subjects: Gender, Citizenship, and Law in Native American Literature* (New Haven, Conn.: Yale University Press, 2013), 4–5.

8. Akim Reinhardt, *Ruling Pine Ridge: Oglala Lakota Politics from the IRA to Wounded Knee* (Lubbock: Texas Tech University Press, 2007), 50; Frederick Hoxie, *Parading through History: The Making of the Crow Nation in America, 1805–1935* (New York: Cambridge University Press, 1995); Frederick Hoxie, *A Final Promise: The Campaign to Assimilate Indians, 1880–1920* (Lincoln: University of Nebraska Press, 2001); Thomas Biolsi, *Organizing the Lakota: The Political Economy of the New Deal on the Pine Ridge and Rosebud Reservations* (Tucson: University of Arizona Press, 1992); Brenda Child, *Boarding School Seasons: American Indian Families, 1900–1940* (Lincoln: University of Nebraska Press, 1998); K. Tsianina Lomawaima, *They Called It Prairie Light: The Story of Chilocco Indian School* (Lincoln: University of Nebraska Press, 1994); Robert Trennert, "Corporal Punishment and the Politics of Indian Reform," *History of Education Quarterly* 29, no. 4 (1989): 595–617.

9. Casey, *Getting Back into Place*, 346.

10. Steven Van Wolputte, "Hang on to Your Self: Of Bodies, Embodiment, and Selves," *Annual Review of Anthropology* 33 (2004): 251–69; Karen Tranberg Hansen, "The World in Dress: Anthropological Perspectives on Clothing, Fashion, and Culture," *Annual Review of Anthropology* 33 (2004): 369–92.

11. Clifford, *Political Genealogy*, 43.

12. David Green, "Veins of Resemblance: Photography and Eugenics," *Oxford Art Journal*, 7, no. 2 (1984): 6; Karin Becker, "Picturing Our Past: An Archive Constructs a National Culture," *Journal of American Folklore* 105 (Winter 1992): 3.

13. Siegfried Kracauer, trans. Thomas Levin, "Photography," *Critical Inquiry* 19, no. 3 (1993): 432.

14. Roland Barthes, *Image-Music-Text*, trans. Stephen Heath (London: Fontana, 1977), 25–26; Deborah Poole, "An Image of 'Our Indian': Type Photographs and Racial Sentiments in Oaxaca, 1920–1940," *Hispanic American Historical Review* 84 no. 1 (2004): 38–39.

15. Alan Sekula, "Reading an Archive: Photography between Labor and Capital," in *The Photography Reader*, ed. Liz Wells (New York: Routledge, 2003), 359–60, 446.

16. Homi Bhabha, *The Location of Culture* (New York: Routledge, 1994), 70–71.

17. Christopher Pinney, *Camera Indica: The Social Life of Indian Photographs* (London: Reaktion Books, 1997), 37.

18. Poole, "An Image of 'Our Indian,'" 39–41.

19. For more on photographic archives and the body, see Allan Sekula, "The Body and the Archive" in *The Contest of Meaning: Critical Histories of Photography*, ed. Richard Bolton (Cambridge, Mass.: MIT Press, 1989), 352, 357.

20. Letter, Commissioner of Indian Affairs Charles Burke to All Superintendents and Indian Service Farmers, May 17, 1923, Crow Agency, 1922, Crow Industrial Survey, NARA (D.C.).

21. Kevin Bruyneel, *The Third Space of Sovereignty: The Postcolonial Politics of U.S.–Indigenous Relations* (Minneapolis: University of Minnesota Press, 2007), 97–121. For an explanation of the legal landscape surrounding the Indian Citizenship Act, see Bruce Duthu, *Shadow Nations: Tribal Sovereignty and the Limits of Legal Pluralism* (New York: Oxford University Press, 2013), 87–93. For more on the SAI, see Lucy Maddox, *Citizen Indians: Native American Intellectuals, Race, and Reform* (Ithaca, N.Y.: Cornell University Press, 2005); and Philip Deloria Jr., "Four Thousand Invitations," *Studies in American Indian Literatures* 25, no. 2 (2013): 25–43.

22. Maddox, *Citizen Indians*, 107–8.

23. John Troutman, *Indian Blues: American Indians and the Politics of Music, 1879–1934* (Norman: University of Oklahoma Press, 2009); Christian McMillan, *Making Indian Law: The Hualapai Case and the Birth of Ethnohistory* (New Haven, Conn.: Yale University Press, 2007); Hoxie, *Parading*.

24. Frederick Hoxie, "From Prison to Homeland: The Cheyenne River Indian Reservation before World War I," *South Dakota History* 10, no. 1 (1979): 1–24.

25. Troutman, *Indian Blues*; McMillan, *Making Indian Law*.

26. Hoxie, *Parading*, 172, 227, 295–96, 302; regarding the Crow Act, 253–63; Frank Rzeczkowski, *Uniting the Tribes: The Rise and Fall of Pan-Indian Community on the Crow Reservation* (Lawrence: University Press of Kansas, 2012), 193.

27. Hoxie, *Parading*, 175.

28. Ibid., 302.

29. Glen Mimura, "A Dying West? Reimagining the Frontier in Frank Matsura's Photography, 1903–1913," *American Quarterly* 62, no. 3 (2010): 687.

30. Hoxie, *Parading*, 269.

31. Piatote, *Domestic Subjects*, 109.

32. K. Tsianina Lomawaima, "The Mutuality of Citizenship and Sovereignty: The Society of American Indians and the Battle to Inherit America," *Studies in American Indian Literatures* 25, no. 2 (2013): 337.

33. Patrick Wolfe, "The Settler Complex: An Introduction," *American Indian Culture and Research Journal* 37, no. 2 (2013): 1–2.

34. Martin Berger, *Sight Unseen: Whiteness and American Visual Culture* (Berkeley: University of California Press, 2005), 67.

35. Crow Industrial Survey, NARA (D.C.).

36. Ben Pease, ibid.

37. For a fuller discussion of cars and Native peoples, see Philip Deloria, "Technology: 'I Want to Ride in Geronimo's Cadillac,'" in *Indians in Unexpected Places* (Lawrence: University Press of Kansas, 2004), 136–82.

38. Crow Industrial Survey, NARA (D.C.).

39. Hoxie, *Parading*, 315–16, 324.

40. Allotments to Crow Indians: Hearing before the Committee on Indian Affairs, United States Senate, 66th Cong. 1 (1919). A bill to provide for the allotment of lands of the Crow Tribe, for the distribution of tribal funds, and for other purposes.

41. Hoxie, *Parading*, 299.

42. Ibid., 300.

43. Crow Superintendent C. H. Asbury to Assistant Commissioner of Indian Affairs E. B. Merritt, March 3, 1925, Plenty Buffalo, Crow Industrial Survey, NARA (D.C.).

44. Assistant Commissioner of Indian Affairs E. B. Merritt to Crow Superintendent C. H. Asbury, March 11, 1925, ibid.

45. Janet Carsten and Stephen Hugh-Jones, "Introduction," in *About the House: Lévi-Strauss and Beyond*, ed. Carsten and Hugh-Jones (New York: Cambridge, 1995), 1–46. Although the home can also be a site of violence, abuse, and discord, the larger point holds that homes are the site in which appropriate and inappropriate behaviors become defined or normalized.

46. Adele Perry, "From 'The Hot-Bed of Vice' to the 'Good and Well-Ordered Christian Home': First Nations Housing and Reform in Nineteenth-Century British Columbia," *Ethnohistory* 50, no. 4 (2003): 587–610. For more on domesticity as an ordering concept for imperialism, see Laura Wexler, *Tender Violence: Domestic Visions in an Age of U.S. Imperialism* (Chapel Hill: University of North Carolina Press, 2001).

47. Antoinette Burton, *Dwelling in the Archive: Women Writing House, Home, and History in Late Colonial India* (New York: Oxford University Press, 2003).

48. Piatote, *Domestic Subjects*, 3.

49. Maren Stange, "Jacob Riis and Urban Visual Culture," *Journal of Urban History* 15, no. 3 (1989): 274–303; Amy Kaplan, "Manifest Domesticity," *American Literature* 70, no. 3 (1998): 581–606; George Sánchez, "'Go after the Women': Americanization and the Mexican Immigrant Woman, 1915–1929," in *Unequal Sisters: A Multicultural Reader in U.S. Women's History*, ed. Vicki Ruiz and Ellen DuBois (New York: Routledge, 1994), 284–97.

50. Paul U. Kellogg, "The Pittsburgh Survey," *Charities and the Commons* 11, no. 14 (1909): 518.

51. Maren Stange, "The Pittsburgh Survey: Lewis Hine and the Establishment of the Documentary Style," in *Symbols of Ideal Life: Social Documentary Photography in America, 1890–1950* (New York: Cambridge University Press, 1989), 47–87.

52. John Tagg, *The Burden of Representation: Essays on Photographies and Histories* (Amherst: University of Massachusetts Press, 1988), 63–64.

53. Susan Sontag, "Looking at War," *New Yorker*, December 9, 2002, 82–99.

54. Catherine Lutz and Jane Collins, "The Photograph as an Intersection of Gazes: The Example of National Geographic," in *The Photography Reader*, ed. Wells, 359–60.

55. Sekula, "The Body and the Archive," 350, 360.

56. Lisa Emmerich, "'Right in the Midst of My Own People': Native American Women and the Field Matron Program," *American Indian Quarterly* 15, no. 2 (1991): 201–16.

57. "Interior of the Best Indian Kitchen on the Crow Reservation," ca. 1910, photograph by Richard Throssel. Peggy Albright, *Crow Indian Photographer: The Work of Richard Throssel* (Albuquerque: University of New Mexico Press, 1997), 8, 24–26, 34–35, 37–39.

58. Ibid., 8.

59. Ibid., 144.

60. Jeffrey Anderson, *Arapaho Women's Quillwork: Motion, Life, and Creativity* (Norman: University of Oklahoma Press, 2013), 12–13, 22–25, 73.

61. Bear Ground, Crow Industrial Survey, NARA (D.C.).

62. Hoxie, *Final Promise*, 169–71, 183.

63. Robert Lowie, *The Crow Indians* (New York: Farrar & Rinehart, 1935), 18–32; Rodney Frey, *The World of the Crow Indians: As Driftwood Lodges* (Norman: University of Oklahoma Press, 1987), 40–58.

64. Crow Industrial Survey, NARA (D.C.).

65. Ibid.

66. For more on the use of clothing to mark status or identity, see Terence S. Turner, "The Social Skin," in *Reading the Social Body*, ed. Catherine Burroughs and Jeffrey Ehrenreich (Iowa City: University of Iowa Press, 1993), 15–39; and Alison Guy and Maura Banim, "Personal Collections: Women's Clothing Use and Identity," *Journal of Gender Studies* 9, no. 3 (2000): 313–27.

67. Jane Simonsen, "Descendants of Black Hawk: Generations of Identity in Sauk Portraits," *American Quarterly* 63, no. 2 (2011): 316–17.

68. Frank Goodyear, *Red Cloud: Photographs of a Lakota Chief* (Lincoln: University of Nebraska Press, 2003), 3, 6, 16.

69. Frank Van Nuys, *Americanizing the West: Race, Immigrants, and Citizenship, 1890–1930* (Topeka: University Press of Kansas, 2002); James Barrett, "Americanization from the Bottom Up: Immigration and the Remaking of the Working Class in the United States, 1880–1930," *Journal of American History* 79, no. 3 (1992): 996–1020; Gayle Gullett, "Women Progressives and the Politics of Americanization in California, 1915–1920," *Pacific Historical Review* 64, no. 1 (1995): 71–94; Nyan Shah, *Contagious Divides: Epidemics and Race in San Francisco's Chinatown* (Berkeley: University of California Press, 2001); Mae Ngai, *Impossible Subjects: Illegal Aliens and the Making of Modern America* (Princeton, N.J.: Princeton University Press, 2004); Sam Erman, "Meanings of Citizenship in the U.S. Empire: Puerto Rico, Isabel Gonzalez, and the U.S. Supreme Court, 1898–1905," *Journal of American Ethnic History* 5, no. 4 (2008): 5–33.

70. For other examples of the relationship between clothing and a nation's body politic, see Tina Mai Chen, "Dressing for the Party: Clothing, Citizenship, and Gender Formation in Mao's China," *Fashion Theory* 5, no. 2 (2005): 143–72;

and Mary Lou O'Neil, "You Are What You Wear: Clothing/Appearance Laws and the Construction of the Public Citizen in Turkey," *Fashion Theory* 14, no. 1 (2010): 65–82.

71. Hoxie, *Final Promise*, 180.

72. Francis Paul Prucha, *The Great Father: The United States Government and the American Indians* (Lincoln: University of Nebraska Press, 1995), 881.

73. Albright, 52–53; *Gettysburg Times*, January 5, 1917.

74. Poole, "An Image of 'Our Indian,'" 74–80.

75. Some might also define it as an act of photographic survivance. Ojibwe scholar Gerald Vizenor coined "survivance" to refer to an active resistance toward domination that goes beyond survival. Amy Lonetree applied survivance to Ho-Chunk photographs of the late nineteenth and early twentieth centuries in her essay "Visualizing Native Survivance: Encounters with My Ho-Chunk Ancestors in the Family Photographs of Charles Van Schaick," in *People of the Big Voice: Photographs of Ho-Chunk Families by Charles Van Schaick, 1879–1942*, ed. Tom Jones et al. (Madison: Wisconsin Historical Society Press, 2011), 14.

76. Rayna Green, "Rosebuds of the Plateau: Frank Matsura and the Fainting Couch Aesthetic," in *Partial Recall*, ed. Lucy Lippard (New York: New Press, 1992), 52.

77. Simonsen, "Descendants of Black Hawk," 302.

78. For more on Native women's self-presentation, see Mimura, "A Dying West?" 703–4.

79. Charles Brown, Crow Industrial Survey, NARA (D.C.). See also Joe Sings Pretty; Bird Hat; Cold Wind.

80. Bird Far Away, ibid. See also Shows His Gun, or Joe Gun; Ben Pease; Ben Gardner.

MARGOT FRANCIS

"Bending the Light" toward Survivance: Anishinaabec-Led Youth Theater on Residential Schools

THIS ESSAY EXPLORES an Anishinaabec-led youth theater project on the intergenerational legacy of residential schools to rethink ideas about Indigenous survivance.[1] My aim is to develop a hermeneutics for listening to complex narratives within the play and in interviews with the audience and cast. While there is now a substantial literature on the racist ideological framework of these schools and their traumatic effects, less has been written about former students who considered themselves successfully assimilated graduates. A key story in the production discussed here concerns the legacy of one such student, Marguerite Stella Syrette, who attended St. Joseph's Residential School for girls in Spanish, Ontario, in the 1930s. Her grandson, Teddy Syrette, was the lead writer and actor in this theater project, where he developed a compelling set of auto-ethnographic reflections on his relationship with his grandmother. These stories illustrate the legacy of those who considered themselves successful converts and model citizens as a result of residential schooling, capturing what may be for many readers an unexpected outcome of the residential school project. At the same time, these narratives also demonstrate how students wove complex narratives of appropriation and transculturation in contexts not of their own choosing.

My work draws on Indigenous analysis of survivance (e.g., that of Vizenor) and Figes's study of those who endured the terror of Stalinist Russia, as well as insights from interviews from the cast and audience to explore the ambivalence at the heart of navigating domination. I argue that this performance enacted a risky and important form of Indigenous self-representation, where actors and audience members related anecdotes and shared ephemera which hinted at stories that can never be fully known. Through dramatic monologues, humor, and auto-ethnographic storytelling, Teddy Syrette's performance highlighted both how racial and hetero-gendered norms taught in the schools echoed down the generations within Indigenous families, as well as the grit and determination that enabled Anishinaabec survivance—without papering over the contradictions.

The context for this theater performance is the present-day legacy of boarding schools for Indigenous children. In Canada, as in other settler colonial contexts, residential schools were officially designed to alienate Indigenous children from their family and kinship relations, convert them to Christianity, and assimilate them into the lowest rungs of a settler society. Schooling practices aimed to extinguish Indigenous languages, culture, and spiritualities through representing them as backward and primitive, and many staff employed regulatory practices that ranged from public humiliation to physical and sexual abuse in order to punish students and expunge their Indigenous heritage.[2]

I will start with a brief review of the history of residential schools and then explore the contradictions of "assimilation" through analysis of Teddy Syrette's compelling narratives from the play. The next section draws on interviews with the cast and selected audience members to elaborate on how they made sense of that legacy in order to "bend the light" toward Indigenous survivance. Throughout I highlight the contradictory ways in which Anishinaabec people (re)imagined the assimilative drive of residential schools and theorize the significance of Indigenous theater for navigating the inheritance of education as a racialized program of social control.

Background and Context

Boarding schools for Indigenous children first began to proliferate in Canada in the mid-1800s; while most closed in the 1960s or 1970s, the last institution did not shut its doors until 1996. The schools were jointly run by the churches and the government. They were systematically underfunded and in most cases provided a substandard education geared toward menial work.[3] Yet these schools also provided a key plank in the mission of the Indian Department, which aimed, according to Duncan Campbell Scott, deputy minister in 1920, to get "rid of the Indian problem" through the "gradual civilization" of Indigenous people through education.[4] The purpose of this Canadian policy, as one American Bureau of Indian Affairs official said in 1945, was "the extinction of the Indians as Indians."[5] This was pursued through many avenues, including land seizures, the reserve system, the outlawing of Indigenous spiritual and cultural practices, and state regulation of Indigenous legal status, governance, and economic activities. Schooling, however, was a critical component in that assimilative policy, and it was only with the Report of the Royal Commission on Aboriginal Peoples in 1996 that the state publicly acknowledged this problematic legacy.[6] The Conservative prime minister of Canada Stephen Harper officially apologized for the residential school system and set up a Truth and Reconciliation Commission in 2008.[7]

It is important to note that it has taken well over a century and a half for Indigenous critiques of the residential school system to gain any official recognition. As one of my interviewees, the director of the National Residential School Survivor Society Mike Cachagee, commented, "For years we've had no credibility in telling these stories."[8] From the earliest experiments in church-run boarding schools, Indigenous communities resisted the coercive and assimilative aspects of the schools by withholding their children, to the extent that government officials in 1856 considered the early schools to be a failure.[9] Nevertheless, attendance at an Indian school was made obligatory in 1920, with institutions unevenly distributed across the country and some communities having access to day schools which had similar aims and practices.[10]

Much of the scholarship produced over the past twenty years, including the 2012 Truth and Reconciliation (TRC) report *They Came for the Children* has emphasized Indigenous resistance. J. R. Miller's book-length history of residential schools, *Shingwauk's Vision*, recounts how some parents withheld their children from the schools despite the legal and financial consequences. Similarly, the TRC highlights that Haisla parents boycotted the school in Kitimat, British Columbia, when they believed children were not being treated well.[11] Celia Haig-Brown also described how parents, in at least one case, drove out an instructor who had been accused of abusing a female student.[12] Children in the schools were sometimes able to challenge the rigid disciplinary requirements by continuing to speak their languages despite punishments, or through acts of violence against the staff, or by running away—though some died of exposure or drowning in their attempt to escape.[13] Further, a range of Indigenous authors have stressed the ways children and youth challenged the institutions from within, emphasizing the fact that students were not simply victims of social engineering. For example, Tomson Highway's acclaimed novel *Kiss of the Fur Queen* employs fictional characters to reimagine his and his brother's experience of residential school. Highway emphasizes the brothers' continued connection to both Cree and Christian spiritualities and the creative resistance they displayed as adults when they turned a legacy of pain and loss into dance, theater, music, and art.[14]

Nevertheless, most Canadians continue to be unaware of the schools, and only recently has there been some limited acknowledgment that the schools' objective was a (failed) attempt at cultural genocide. It is important to emphasize that many of the children who attended the schools died there. Government reports confirm that 24 percent of children in the pre-WWII Western schools died from tuberculosis and other diseases, and there were high rates of physical and sexual abuse.[15] Consequently, stories that might be seen to underplay the traumatic nature of residential school experiences have been less often told. Despite this, the Anishinaabec actors and audience members involved in the theater production highlighted a range of more ambivalent narratives emphasizing the contradictory ways that Indigenous parents, children, and communities navigated their residential school experiences. Listening to their analysis, it seemed to me that they were asserting the importance of survivance as a politics of interpretive autonomy and discursive agency in ways that invited me, as a researcher, to rethink what might be understood by the very words "assimilation" or "resistance" in the first place.

The 2011 theater production on which this essay is based was developed by an Anishinaabec-led group of actors who were participants in summer community theater projects in Batchewana and Garden River First Nations. The actors wrote the script based on interviews with their extended family, other survivors of the schools, and research from the Shingwauk Residential School archives.[16] The play, *No Choices, Different Voices*, was first presented at the National Residential School Survivor Society biannual conference from July 1 to 3, 2011, and performed for a wider audience in August 2011 in Sault Ste. Marie, Ontario. The youth actors were mentored by Debajehmujig Theatre, one of the most accomplished Indigenous dramatic groups in Canada. The show itself staged a series of dramatic narratives to retell the legacy of residential schools primarily from the perspective of children attending those institutions, and each of the actors also constructed an auto-ethnographic response to these narratives. For some this meant speaking in their own voices as Indigenous youth who were, for the first time, grappling with the impact of this legacy in their family and community. For non-Indigenous youth the focus was on attempting to make connections with this traumatic history through related experiences of marginality,[17] as well as confronting their responsibility as citizens in a settler state through their involvement in this project and through inviting audiences to consider the importance of this difficult legacy.[18] In the next section I highlight a series of auto-ethnographic vignettes by Teddy Syrette, the lead writer and actor in this project, and theorize these in conversation with interviews with other Indigenous actors and community members.

Anishinaabec Performance: "I'm a Friggen Indian"

In the opening monologue of *No Choices, Different Voices*, Teddy Syrette introduces the audience to his gradual realization of the schools' impact on his family, starting with his visit to the St. Joseph's Residential School in Spanish, Ontario, in May 2011:

> I see the building standing across a field and through the trees. This place is closed off to the public, but I'm fascinated by the discovery. . . . It is early eve-

ning and the sun shines from the southwest, pouring through the open holes of windows and doorways, so the air flows through its ribs and bones. The building stands thirty feet tall and it breathes... I grab my phone and snap a picture.

The visit to St. Joseph's Residential School where Teddy snapped this picture was originally a brief side tour on his trip to meet with Debajehmujig Theatre, the future mentors of the project documented here.[19] Later in this monologue, Teddy describes arriving home and showing his father the picture taken on his cell phone. While he is aware of the existence of residential schools and is proud of his discovery of a "cultural ruin," what he doesn't know is that this school is part of his own family history. Indeed, the discussion with his father reveals that his grandmother attended this very institution. As Teddy notes later, the "discovery of the building" means that he is, in a certain way, meeting his grandmother "for the first time." Indeed, this photograph is the start of a process through which Teddy reimagines a long-estranged relationship. Within his family there had been no discussion about how his grandmother's school experience was sealed off from the everyday realm of familial and community memory.

Interestingly, questions about the ways the residential school legacy is invisible *within* Indigenous families and communities, as well as in the dominant society, were raised by all the Indigenous actors in the show. For example, a mixed-race Anishinaabec youth who lived off-reserve and who had been, up until his involvement in this project, disconnected from Anishinaabec history and culture, noted that family stories of his grandfather's traumatic flight from Hungary prior to WWII were well-known. In contrast, although he had three uncles and two aunts who were in residential schools, he knew nothing of that legacy.[20] Similarly, two other actors (Anishinaabec and Cree) talked about how they had some superficial understanding of the schools, but prior to working on this show, as Tazz McCloud put it, "residential schools were not really on my radar.... Everything the audience learned I also learned in the last few months."[21] Actor Chase Neveau also remarked on this absence, suggesting that the lack of discussion was "eerie" in a community where many families had been profoundly affected by this legacy.[22]

For these youth, however, the "eerie" silence was not just about the legacy of residential schools: it was also about the meanings associated with being Indigenous. Midway through the first act Teddy speaks to this issue directly:

For the longest period of my life I always thought I was either Italian, or what Cher likes to call a "half breed." Then my aunty told me that I was an Indian.... "AN INDIAN!?!" Holy man! I'm a friggen Indian. I was so excited to discover I was an Indian. However, as a little boy I never knew what being Indian, Nish, Native, Aboriginal, or my favorite, only because it sounds fancy IN-DI-GE-NOUS actually meant... Hmm... Indigenous. That one always used to make me stutter if

> I talked too fast. "Hey look at all those IN-DI-GE-NOUS . . . IN-DI-DI-GE-GE-NEE . . . IN-DI-GE-GE-NEE, oh whatever, 'Aanii Niishnaabs!'"

Teddy grew up in the Batchewana First Nation, on the outskirts of the mid-sized northern Ontario community of Sault Ste. Marie, and while the young actor realized this territory was "different," the significance of this was unclear. In his opening monologue Teddy dramatizes the discovery of his "Indian" or Nish (short for Anishinaabec) status, and then turns to a satirical commentary on the politics of naming oneself. While "Indigenous" has recently become an umbrella expression signifying an international politics connecting Native communities, Teddy describes it, somewhat mockingly, as "fancy." Employing a quirky sense of humor, he turns his point of address back to his community, "Aanii Niishnaabs!" (Aanii means "hello" in the Anishinaabemowin language), thus invoking a shared sense of cultural solidarity. In these ways, Teddy's monologue uses humor as a flexible performative strategy which both acknowledges his sense of disconnection from "Nish" history and identity, and asserts his clear affinity with that same project. In this next excerpt, Teddy elaborates on that conflicted legacy:

> One thing that always confused me as a child was that I always thought one side of my family wasn't Aboriginal. My father said we were, but everyone on his side of the family has fair skin with light-colored eyes and hair. . . . I, on the other hand, was always brown: hair, eyes, and skin tone. I felt like the black . . . no wait, the *brown* sheep of the family. They even acted like, well how can I say this without using the "Z" word? Oh! I know, "like non-Aboriginal people." I just always felt different and sometimes I thought I was treated differently.

The "Z" word refers to Zhaagnaash, which means "white people" in Anishinaabemowin.[23] When Teddy traces back this sense that his father's side of the family seems "non-Aboriginal," the place he lands is with his grandmother, Marguerite Stella Syrette, who attended St. Joseph's Residential School. This estrangement is illustrated in a story that closes the first act of the play. Here Teddy describes the tension between himself and his grandmother through a series of binaries: she was a devout Roman Catholic, while he was a boy who "cried" when he "had to go to Sunday School"; she was a "flawless seamstress" who worked for the finest dress shops in Sault Ste. Marie, while he was "a curiously confused boy who tried on the dress when she left the room." Despite all this, Teddy decided to tell her a secret. The occasion was a visit in the hospital, where his grandmother was recovering from a fall. Teddy chatted with her about the "crappy food" and whether he would return to finish high school:

> But after a while I was ready to tell my grandmother, the one person I wasn't close to, that I, her brown sheep grandson was GAY! However, before I could

speak she reached over to grab a magazine, pointed to the headline: 'Rosie O'Donnell Marries Longtime Girlfriend' and said, 'Did you see this? Tssk, tssk, disgusting!' I lied and told her I was going back to school then left.

As might be expected, after this conversation the rift between Teddy and his grandmother "grew wider"; she died a year before the performance documented here. Given the hetero-patriarchal religious ideology which characterized residential schools, it is not surprising that Marguerite Syrette was not familiar with the traditions that honored "two-spirit" people *within* many Indigenous communities.[24] Despite this painful schism, Teddy used his discovery of St. Joseph's Residential School as the starting point for "a journey to find out more about the grandmother" he "never understood."

Teddy's first opportunity came during his three-week internship at Debajehmujig Theatre in Wikwemikong (Wiki) on Manitoulin Island in the spring of 2011. He describes the incident in the second act of the play, highlighting how a casual conversation allowed him to reconnect with his grandmother's family on the island, whom he had never met:

> When I met my other family members in Wiki what struck me more than anything was that almost all of them were visibly Aboriginal, they looked like me. The brown sheep of the family had finally found his matching flock. They mentioned to me that my gram was always a bit different from the rest: reserved, introverted, and kept to just her immediate family. My cousins talked about how she had a sister who passed away in Spanish Residential School [St. Joseph's Residential School in the community of Spanish] and that after she had returned to Wiki, she had changed. She was even more distant and the only people she really socialized with were other students who attended school.

While Teddy's grandmother was raised in Anishinaabemowin before being sent to residential school, when she returned she no longer spoke the language. Most striking for Teddy was that despite the many horror stories associated with these schools, his grandmother's "feelings . . . were of gratitude and personal growth." Indeed, Marguerite had "fond memories" of "playing baseball with her sister and sending notes to her brother Morris by hiding them in the brim of the Father's hat." Later, when Marguerite herself was a mother, she would have preferred that her own children went to a residential school, a perspective that seemed to fit with what Teddy described as her "drill sergeant" approach to her own children and grandchildren. Complaining about the distance her children had to walk to school, Marguerite noted that *her* classroom had always been "just down the stairs."[25]

Teddy ends this sequence by asking himself, and implicitly the audience, the following question: "'Did the government and church manage to kill the Indian in my grandmother through assimilation?' or 'Was my grandmother always open to the idea of identity [as a process of] adaptation?'" While the only person who might address this question is no longer alive, Teddy used the development of the play to explore this unanswerable query.

As the audience for this production was primarily composed of members of Garden River and Batchewana First Nations, some of them knew Marguerite Syrette, and one of my interviewees, Alice Corbiere, commented on her representation in the play. Corbiere is a member of Batchewana First Nation and was the administrator for the band council from 1966 to 1978. While I did not specifically ask her about the representation of Marguerite Syrette, she raised this issue in response to a question about the schools' intergenerational effects:

> Marguerite was a great woman, very strong. I think Teddy presented it quite well. Everything was black or white with her. The strictness of the residential school came out. She was a fantastic seamstress and she worked for the top shop here in Sault Ste. Marie. She was well respected in the city for her skills. When we are talking about the intergenerational effects—it is the lateral violence that is within our First Nations members. I really think that residential schools taught this. We were taught that you're not Indian. So we were taught, "I'm not as Indian as you are. You're more Indian than me." And on and on it went.

Here Alice Corbiere reflects on the legacy of a colonial education where the objective was to "kill the Indian in the child" and theorizes that this demeaning context contributed significantly to students internalizing negative ideas about "Indian" identity. The term "lateral violence" refers to the ways that people who are survivors of colonization, intergenerational trauma, and ongoing oppression may lash out against members of their own community. As Mick Gooda, the social justice commissioner for Aboriginal and Torres Strait Islander communities in Australia, remarked in 2011, the "concept of lateral violence has its origins in literature on colonialism from Africa and Latin America, as well as on the oppression of African Americans . . . and women. The process of colonisation . . . has its roots not only in the violent subjugation of groups but also more insidious forms of social control."[26] Theorists such as Frantz Fanon have argued that despite many expressions of resistance, the experience of ongoing oppression leads some colonized people to internalize the values of their oppressors.[27] In this context, lateral violence is understood as lashing out at your "own" rather than at those who are above you in the hierarchy of power. Or, as Mick Gooda explains, the "overwhelming position of power held by the colonizers, combined with internalized negative beliefs, fosters the sense that directing anger . . . toward the colonizers is too risky. . . . In this situation we are safer and more able to attack those closest to us."[28] The exercise of lateral violence, then, must be located within the context of the redemptive narrative taught in most residential schools which asserted that Indigenous people needed to expunge their own cultures, languages, economies, and spiritualities—indeed, their own people—in order to gain a place within the modern social order.

I suggest that theories about the internalization of settler colonial values might productively be linked to other analyses about the impact of power in ways that produce additional shadings to this history. Here I draw on Orlando Figes's study of those who endured the terror of Stalinist Russia, in the hope that this perhaps surprising source might generate additional possibilities for understanding the complicated forms of survivance developed by those facing overwhelming state power. Figes explores oral-history accounts of the private lives of those who lived through the Stalinist terror, including interviews with people whose family members were arrested by the NKVD or who were deported to labor camps in the Gulag, and others who denounced their friends and family or were informers for the state. In all these instances, Figes is interested in how people speak about their "strategies for survival, the silences, the lies, the friendships," and the ways people "preserved their traditions and beliefs . . . if they were in conflict with the public values of the Soviet system . . . [in short] how did living in a system ruled by terror affect intimate relationships?"[29] His research details the complex ways people accommodated themselves to the Soviet ideals through individualized narratives of personal accomplishment, self-discipline, and stoicism, in order to assert a pride in their "way of life," despite the overwhelming context where they lacked control over foundational aspects of daily life.

I am interested in the ways Figes's analysis might be relevant for understanding Indigenous parents and children whose lives were also ruled by the overwhelming power of the state as they navigated the residential school system. In order to understand these narrative strategies in relation to Marguerite Syrette, it would be helpful to know more about her life history. As Alice Corbiere remarked, one could develop "a whole story" based on Marguerite, "and her marriage to a former war veteran, and what he came home to, and her own family from Manitoulin Island, and what they went through."[30] While I am not familiar with all the family history, I can provide a few additional details to flesh out this picture. Marguerite was taken from her family home on Manitoulin Island to the residential school on the mainland in the town of Spanish when she was six years old; she did not return until she was a teenager, after her mother had died, to help raise the younger children. As Mike Cachagee noted, "If your [non-Aboriginal] child doesn't go to school, they send a truant officer. But if I ran away from the residential school, they'd send the police after me."[31] Thus any understanding of the "voluntary" release of children needs to be considered within the context of the legal control that governed the lives of Indigenous people during this period. Marguerite left her family home to marry an Anishinaabec veteran after WWII. The Royal Commission on Aboriginal People has said that after the war, veterans returned to blatant inequalities in accessing medical benefits and funding for education or small businesses—all of which were offered to non-Aboriginal veterans.[32] In this context, Marguerite Syrette developed her skills as an expert seamstress, learned in St. Joseph's Residential School, while also raising children and supporting her family. Marguerite also contributed to Anishinaabec governance by serving as the secretary for the Batchewana band council, and as a band councilor in the 1950s and 1960s.

Marguerite's early life story after she left residential school illustrates the gendered responsibilities that accrued to older girl children for social and familial reproduction. Her departure from the school she had been compelled to attend, but which she seemingly valued, was based entirely on the gendered assumption that she would take over the role of her mother in caring for her younger siblings. Later, as an adult, Marguerite faced a colonial system where Indigenous people were considered wards of the state (lacking the franchise until 1960) and systemic racist inequalities in gaining employment. Despite this, Marguerite worked her way up to becoming one of the most respected seamstresses in Sault Ste. Marie and was active in Anishinaabec band council administration and politics. Thus, throughout her life, she contended with and contested gendered racial and colonial discourses: being sent to school at age six, then being removed to raise her siblings; and as an adult making sustained contributions to the economic livelihood of her family as well as through her work in Anishinaabec governance.

In the final monologue of the play, Teddy pays tribute to this grandmother who remains an enigma for him. He reflects on her self-discipline, stoicism, and strength of spirit as qualities through which she developed a hybrid "way of life," excelling in a small-town economy meant to exclude her. He comments,

> In one of my many adventures while interning at Debaj . . . I stumbled across a waterfall. Near the falls some trees are being prepared to be cleared. The lower branches have all been removed, but the trees still stand. As I look at the trees I have a moment of clarity and think of my grandmother and other people who also have been affected by residential schools. . . . Like these trees, they have been cut but continued to live on.

Here Teddy uses a land-based metaphor to describe how those wounded by Canadian state policies that "cut off" their language and familial connections may still engage in a process of negotiation which, as Homi Bhabha suggests, "is neither assimilation nor collaboration."[33] Teddy's description of trees being cleared from the land as an allegory for the removal of Indigenous people can be compared to Vizenor's concept of the trace, which he also used in combination with Anishinaabec natural metaphors. For Vizenor, the trace could be connected with the word "agawaatese," which "could mean a shadow, or casts a shadow. The sense of agawaatese is that the shadows are animate entities. The shadow is the unsaid presence in names, the memoires in silence."[34] These shadows remind us that trees stripped for clearing can nevertheless carry a trace of their former presence. While these traces may frequently be overlooked, Teddy uses his memory of the trees to "story up"[35] that legacy in ways that allow him to understand the brutal context for his grandmother's survivance.

Teddy ends the play by acknowledging Marguerite as "a respected woman in her trade, a devoted person of faith, a council woman for Batchewana First Nation . . . My grandmother." In the final stanza he performs a simple but powerfully enacted story about how Marguerite adapted the technologies of sewing, taught at the residential school, for other purposes: "When I was a boy my grandmother made me a ribbon shirt[36] when I began to attend pow-wows. I am grateful that she did this and I am also grateful I was a chubby kid, because today I can still wear it. Miigwetch Nokomis, Miigwetch." Teddy closes with the honorific "Miigwetch Nokomis" (Thank you, Grandmother). At the same time he dons the ribbon shirt—brought up to the stage by his parents, who sat in the front row at every show—and indeed, that shirt had weathered his transition from chubby child to a well-built young man, and still fits.

The enigma of Marguerite Syrette's life remains at the end of this performance. But the play has taken the youth cast and the audience members present on an imaginative passage, which highlights both the oppressive violence of the schools and the ways that some survivors redeployed the skills learned there to remake their own lives, despite a system which taught them they were unfit to govern themselves and their communities. Through dramatic monologues, humor, and auto-ethnographic storytelling, Teddy's story of Marguerite Syrette juxtaposed the coercive relations of power that structured the schools with narratives about the grit and determination that enabled Anishinaabec survivance without papering over the contradictions. In the next section I turn to reflecting on how cast, audience, and interviewees responded to this performance and then explore how these narratives "bent the light" toward other, equally conflicted, themes of survivance.

"Storying Up" the Responses: Survivors and Survivance

No Choices, Different Voices constructed a dramatic container which invited the audience into an intimate relationship with the performers and provoked strong affective responses. These reactions were given careful attention in audience feedback and debriefing sessions after each performance.[37] Thus, in contrast to the "eerie silence" about residential schools that cast members noted at the start of their work, the process of writing and witnessing the play peeled back layers of raw emotion, including deep "frustration, sadness, anger."[38] These emotions were particularly evident in some of the post-show interviews and discussions. For example, in my post-show conversations with Teddy Syrette he highlighted additional reflections about his grandmother that he had chosen not to discuss in the public performance. These included his perception that his grandmother harbored deep discomfort with his gendered "flamboyance" and sexuality, and a persistent uneasiness with people who did "not look white."[39] While these reflections are consistent with Teddy's narrative in the play, they provide a more pointed critique of the ways white supremacist and hetero-gendered norms taught in residential schools echoed down through the generations, and their impact on intimate and familial relationships.

Difficult emotions were also evident in my follow-up interviews with audience members. Carol Nolan talked about the corrosive power of the churches in "brainwashing" parents "into believing that the schools could offer a better life" for their children.[40] This theme was also evident in Joe Corbiere's interview, although he noted that some parents did try to protect their kids by disappearing into the bush, moving to other communities, or going to the United States.[41]

Other members of the audience, however, challenged the youth actors' representations. For example, women at two different performances made a point of standing, after the show, to say that while they appreciated the play it could not reproduce the torment they had experienced in their time at the schools.[42] Indeed, the overwhelming majority of Indigenous audience members interviewed after the performance told stories which testified to cultural, physical, and sexual abuse and numerous attempts by parents and children to enact active and subterranean resistance. This multiplicity of stories served to highlight how the play provoked a profoundly difficult reckoning: as one Anishinaabec audience member noted, although she had been alive at the time when the Shingwauk Residential School in Sault Ste. Marie was in operation, seeing the play "just sent chills through me. The shock of it hit me more, what actually happened."[43]

Other interviewees noted that many students used the education they obtained from the schools, and the bonds they forged with other students, in future community work and sometimes for political activism.[44] This theme is evident in Teddy's narrative insofar as his grandmother used the skills learned at St. Joseph's school, both in her involvement in the Batchewana band council and also in making regalia for his participation in powwow performances. Some audience members, however, highlighted more directly activist responses. Alice Corbiere, for example, noted that her husband, John Corbiere, chief of Batchewana First Nation (1966–78 and 1994–96) and the plaintiff in the *Corbiere* case (a 1999 constitutional challenge to the Indian Act based on the Charter of Rights),[45] used the connections he forged in residential school to build Anishinaabec solidarity. These activities were, to say the least, very different from those intended by school officials. Alice noted, "Whenever we were meeting in groups, there were so many people from other communities [who] knew each other . . . from residential school. And that certainly helped in their dealings, because they already had trust and respect built."[46] As J. R. Miller also noted in his history of the schools, it was former residential school students who provided "the most vociferous criticism . . . and the most effective political leadership" to eliminate that system. Similarly, according to Miller, many who had attended the schools were also energetic proponents for preserving and reviving the cultural and spiritual practices that the schools were meant to eliminate.[47]

Thus the overwhelming theme in most research about residential schools and in my interviews with audience members was the systemic violence of the residential schools. We can see, however, a more ambivalent narrative in Teddy Syrette's representation of his enigmatic grandmother. This ambivalence was echoed in my conversation with Anishinaabec activist and community historian Alan Corbiere,[48] who has organized events for residential school graduates from Manitoulin Island, where he noted some "reaction against the 'survivors' narrative."[49] While these residential school graduates were critical of students being taken from their family home, the physical punishments, and being forbidden to speak their language, they nevertheless asserted that "we're not 'survivors,' we went to school."[50] This response certainly highlights that some schools equipped students for their future lives, as in Corbiere's community of M'Chigeeng First Nation on Manitoulin Island, where "it was the kids who went to school who went on to become the chiefs, teachers, and traditionalists."[51] This testimony could suggest some heterogeneity in the schools over time, where shifts in the management, personnel, and curricular structures could have modified aspects of the ideological violence at the heart of the system. However, it also implies that the discourse of "survivors" itself may impose a kind of "victimry" role, which emphasizes a confined helplessness rather than the vital survivance strategies that enabled these graduates to become leaders within their communities. Indeed, in Alan Corbiere's observation, many of the elders in his community seem to refuse a collective identity based on victim typifications that might set them apart as forever marked by that experience. This ambivalence about the discourse of "survivors" may be particularly important in a context where anti-Indigenous racism is frequently articulated through stereotypes which stigmatize Indigenous people as "whiners" forever locked in a history of injury or injustice instead of people who are mobilizing to re-create their collective cultural identity and sustain their communities. Vizenor himself has emphasized a related critique noting that the concept of survivance is itself meant to suggest a "quality of action" that creates a sense of "native presence over absence, nihility, and victimry."[52]

We might also speculate that the discomfort with the discourse of survivorship—which does imply a critique of the schools as places where only some, literally, *survived*—could have stemmed from the very real dangers of resistance. Indeed, it is important not to romanticize the impact of activist political protest, as sometimes these efforts were met with a backlash from religious authorities, the ramifications of which lasted for generations. For example, when I interviewed Alan Corbiere, he made a point of telling me the following story. In 1885, the Catholic day school for Anishinaabec girls in the town of Wiki was destroyed by fire. The Jesuits who ran the school initially planned to rebuild on the same site and hire local Anishinaabec men for the construction. The wages offered to the Anishinaabec laborers, however, were lower than those paid to non-Indigenous workers, and the Anishinaabec men mounted a strike in protest. According to Corbiere, the Jesuits retaliated against the strike by deciding to move construction of the new school to the mainland.[53] This new school site in the town of Spanish punished the strikers by denying them the work, and also limited what the Jesuits considered the excessive control of the Anishinaabec parents and chiefs who had been attempting to intervene in the running of the school in Wiki.[54] Indeed, Anishinaabeg parental protests about corporal punishment, starvation, and bed bugs in the earlier school in Wiki have been confirmed in other scholarship.[55] It was in the newer St. Joseph's Residential School in the community of Spanish, far from the oversight of her parents, that Marguerite Syrette would be sent in the 1930s, and it was the shell of this building that Teddy Syrette, her grandson, photographed in 2011.

Conclusion

How then might I draw together the contradictory forms of survivance chronicled in the theater production and interviews highlighted here? It should be evident that neither the discourses of passive victim nor those of resilient graduate are sufficient for understanding these contradictory experiences, as both ends of the binary reduce, rather than add, complexity. Instead, I hope that Teddy Syrette's efforts to "story up" his enigmatic grandmother, Marguerite Stella Syrette, have "bent the light" toward the shadows of a colonial project whose impact is still unfolding. We can certainly say that sometimes, after long periods away from their family, children like Marguerite Stella Syrette grew up to take an individual pride in their stoicism and self-discipline and in the success they achieved in a small-town economy meant to exclude them, while also maintaining fond memories of the schools. This perspective might have been a strategy for transcultural appropriation, as Bhabha asserts; or a form of internalized oppression, as Alice Corbiere argued; or it could indicate strategies of survivance which themselves may have necessitated forgetting. Teddy Syrette's representation of his grandmother suggests it was all of the above.

More broadly, this theater performance provided an opportunity for Anishinaabec youth to articulate the contradictory effects of a profoundly corrosive education policy. This legacy will never be "overcome," but through this Anishinaabec project some youth did establish a different relationship to that history and created space for articulating new ways to make sense of this inheritance. My interviews with the cast and audience also hinted at the ways that Indigenous survivance affected, and continues to affect, white settlers, sometimes deeply and irrevocably: from the white managers of elite dress shops in Sault Ste. Marie, who acknowledged Marguerite Syrette as their most talented seamstress; to the non-Indigenous actors and audiences who participated in this contemporary theater performance on the legacy of residential schools and found themselves profoundly changed. This final aspect of Indigenous survivance is also critical, for if researchers fail to see Indigenous performance as having real effects then survivance is still seen as damaged and ineffective. Instead, we might take seriously the profoundly complicated affective responses to this production. As one white audience member from Sault Ste. Marie noted in my interview with her, now that she is aware of that history it is the "elephant in the room" when she is with Indigenous friends: "I can't ever seem to shake that feeling."[56] A non-Indigenous actor of mixed Roma and Romanian heritage reflected on a similar point in her monologue in the second half of the performance, commenting that she had grown up "obsessed with atrocities" in other places—"the Holocaust, Vietnam, Rwanda"—and yet she "had no idea" about the history of residential schools in Canada, nor that the Shingwauk Residential School stood just a few blocks from where she was raised.[57] It was her participation in this theater project which led her to hear the testimony of survivors and to build alliances with Indigenous actors; becoming acutely aware, for the first time, of the spaces of violent absence and constrained presence closer to home.

MARGOT FRANCIS is associate professor at the Centre for Women's and Gender Studies, cross-appointed to the Department of Sociology at Brock University. She is author of *Creative Subversions: Whiteness, Indigeneity, and the National Imaginary.*

Notes

1. I borrowed the phrase "bending the light" from Lee Maracle, "Oratory on Oratory," in *Trans.Can.Lit.: Resituating the Study of Canadian Literature*, ed. Smaro Kamboureli and Roy Miki (Waterloo, Can.: Wilfred Laurier Press, 2007), 59.

2. John Milloy, *A National Crime: The Canadian Government and the Residential School System, 1879 to 1986* (Winnipeg: University of Manitoba Press, 1999).

3. Ibid.

4. Quoted in J. R. Miller, *Skyscrapers Hide the Heavens: A History of Indian–White Relations in Canada* (Toronto: University of Toronto Press, 2000), 281.

5. Ibid., 282.

6. The report is online at AADNC-AANDC.gc.ca.

7. For the official apology see "Prime Minister Stephen Harper's Statement of Apology," *CBC News*, June 11, 2008, CBC.ca.

8. Mike Cachagee, personal communication with the author, August 2011.

9. Miller, *Skyscrapers Hide the Heavens*, 143.

10. Thanks to an anonymous reviewer at NAISA for clarifying the history for compulsory school attendance.

11. J. R. Miller, *Shingwauk's Vision: A History of Native Residential Schools* (Toronto: University of Toronto Press, 1996), chap. 12; TRC, *They Came for the Children* (Winnipeg, Can.: Truth and Reconciliation Commission of Canada, 2012), 50.

12. Celia Haig-Brown, *Resistance and Renewal: Surviving the Indian Residential School* (Vancouver: Tillicum Library, 1988), 102.

13. Miller, *Shingwauk's Vision*, 365–68.

14. Tomson Highway, *Kiss of the Fur Queen* (Toronto: Doubleday Canada, 1998), 38. For a literary analysis of Highway see Sam McKegney, *Magic Weapons: Aboriginal Writers Remaking Community after Residential School* (Winnipeg: University of Manitoba Press, 2007).

15. See Milloy, *National Crime*, 91–92; and Suzanne Fournier and Ernie Crey, *Stolen from Our Embrace* (Vancouver: Douglas & McIntyre, 1997), 49. See also the 2004 report *Historic Trauma and Aboriginal Healing* from the Aboriginal Healing Foundation, AHF.ca.

16. My involvement in this project first began in 2005–6 when I accepted a faculty position in the Sociology Department at Algoma University, located in Sault Ste. Marie, just adjacent to Garden River and Batchewana First Nations. As a white scholar focusing on settler–Indigenous relations I became interested in Garden River and Batchewana's history of intercultural theater, which spanned the period from 1900 to 1968, a legacy about which I have written elsewhere

(see chap. 5 in Francis, *Creative Subversions*, Vancouver: University of British Columbia Press, 2011). In 2005 Alice Corbiere and I cofounded the Garden River Arts Committee, and from 2006 to 2011 this group worked with Anishinaabec and Cree scriptwriters and with a local white director Sue Barber, to revive and reinvent Anishinaabec theater in that region. These productions have been supported by the Garden River Band Council and provincial and federal arts councils. From 2007 to 2011 this research was funded by a Social Sciences and Humanities Research Council Strategic Grant, whose principal investigator was the Anishinaabec scholar Karl Hele, director of First People's Studies at Concordia University and a member of Garden River First Nation. I attended each of the performances and interviewed all the youth cast and sixteen audience members, including people from the local Anishinaabec communities and various white audience members who heard about the play through local media.

17. The actors who identified as non-Indigenous included a youth who was raised as white who had non-status Indigenous heritage which had been covered up in his family history, and one actor with mixed Roma and Romanian heritage. Several actors identified as gay or two-spirit.

18. While the most developed narrative in the play focused on the life story of Marguerite Stella Syrette (née Fox), from the perspective of her grandson, many other short narratives highlighted a range of traumatic stories. These included tales of child abduction by the Indian agents and the Royal Canadian Mounted Police, brutal discipline and punishment in the schools, being forbidden to speak Anishinaabemowin, the separation of siblings, child abuse and child rape, the alienation and despair of the young adults returning to their reserves, and the prevalence of alcoholism and suicide to deal with this legacy.

19. This "side trip" was organized by Joe Corbiere, one of the longtime supporters of this youth theater project from Batchewana First Nation. He drove Teddy and several other members of the team to Manitoulin Island and, owing to his many years of work as a community-based lawyer on the island, organized a tour of key sites.

20. Isaac Rendell, personal communication with the author, August 2009.

21. Tazz McCloud, personal communication with the author, August 2011.

22. Chase Neveau, personal communication with the author, August 2011.

23. See "An Ojibwe Language Word List," n.d., NativeTech.org.

24. The term "two-spirits" gained prominence in the early 1990s as an alternative to Western labels such as lesbian, gay, bisexual, or transgendered. For more information see "Who Are the Two Spirits? Q&A with Will Roscoe," n.d., WillsWorld.org. The erasure of the gender-diverse legacy within Indigenous communities is not uncommon. See K. Balsam, H. Bu, K. Fieland, J. Simoni, and K. Walters, "Culture, Trauma, and Wellness: A Comparison of Heterosexual and Lesbian, Gay, Bisexual, and Two-Spirit Native Americans," in *Cultural Diversity and Ethnic Minority Psychology, Special Issue: Lesbian, Gay, and Bisexual Racial and Ethnic Minority Individuals* 10, no. 3 (2004): 287–301.

25. Teddy Syrette, personal communication with the author, August 2011.

26. "Social Justice Report 2010," HumanRights.gov.au. References in this document include Frantz Fanon, *The Wretched of the Earth* (1963; London: Pen-

guin Classics, 2001); Paulo Freire, *Pedagogy of the Oppressed* (New York: Continuum, 2006); S. Carmichael and C. Hamilton, *Black Power* (New York: Vintage Books, 1967); and J. Miller, *Toward a New Psychology for Women* (Boston: Beacon Press, 1976).

27. Frantz Fanon, *Black Skin, White Masks*, trans. Charles Lam Markmann (New York: Grove Press, 1967).

28. "Social Justice Report 2010."

29. Orlando Figes, "Private Life in Stalin's Russia: Family Narratives, Memory, and Oral History," *History Workshop Journal* 65 (2008): 120.

30. Alice Corbiere, personal communication with the author, August 2011.

31. Mike Cachagee, personal communication with the author, August 2011.

32. Chapter 12 on Veterans in the Royal Commission on Aboriginal People, 523–76. Available at https://qspace.library.queensu.ca/bitstream/1974/6874/5/RRCAP1_combined.pdf.

33. Quoted in Gautam Premnath, "Remembering Fanon, Decolonizing Diaspora," in *Postcolonial Theory and Criticism*, ed. Laura Chrisman and Benita Parry (Cambridge, U.K.: English Association, 2000), 63.

34. Gerald Vizenor, *Manifest Manners: Postindian Warriors of Survivance* (Hanover, N.H.: Wesleyan University Press, 1994), 72–73.

35. I borrowed the phrase "storying up" from Lee Maracle, "Oratory on Oratory," in *Trans.Can.Lit*, ed. Kamboureli and Miki, 58.

36. For a description of the history and meaning of ribbon shirts see "Some History: Ribbon Work and Ribbon Shirts," March 23, 2010, BeyondBuckskin.com.

37. Here credit should go to Jeff Arbus, who trained the cast in effective strategies for post-performance discussion.

38. Joe Corbiere, personal communication with the author, August 2011.

39. Syrette, personal communication with the author, August, 2013.

40. Carol Nolan, personal communication with the author, August 2011.

41. Joe Corbiere, personal communication with the author, August 2013.

42. I witnessed these challenges by elder Anishinaabec women in the discussion following two performances.

43. Alice Corbiere, personal communication with the author, August 2011.

44. For a complicated analysis of the gendered dimension of this resistance, see Jo-Anne Fiske's fine article "Gender and the Paradox of Residential School Education in Carrier Society," in *Women of the First Nations*, ed. Christine Miller and Patricia Marie Chuchryk (Winnipeg, Can.: University of Manitoba Press, 1996), 167–82.

45. See *Corbiere v. Canada*, 1999. Available at http://ualawccsprod.srv.ualberta.ca/ccs/index.php/constitutional-issues/the-charter/equality-rights-section-15/687-corbiere-v-canada-1999.

46. Alice Corbiere, personal correspondence with the author, August 2011.

47. Among the Anishinaabec this included drumming, on the Plains it was dancing, and among those on the Pacific Coast it was the potlatch.

48. Alan Corbiere is a distant relative of Alice Corbiere and Joe Corbiere.

49. Alan Corbiere, personal correspondence with the author, May 2013.

50. Ibid..
51. Ibid.
52. Vizenor, *Manifest Manners*, 1.
53. Alan Corbiere, personal correspondence with the author, May 2013.
54. Ibid.
55. Miller, *Shingwauk's Vision*, 356.
56. "Dorothy," personal communication with the author, August 2011.
57. Sarina Merling, personal communication with the author, August 2011.

ERIC STEVEN ZIMMER

Building the Red Earth Nation: The Civilian Conservation Corps— Indian Division on the Meskwaki Settlement

"THIS TRACT OF LAND, upon which my tribe dwells," John Tataposh wrote to President Franklin Delano Roosevelt in 1938, "is communally owned by the [Meskwaki] Indians, purchased with their ancestors' own money. Therefore, we have the right to, through the right of ownership, decide how our affairs should be handled. Every member of my tribe has a right, a right of ownership of the land on which we live, to the disposal of our affairs as he sees fit."[1] Tataposh penned this letter in protest of the Meskwaki Nation's new constitution, which his community had ratified the previous November. Because he and others believed it a deviation from their rightful form of governance, Tataposh asked Roosevelt to annul the document. This request, of course, strikes a starkly political tone. But questions about land ownership and environmental control lay at its core. Indeed, when read within the context of the widespread political and environmental action that took place across Native America in the 1930s, Tataposh's letter reveals the close link between Meskwaki land and its people's vision of tribal sovereignty.

This essay examines the ways in which the members of the small Meskwaki Nation used the Civilian Conservation Corps—Indian Division (CCC—ID) to act on the political changes embedded within the Indian New Deal and improve their most valuable asset—the land they call home.[2] It exposes the ways in which a small Native community gleaned more than dollars from New Deal programs. In the CCC—ID, for example, the Meskwaki found opportunities to develop their environment and affirm their tribal sovereignty. The tribe used the CCC—ID to strengthen their cash economy as well as the natural and built environments on their land. They also worked within the Indian Division, leveraging political authority and influencing Office of Indian Affairs (OIA) decision making in environmental projects and personnel matters.[3] Until only recently, historians of Native America have tended to overlook tribal political maneuvering in the twentieth century.[4] Indeed, the Meskwaki experience offers a case study for understanding how oft-ignored federal programs afforded even small Native communities opportunities to assert themselves politically and capitalize on the national policy shifts of the 1930s.

The dramatic changes in federal Indian policy that came about in this decade—collectively known as the "Indian New Deal"—have received a great deal of scholarly attention. For generations, the federal government forcibly removed Native peoples from their homelands; engaged in duplicitous treaty making and breaking; and advocated aggressive assimilation and allotment of tribal peoples. All of this aimed to eradicate Indian economies, lifeways, and forms of governance. But the tide of U.S. Indian policy started turning in the late 1920s.[5] Rampant poverty in Indian Country spurred a federally sponsored, two-year study of reservation conditions that was published in 1928. This document, called the "Meriam Report," detailed the many systemic failures of Indian policy. The report "recommended badly needed changes in virtually every aspect of Indian policy," according to Virginia Davis, "and advocated for increased funding of Indian programs."[6] In 1933 the newly inaugurated Roosevelt appointed John Collier as Commissioner of Indian Affairs. During his twelve-year tenure at the Indian Office, Collier oversaw the implementation of Indian New Deal programs that mirrored the broader shifts toward social welfare brought on by the Roosevelt administration.[7] The core component of the Indian New Deal was the 1934 Indian Reorganization Act (IRA), which abolished allotment, emphasized tribal cultural autonomy, and offered Native communities a return to self-governance through the development of tribal constitutions. It thus marked a watershed in federal Indian policy.[8]

Scholars, though, have largely ignored programs like the CCC–ID, which had a significant impact in Indian Country. When historians mention the CCC–ID at all, they have tended only to emphasize the program's economic benefits and the professional training Native enrollees received from their work.[9] Indeed, the CCC–ID was one of the most successful programs of the Indian New Deal, insofar as it made gains toward ameliorating the Depression's effects in Native communities. Initiated in 1933, the program employed over twenty-six thousand Native Americans within only a few years. Historian Calvin Gower depicts the CCC–ID as giving "poverty-stricken Indian employees and their families a financial boost when they probably needed it most." So extensive were the program's benefits, he continues, that its end in 1942 brought along "a severe setback to the American Indian."[10] Moreover, Collier's use of various New Deal programs, including the CCC–ID, "enabled him to greatly expand the scope of federal services available to Indians."[11] But the program also had its downsides. While conservation projects gave professional training to tribal members, historians have pointed out how this ultimately led some Natives to leave their communities in search of off-reservation employment. Ironically, perhaps, this resulted in furthered assimilation and may have alienated some tribal members from their communities.[12] In a 1980 *New York Times* opinion piece, the venerated Lakota author

Vine Deloria Jr., wrote wryly that, if nothing else, CCC–ID paychecks allowed his people to "climb from absolute depravation to mere poverty."¹³

No matter one's read on the economic benefits of the CCC–ID, an emphasis on financial relief has led many historians to overlook Native attempts to work within the Indian New Deal and enhance both their physical environment and their claims to local control over tribal affairs. Most historians of the CCC–ID recognize that the bulk of Indian conservation focused on environmental work, such as "erosion control, forestation, and range management."¹⁴ Some have also shown that "Indians were given a role in determining how conservation programs were to be operated" in their communities.¹⁵ Jennifer McLerran even argues that Collier wanted the CCC–ID to be the "Indians' own endeavor" and intended for tribal members' active involvement in the establishment and execution of Indian Division projects.¹⁶ Yet these nods toward Native participation in CCC–ID planning fail to recognize how the larger politics of the Indian New Deal era—such as contestation over the IRA and power struggles with federal administrators—overlapped with efforts to improve tribal lands at the same historical moment. In the Meskwaki case, for example, the CCC–ID receives passing mention in several works, all of which note the program's mediocre and short-term cash benefits before moving on to the more frequently studied events of the 1930s, like the formation and ratification of their tribal constitution.¹⁷

Meskwaki tribal members consciously improved their land by planting trees, digging wells, laying telephone lines, and pursuing dozens of other environmental projects over the course of the decade. Throughout, they struggled to influence CCC–ID decision making by selecting project locations, approving agency plans, and at one point forcing the removal of a federal administrator who had a tense relationship with some tribal members. Examining these moments yields a window into the ways in which Depression-era programs did not merely offer Native communities some ephemeral economic opportunities. Quite the opposite, this small, midwestern Native nation blended an interest in improving their land base—an environment of forests, farmlands, and wetlands, all interspersed with members of a closely knit community—with a clear understanding of the opportunities presented by the CCC–ID and other relief programs.

Meskwaki leaders had a prescient knowledge of the political opportunities embedded within shifting Indian policies of the 1930s. They simultaneously developed their people's land and negotiated for greater control over tribal affairs during the Indian New Deal. They did so to improve the cultural and physical resources at the heart of their community and to survive the economic and political turmoil of a tumultuous decade.¹⁸ Indeed, Meskwaki leaders and CCC–ID workers made deliberate decisions about improving their land in particular ways and used the process of that development to strengthen their political position vis-à-vis the federal government. More than seventy years after the CCC–ID shut its doors, similar endeavors are still underway on Meskwaki land.

The Settlement and Sovereignty

Today, the Meskwaki Nation—officially recognized as the Sac and Fox Tribe of the Mississippi in Iowa—owns a nearly eight-thousand-acre "settlement" about three miles west of the town of Tama in central Iowa. How the tribe, whose name translates to the "People of the Red Earth," came to own that property is a story unique in the history of Native America. It begins when the federal government removed the tribe to the Indian Territory of present-day Kansas in the 1840s.[19] While some tribal members never left Iowa, a small group returned to the state in the early 1850s and eventually negotiated with the state legislature for the ability to purchase a land base on which they could rebuild their community. Removal-era treaty stipulations combined with the fact that most Natives—including the Meskwaki—were not American citizens at mid-century blocked the tribe from purchasing land outright. But through persistent negotiation with the state legislature, the tribe secured permission to remain in Iowa in 1856. The next year, they arranged for Governor James Grimes to purchase their original eighty-acre parcel with Meskwaki money and to hold it in trust for the tribe in perpetuity, as long as tribal members followed state laws and paid their property taxes. This settlement is not a reservation, as most tribal lands are called, because it was never assigned by the federal government. Rather, it was independently selected by tribal members. After 1857, the settlement remained in a state-tribal trust for four decades, as the tribe subsisted, self-governed, and used annuity payments from the federal government to continually purchase additional land.[20]

The settlement is the modern Meskwaki homeland, and in this environment tribal members rebuilt their community and prepared for future growth. Because of the resources it has long furnished and its importance to maintaining tribal sovereignty, the settlement occupies a central position in the Meskwaki economy and political culture. An oral history by Meskwaki historian Johnathan Buffalo imparts one perspective on the centrality of the settlement to tribal life. As he notes, the settlement is the physical environment the Meskwaki inhabit—where they have subsisted in one way or another for several generations—as well as the space on which they rebuilt their community after removal. But this environment also plays an important role in a Meskwaki creation story, which, according to Buffalo, is still underway:

> Eventually, [the Meskwaki] were removed to Kansas [after the Black Hawk War of 1832], which is out of our environment. Iowa was at the edge of our environment, but Kansas was a different type of environment, a different grass. Even the buffalo behaved differently, because we were used to the woodland buffalo. We were used to our . . . swamp rattlesnakes. Prairie rattlesnakes are different. So everything was different . . .
>
> Then we wanted to come home, to Iowa, our newest home. But traditionally as Meskwaki whenever we say "home," we mean east to our creation place, wherever that is. No Meskwaki knows where that is, but we'll know where it is when the time comes—that very spot. Someday we know we'll go home.
>
> [Long ago,] [w]hen our creator shot [an arrow into the sky], he shot it towards the West. Then he said, "See that arrow?" People looked at it. "Someday you will be going that way." People said, "No, this is home, by the sea." He said, "No, someday you will have to go." Then he said, "You will be able to come back someday, you will be back." That is what we are doing. We are in the process of going back home. Iowa has been our home for more than a hundred years, longer than [our people were in other midwestern states like] Wisconsin. Iowa has become our home because Iowa has become a place of safety . . . We started coming home in the 1850s and purchased land in 1857. We have been there since, in our home, in our settlement.[21]

As Buffalo notes, the settlement forms the bedrock of the modern Meskwaki community and was the key to their political and economic survival through some of the most onerous years of American colonialism. By remaking Iowa as their chosen, if temporary, homeland in 1857, Meskwaki people reinforced their ability to harness and engage the physical environment. They did so not only to survive off its flora and fauna, but because the land created a buffer between the Meskwaki and non-Meskwaki worlds.[22] In the CCC–ID years, they would take that project even further, utilizing a unique administrative and political opportunity to manage the resources endemic to their environment.

Throughout the late nineteenth century, the settlement remained the physical space on which tribal members hunted, farmed, and subsisted. But by 1900 its legal status had shifted dramatically from the relatively autonomous state/tribal trust the Meskwaki had enjoyed in the latter half of the preceding century. Bowing to pressure by assimilationist whites, the Iowa state legislature transferred jurisdiction over the tribe and its lands to the federal government in 1896.[23] Although it took more than a decade before this jurisdictional transfer fully took place, the Meskwaki increasingly found themselves under the political control of an oppressive and manipulative Indian Office.[24] Over the next several decades, the tribe struggled to retain control over tribal affairs and was all but subsumed under the weight of federal authority.[25]

Within this changing political landscape, Meskwaki men and women also faced pressures to assimilate into the mainstream of American culture and economy. Their settlement ownership protected the tribe from the ravages of the allotment program, which aimed to turn American Indians into yeomen farmers. Initiated by the 1887 Dawes Act, allotment resulted in a net loss of over eighty million acres of Native land nationwide by 1934. Meskwaki tribal members, however, still transitioned to the new technological, economic, and social practices brought on by their increasing contact with outside communities in the early twentieth century.[26] Like members of other Native nations, the Meskwaki sought ways to selectively participate in new industries by utilizing the natural resources at their disposal. Larry Nesper and James H. Schlender have demonstrated how, during this same period, Anishinaabeg (Ojibwe) peoples in Wisconsin used their most valuable environmental resource—walleye—by offering guide services to white fishermen as a "creative response" to the pressures of economic assimilation.[27] Similarly, many Meskwaki began blending day labor on local farms with their hunting and gardening practices to earn cash while supplementing their subsistence needs.[28] But periodic flooding plagued the settlement lowlands, making it difficult to maximize the land's potential and occasionally pushing residents, many of whom lived near the water's edge, away from their homes when the Iowa River, as it did every year or so, crested its banks.

The Great Depression, the CCC, and the Indian Division

The Indian Division was a discrete part of the broader Civilian Conservation Corps (CCC), one of several federal programs established during the first months of the New Deal. As with other federal ventures, the Roosevelt administration designed the CCC to provide economic relief to an American economy decimated by the Great Depression. Roosevelt and his team launched the program in 1933, when the national unemployment rate hovered around 25 percent. By the end of its tenure in 1942, the CCC had employed some 2.5 million men nationwide. Along with other programs, the CCC sought to improve the country's infrastructure and natural resources by building hospitals, roads, and bridges; erecting dams; planting trees; and fighting erosion.[29] At the same time, the CCC was supposed to improve the men themselves. Policymakers believed that by conducting manual labor in military-like camps, CCC enrollees would learn how to become productive citizens and family men. Historian Margot Canaday details how the CCC focused specifically on administering workers under a strict moral code. This would, administrators believed, shape laborers into idealized American breadwinners who could provide for heteronormative families.[30] Neil M. Maher, moreover, argues that within this milieu of sweat and conservation the CCC "link[ed] landscape, labor, and politics in new ways during the New Deal."[31]

Indeed, the CCC–ID appeared within a particularly contentious era in Meskwaki political history. As Collier launched the Indian New Deal, intense debates over the meanings and form of Meskwaki governance dominated the tribal political discourse. When the OIA presented the IRA in 1934, tribal members struggled to determine whether their best chance for stronger tribal sovereignty lay within their customary chief/council system or within a new order undergirded by a written constitution. In November 1937 the tribe ratified its constitution in a close election, formally reorganizing the tribal government into a democratically elected council that governed through written bylaws. This document remains in effect today but has been controversial for generations.[32] In addition to the IRA debates, tribal members also engaged local and federal governments over issues surrounding the schooling of Meskwaki children in the 1930s. In 1934 the federal government attempted to close two settlement day schools and transport Meskwaki students to the nearby town of Montour. Tribal members opposed this action, especially after hearing reports of unfair treatment by white teachers and students. Meskwaki families organized a "Student–Parents Association" and argued that the decision to bus their children off the settlement infringed on tribal sovereignty because it had been made "without consulting the tribe." Eventually, tribal members negotiated a solution in which Meskwaki children would attend a new day school through eighth grade, and older students would attend a high school much closer to the settlement.[33]

Even in this tempestuous political environment, the Great Depression probably sat at the forefront of most Meskwaki minds. The Depression's effect on the settlement was somewhat paradoxical: On one hand, Meskwaki families continued to subsist as they had for generations, satisfying basic needs by hunting and farming. In this sense, as historian Richard Frank Brown writes, even before the Depression—the era in which the Meriam Report documented rampant poverty across Native America—Meskwaki tribal members "were poor," by white standards, but "experienced no actual destitution."[34] But on the other hand the Depression wiped out the local cash economy, stripping tribal members of any opportunities to hold jobs as farm hands, day laborers, or any of the other roles they frequently filled in surrounding communities.[35] Meskwaki families lost what little cash and opportunities they previously had, and the shock of the Depression inflicted further damage on the tribe's most vulnerable members. During the harsh winter of 1930, for example, tribal members contacted several charities in Des Moines for support.[36]

The CCC–ID may have been, as Gower writes, "the first effort to bring material aid" to Depression-ridden Native communities, but it certainly was not the only one.[37] Responding to the plummeting national economy, the Roosevelt administration dumped huge amounts of money into relief and recovery programs. Historian Jason Scott Smith estimates that between 1933 and 1939, a full two-thirds of such spending went to public works programs like the CCC.[38] In Iowa alone, thirty-six CCC camps (not including the Indian Division), a variety of Works Progress Administration (WPA) projects, and other relief programs supported state citizens.[39] Although the Indian Division served fewer people, its impact was significant: at the end of its first season, the CCC—ID employed fifteen thousand Native workers nationwide, and administrators estimated that more than one hundred thousand family members of Indian program employees benefited from the projects. By the time the CCC—ID ceased operations in 1942, "around 77,000 Indians had obtained work in the Indian division" across the United States. Their income improved the quality of life, however marginally, for hundreds of thousands of their relatives and community members.[40]

The Meskwaki program was comparatively small. The OIA budgeted only enough funding for twenty Meskwaki men during the program's inaugural 1933 season, the lowest of any of the eighteen states receiving program funding that year.[41] The Meskwaki CCC—ID grew steadily from there. By winter 1933 the number of enrollees rose to forty-two, and by early 1934 sixty-one Meskwaki men worked on a variety of conservation projects, though administrators staggered their employment and allowed men time to tend their personal crops.[42]

On the Meskwaki settlement, other programs also aided tribal members. The Indian Relief and Rehabilitation Program, "the first major federally funded program specifically aimed at improving housing conditions for reservation Indians," lent funding to several Meskwaki families, like those of George Buffalo and Frank Eagle, who used federal money to repair their homes in 1937.[43] Six elderly tribal members also received direct payments from the newly founded Old Age Assistance program, and by 1936, forty-three of the ninety-one families on the settlement received some form of relief.[44] While CCC—ID work was only open to Native American men, Meskwaki women also participated in government-funded relief programs. Meskwaki women canned over twelve thousand quarts of vegetables as part of a WPA project in 1941 alone.[45] Because the settlement was (and remains) collectively owned, administrators considered it one large, privately owned farm for the purposes of the Agricultural Adjustment Act (AAA), a New Deal program that controlled farm production and prices by offering cash payments to farmers to control their planting. This decision capped AAA payments to the tribe at about $1,000 annually. In 1939 several Meskwaki discovered that they could register their farming plots under individual AAA accounts, thereby increasing the total agricultural aid paid to tribal members to about $2,500.⁴⁶

Beyond these federal programs, Meskwaki tribal members also bought and butchered hogs for food and manufactured maple syrup from settlement trees—a long-standing custom in their community—which they traded to regional tribes for a variety of foods and other goods.⁴⁷ In these and other ways, New Deal programs and other opportunities certainly benefited the settlement's residents. But "even with the assistance of the Indian New Deal," as historian Judith Daubenmier writes, "Meskwaki families only had about $500 a year to live on in the mid-1930s, less than a quarter of the $2,085 average gross income for white Iowa farm families."⁴⁸

Meskwaki employees lived and worked on the settlement throughout the CCC–ID program. Administrators designed the regular CCC "around a residential camp program [in which] CCC camps were intended almost exclusively for unmarried men" between seventeen and twenty-eight years of age. Indian Division programs, in comparison, tended to include adult men of any age, as long as enrollees could pass physical examinations.⁴⁹ CCC–ID camp structures were less rigid and followed three basic models. The first, called "boarding camps," most closely "resembled the installations of the regular CCC." At these camps, tribal members lived away from home in on-site bunkhouses and received pay as well as room and board for the days they worked. In "married camps," "entire Indian families . . . lived in either tents or shacks near their work," and tribal members received a meager stipend for food and

FIGURE 1. Meskwaki CCC–ID employee Amos Morgan collects maple syrup from settlement trees. Tribal members used a variety of strategies—including paid work in federal programs and long-held subsistence practices like that shown here—to overcome the Great Depression's hardships. Photograph courtesy of the Meskwaki Historic Preservation Department.

shelter in addition to their monthly salary. The Meskwaki fit into the third and rarest camp type. They lived at home and met each morning at a designated location, received their daily work assignments, and drove to their project site.[50] Meskwaki enrollees received sixty cents per working day in lieu of room and board in addition to their salary. Wages averaged around thirty dollars per month for most employees, the same amount paid to regular Corps enrollees.[51]

When the Indian Division work started in July 1933, the Meskwaki settlement encompassed over three thousand acres, and a wide variety of projects altered that landscape over the course of the decade.[52] Only two stands of pine trees and the "stonehouse," a limestone facility constructed adjacent to Highway 30 in 1941, are widely remembered today.[53] Yet the sheer number of projects and their overall effect on the settlement's natural and built environments far outstretch modern memories. One map illustrating the locations of CCC–ID developments reveals that by April 1935—merely two years into the program—over seventy projects ranging from trail development to dam construction and the building or repair of fences along the settlement's perimeter had been completed. Another map points out nearly ninety new tasks planned for the remainder of the 1935 work season. Each of these maps, moreover, indicates that virtually every portion of the settlement was altered in some way during the CCC–ID years.[54]

The Indian Division thus offered an opportunity for tribal members to build up their environment—the tribe's single most important physical resource in terms of both economic vitality and political leverage—in important ways. Analyzing the successes and failures of the New Deal as a whole, historian David M. Kennedy argues that "decidedly frenzied and much ballyhooed" New Deal programs—like the CCC—"were short lived and ultimately inconsequential."[55] But from an environmental perspective, this is far from accurate. Conservation projects had a significant impact on the physical infrastructure of local communities. For the Meskwaki, the CCC–ID offered the organizational, educational, technological, and financial means to improve their environment. By curbing the problems associated with annual erosion and flooding and by developing their roads and buildings, tribal members hoped to enrich their settlement and thereby position their community for more effective transportation, communication, and resource management in coming decades.

Nationwide, CCC–ID projects focused on "some phase of forestation, range development, or soil erosion control," and the Meskwaki settlement fit this mold.[56] According to the final report completed at the program's end in 1942, Meskwaki environmental work fit into several major categories: From 1933 to 1935, tribal members tended 565 acres of hardwood forest, which

FIGURE 2. Assembled from two archival maps illustrating the locations of CCC—ID work in 1935, this map shows the high density of work relief projects on the Meskwaki settlement. (Dots outside the settlement boundaries refer to perimeter fence construction and repair.) Tribal employees altered large portions of the settlement's natural and built environments that year, revealing the extensive infrastructural improvements of the CCC—ID era. While the map appears in black and white here, a color-coded version can be found in the article available online in JSTOR. The color coding reveals the various types of Indian Division projects that occurred on Meskwaki land. Map by the author, 2014.

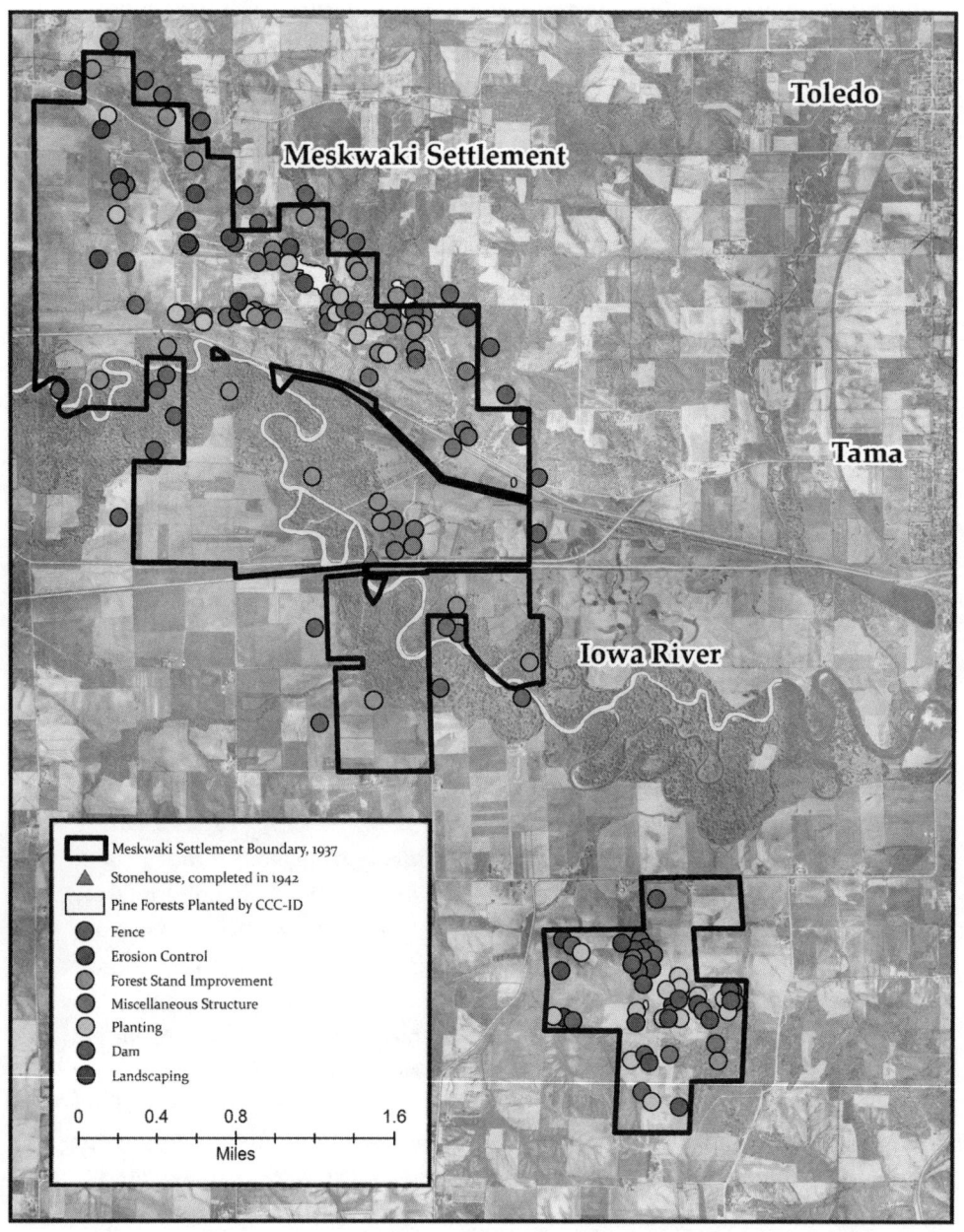

covered about a fifth of the settlement's total area, pruning and shaping live trees while slashing and burning dead and diseased ones. CCC—ID workers produced over four million board feet of lumber, along with an additional four million board feet of cordwood before 1942, and also continued a timber production project begun in 1921. General reforestation occupied much of the tribe's enterprise, and Meskwaki enrollees planted 116.4 acres of pine, black ash, and miscellaneous hardwood trees during the program's ten years—some twenty-eight thousand saplings in 1939 alone. Planting contributed to the dozens of erosion-control projects designed to speed up the drainage process when the Iowa River, which bisects the settlement, flooded farmlands or encroached on residential areas. When waters pooled beyond the river's banks, tribal members hitched horses to wooden planks and pushed water into the ditches. Meskwaki laborers also developed three natural springs, dug seven wells, built drainage ditches, and revegetated the pastureland along the hundred-acre area known as Whiskey Bottom in the central portion of the settlement.[57]

Tribal members also enhanced the settlement's built environment. In 1933 they laid 1.5 miles of telephone line connecting an agency office to two settlement day schools. Meskwaki men reconditioned the settlement's perimeter fence in 1935 and again in 1942 and laid a 1.5-mile-long road connecting the central portion of the settlement to a farm and timber stand on its southern edge. Landscaping projects conducted in conjunction with the WPA developed the area around one of the day schools, as well as the Indian Office headquarters and sanatorium located off-settlement in the nearby town of Toledo. Tribal laborers also improved the settlement's recreational areas. In 1935 they constructed toilets, fireplaces, tables, benches, and a baseball diamond on the powwow grounds where the tribe held its annual festival each August, along with a storage facility built a few years later.[58]

The early twentieth century was a tumultuous time for the members of the Meskwaki Nation, characterized by disruptions of their political, social, and economic lives. As the Great Depression bore down on them, tribal members turned to their own ingenuity and also sought reprieve from available federal relief programs, like the CCC—ID, for survival. But inherent to their Indian Division work was a kaleidoscopic process of environmental enhancement that reshaped almost every corner of their settlement, making it more livable, more navigable, and better able to serve their nation over the course of the decade. Regardless of whether they recognized its long-term implications, augmenting the homeland they had remade in Iowa in 1857 allowed the Meskwaki to demonstrate that they could use their settlement not only to insulate themselves from marauding policies like allotment or to produce basic subsistence—they could also harness the environmental opportunities presented by the CCC–ID, and in so doing, improve their land and secure their community's long-term infrastructural viability.

Bolstering Sovereignty

Aside from improving their shared property, members of the Meskwaki Nation also used the CCC–ID to test the promises of a return to self-governance embedded in the Indian New Deal. In his examination of CCC–ID programs in South Dakota, historian Roger Bromert tempers claims that the Indian Division offered opportunities to Native peoples to enlarge their political authority. He argues that while tribal leaders had the power "to help select projects" and "were given virtually independent action on the reservations, the Indian program had to meet most of the regular CCC regulations, and when disagreements arose, the white CCC rules prevailed."[59] On the Meskwaki settlement this was sometimes the case. Twice, OIA administrators held the badly needed relief work hostage when tribal members behaved in ways the administrators deemed inappropriate. In September 1934 the Indian Office temporarily laid off nine workers for drinking alcohol, and briefly suspended the entire program in the spring of 1935 when a few men quarreled with a program supervisor.[60]

Yet the Meskwaki tribal council held sway over many aspects of their land use, as well as various CCC–ID decisions. The tribal council had many functions, but in the context of the CCC–ID it selected project locations and approved program plans. Before the ratification of the tribal constitution in 1937, a group of elders had appointed themselves to an acting council. This body exerted influence over the CCC–ID program, for example, by delaying several projects in April 1935 as its members discussed the best locations for timber planting.[61] The constitutionally backed tribal council continued this practice upon its inauguration in 1938 and also set about evaluating and directing CCC–ID work. In September of that year, the council members requested surveys of various tracts of land so they could determine which sections to lease to outsiders and which to improve with available Indian Division work.[62] For several decades, the tribe had leased various portions of its land to nearby farmers and used the rental fees to pay their property taxes.[63] The council spent six weeks negotiating a higher rental fee for one such lease.[64] Similarly, in 1941 it selected the location for a roadside park and the "stonehouse" along Highway 30, intended as a site from which tribal members could sell crafts to passing tourists. The council authorized an agreement with the U.S. government for its construction and negotiated with tribal member Peter Morgan to use his portion of the settlement for the project.[65] The body also annually reviewed and agreed to all the CCC–ID

FIGURE 3. Several Meskwaki women occupy the roadside park built outside the Meskwaki stonehouse (visible at rear left) in this photograph from the mid-twentieth century. Constructed along Highway 30 between 1941 and 1942, this plaza was intended for community gatherings and, as the sign at left shows, as a base from which tribal members could sell arts and crafts to passersby. Photograph courtesy of the Meskwaki Historic Preservation Department.

work and was grateful for the opportunities it offered. As council president Edward Davenport—who also served as the head of the CCC—ID Safety Board—wrote in 1941, the tribe "express[ed] our most sincere appreciation" to the OIA and CCC for the "training and education in forestry, conservation, construction and surveying, as well as the many improvements made possible on our tribal property."[66]

Meskwaki need for, and appreciation of, CCC—ID employment did not dissuade the workers from expressing dissatisfaction when it arose. It was a standard CCC practice to save large percentages of workers' wages at each monthly pay period, providing only partial payment up front and holding the rest for distribution to employees' families. On the settlement, program administrators, following CCC protocols, paid Meskwaki workers only

60 percent of their wages, "placing [the remaining 40 percent] to his credit for future use." Tribal members disagreed with this policy and in October 1933 agitated to receive their full installment each month.[67] This small victory shows how tribal members held the power to push the Indian Office into altering its policies to meet tribal demands, and in this case, to give Meskwaki workers control over their wages.

But perhaps the most significant point of contention between tribal members and Indian Division administrators—and certainly the one with the greatest impact over the long term—involved the dismissal of Fred Anderson, the forester who oversaw much of the settlement work. Originally stationed at an OIA central office in Minneapolis, Anderson arrived at the settlement in May 1934 and replaced the outgoing forester.[68] By February 1935 Sam Slick and Young Bear, both members of the self-appointed tribal council, met with the Indian Office superintendent Ira D. Nelson to discuss Anderson's position and an altercation between him and a tribal member. The precise details of this incident remain murky, but it is clear that Frank Mitchell, a Meskwaki, engaged Anderson in a heated exchange. Their disagreement proved severe enough for Nelson to suspend all relief work until the tribal "council would guarantee no more disturbances" from Meskwaki workers.[69] Nelson blamed the disruption on two causes. First, he suspected that certain tribal members were jealous of others over the pay that two workers, Albert Davenport and Oscar Kapayou, received in their capacities as project foremen. These "straw bosses," as they were called, received significantly higher pay than did the average workers, earning forty-five and thirty-six dollars per month respectively.[70] Nelson also suspected that political vitriol over the pending IRA election had spilled over into CCC–ID work, as both of the foremen were politically opposed to members of the self-appointed council. When several Meskwaki requested that Davenport, Kapayou, and Anderson be relieved of their duties, Nelson assumed that the group was motivated by either financial or political greed.[71]

The full details of this incident are lost to history. It is possible, as Nelson suggested, that some level of personal or pecuniary rivalry drove the removal petition. Its authors, however, cited Anderson's "fail[ure] to cooperate with the acting tribal council" as the chief cause of their discontent, revealing that they viewed some of his managerial decisions as encroachments into tribal matters. Nelson defended Anderson and maintained that, as forester, Anderson had considered the council's input when making decisions. "I feel," Nelson wrote to Collier, "that this petition has been fostered by those who are jealous of the sub-foreman and assistant leaders."[72] Their motives aside, the fact remains that the acting council and their fellow petitioners held sufficient influence within the Indian Office and the CCC–ID's administrative system as to effect an immediate resolution. To get relief work up and running again, Slick and Young Bear agreed to hold a public meeting to discuss the issue and discourage further CCC–ID disruptions. Nelson initially argued that he would not make personnel changes on demand and continued defending Anderson to the Indian Office administrators in Washington, D.C. He also focused the blame on political rivalries within the tribe. Nonetheless, the Meskwaki won out, and Anderson was transferred to Fort Yates, North Dakota, the following month.[73]

Anderson's removal from the settlement may have been a victory for Meskwaki home rule in the short term, but its consequences resounded for the duration of the tribe's Indian Division projects. After he left, the Meskwaki CCC–ID program did not receive another forester until 1941. Instead, R. W. Hellwig, an OIA employee based in Minnesota, oversaw projects from a distance. He and other officials made occasional visits to the settlement, reviewing progress and directing operations.[74] Combined with budget cuts that hampered CCC–ID programs nationwide in 1937, the lack of an on-site forester made it difficult to develop and administer new projects. This resulted in a severe curtailment of the amount of work available to Meskwaki residents.[75] Despite the Meskwaki council's continued demonstrations of their interest in and concern for environmental projects, CCC–ID administrators did not consider any tribal members qualified to oversee the work on their own land. Accordingly, with "no one capable of preparing" program plans, as one official wrote, projects were staffed on a case-by-case basis through the end of the 1930s. They were canceled entirely for half of the fiscal year in 1941, because the "district office at Minneapolis, Minnesota ha[d] been unable to supply foremen to supervise the work on projects which ha[d] already been approved."[76] Adding to the hardship, the scale-back cut monthly salaries to fifteen dollars in March 1939, and the OIA cancelled subsistence payments.[77]

By the time the OIA hired R. T. Mitchell as junior engineer to oversee CCC–ID work late in 1941, the tribe had undergone seven long years of progressively sporadic work relief.[78] Unemployment remained a challenge for the Meskwaki community throughout this time. The demand for work was so high that Indian Office administrators began rotating work schedules in various relief programs to spread wages as evenly as possible across the tribal population, while the shortage forced many tribal members to draw direct relief.[79] Though CCC–ID projects continued through this later period, they were rare. This further weakened the struggling tribal economy. This reality underscores an important lesson of the Meskwaki CCC–ID experience. Even as the Indian Division programs offered increased local control to the tribe, consequences born from their decision to remove Anderson would reverberate through the remainder of the Great Depression.

Connecting Past and Present in Native Environmental History

On May 16, 1941, Meskwaki elders John Tataposh, Young Bear, Jim Poweshiek, and Peter Morgan laid the cornerstone for the new stonehouse to be constructed along Highway 30. The day's celebrations included a parade through the towns of Tama and Toledo, as well as a feed and ceremony at the project site, music performed by tribal members Bill Leaf and John Buffalo, and a small powwow.[80] Planning for the project began the previous fall, as tribal members envisioned a more permanent facility for the sale of their wares to passing tourists along the busy route. The plan included the development of a residential park, replete with the thirty-by-sixty-foot stonehouse, modeled after a similar CCC rock shelter built in Portage, Wisconsin, and a well for drinking water, each erected from limestone imported from a WPA quarry in nearby Legrand. The area included spaces for visitor parking, as well as tables, benches, toilets, and outdoor fireplaces.[81] Such a large project boosted the number of available work positions from ten to thirty-five, bringing enrollment to levels not seen for months.[82] Originally slated for completion by mid-summer, rainy weather, a lack of skilled stonemasons, and the need for laborers to tend to their crops delayed the project's completion until the following spring.[83]

But prior to that time and, indeed, even before the attack on Pearl Harbor drew the United States into World War II, program administrators foresaw the closing of Indian Division operations on the Meskwaki settlement.[84] As the United States entered the war, many Meskwaki men enlisted in the military.[85] According to one edition of *Indians at Work*—a magazine that chronicled Native emergency conservation work nationwide, published by the OIA until 1945—at least two young Meskwaki women, Ada Old Bear and Marie Jefferson, "turned from the making of beadwork to inspecting ammunition at the Des Moines ordinance plant" in support of the war effort.[86] As the conflict ramped up, CCC programs across the nation wound down, and operations ceased on the settlement in July 1942.[87]

The stonehouse endures as the literal and figurative capstone of the Indian Division projects on the Meskwaki settlement. Over seventy years have passed since tribal members laid its cornerstone, and like the memory of the CCC–ID itself, overgrowth has obstructed much of the structure from sight. Over the generations, as current Meskwaki economic development director Larry Lasley writes, "from 'Trading Post' to 'Community Center' to 'Recreational Building' to 'Boxing Gym' . . . the Stonehouse [did] it all for about 50 years before it was completely abandoned" following a fire some three decades ago.[88] Today, a few tribal members have discussed the possibility of placing the structure on the National Register of Historic Places or finding a

FIGURE 4. (From left) John Tataposh, Peter Morgan, and James Poweshiek attended a brick-laying ceremony at the Meskwaki stonehouse in May 1941. The event celebrated the construction of the building and roadside park, which tribal members hoped would bolster the tribal economy. The project was—and is—emblematic of the changes the CCC–ID made to the settlement's natural and built environments. Photograph courtesy of the Meskwaki Historic Preservation Department.

new use for it. Whether functional or interpretive, a rehabilitated stonehouse would stand as a monument to a transformative era for the Meskwaki Nation.

A coterie of scholars recently wrote that "for Native American cultures, land is a hallmark of identity, a barometer of community integrity, and a resource for ongoing cultural and socioeconomic recovery."[89] The Meskwaki settlement was all of these things during the New Deal, and improving the tribal land base through CCC–ID programs became a way to tap into all these notions at once. The CCC–ID, of course, lessened the hardship of the Great Depression. Many of these results reflect the themes outlined in previous scholarship. According to Meskwaki elder Donald Wanatee, who as a child delivered lunch and water to CCC–ID workers on the settlement, the Indian Division was the first opportunity many tribal members had to earn a regular wage for their labor. After gaining vocational skills, he continues, some tribal members would get a job with the railroad or go to nearby towns and stay there.[90] Yet many remained on the settlement, and the aftereffects of the Indian Division extended far beyond tribal members' pocket books.

FIGURE 5. The foundation and walls of the stonehouse, completed by the CCC—ID in early 1942, remain strong. The building served a variety of purposes before being gutted by a fire in the late 1970s or early 1980s. The roof has since collapsed and trees obscure it from sight. The Meskwaki economic development office is currently considering plans to rehabilitate and preserve this historic building. Photograph courtesy of Suzanne Buffalo, 2014.

The experience of the Meskwaki work group illuminates a few of the ways a small American Indian tribe melded their appreciation for their land with the drive to reaffirm control over local affairs within the rapidly changing policies of the Indian New Deal. The Meskwaki Nation combined a very real "knowledge of their functional environment" with a series of opportunities to improve their resources and bolster their sovereignty.[91] But the Meskwaki are only one of 566 federally recognized tribes today. Dozens of these nations participated in the CCC—ID and similar Depression-era relief programs. Although the nuanced debates over the relationship between Native peoples and their environments lies beyond the scope of this essay, the Meskwaki CCC—ID experience paves new avenues for research and discussion toward those ends. Rethinking the connections between environment and sovereign strategizing in the twentieth century, for instance, can strengthen scholarly understandings of the historical relationship between American Indians and their environments. Such work can add to the robust literature on Native environmental activism while breaking from superficial tropes that have painted tribal members as either simplistically or illegitimately connected to nature.

Entwining studies of twentieth-century Native political and environmental history also offers a metric by which modern Native nations might measure and improve contemporary plans to harness their natural resources for their communities' sake. The Meskwaki natural resources office now raises a small herd of about twenty bison on the settlement's southern edge. Though the tribe maintains these animals for primarily cultural purposes, it periodically distributes buffalo meat to settlement families.[92] In a another endeavor—and one strikingly similar to their navigation of the CCC–ID—the tribe partners with federal AmeriCorps volunteers in the Meskwaki Food Sovereignty Initiative (MFSI), a community gardening project which seeks to "provide those conditions and resources, on a continual basis, that allow the Meskwaki to survive as a viable people and culture."[93] Seeing this movement as one incarnation in a longer pattern of Meskwaki environmental maneuvering might provide lessons that MFSI organizers can use to improve the tribe's physical and political yields. By situating projects like the bison program and the MFSI within the context of their CCC–ID experience, tribal leaders could begin to see that such environmental projects often start with a specific set of goals but can evolve into mediums through which far more diverse feats may be achieved.

The CCC–ID started as an economic relief measure and ultimately gave short-term employment to a total of 112 Meskwaki men between 1933 and 1942.[94] But by the time settlement operations shut down, the program offered far more than just a few paychecks. When laid over the sweeping changes to Native America that occurred in the 1930s, one sees that as the Meskwaki people laid the legal framework for their Red Earth Nation, the Indian Division became a site within which the tribe achieved a series of seemingly small but undoubtedly significant political victories.

Moreover, the CCC–ID allowed the Meskwaki to make the best of their land and political position while they waited, as Johnathan Buffalo says they still do, to take the next step in their collective journey. After all, their resources and future were—and are—at stake. Or, put more simply by a Meskwaki elder to an Indian Office official in 1935, "We own our own property and we got our own resources [and] our money [is] invested in our own land."[95]

ERIC STEVEN ZIMMER is a PhD candidate in history at the University of Iowa.

Notes

The author presented versions of this work at the American Indian Studies Association annual meeting and in lectures at the State Historical Society of Iowa and the Meskwaki Tribal Library and Museum in 2014. He would like to thank the participants in these talks and the anonymous reviewers at *NAIS* for their substantive feedback, as well as Jacki Thompson Rand, R. Tyler Priest, Mary Bennett, Donald Wanatee, Johnathan and Suzanne Buffalo, Mary Young Bear, the staff at the National Archives and Records Administration in Chicago, Joshua Sales, Sam Hurst, Robert Wellman Campbell, Paul Mokrzycki, Allison Wells, and Samantha Zimmer for their help reading, commenting on, or otherwise assisting in the research and writing of this essay.

1. John Tataposh to Franklin Delano Roosevelt, February 2, 1938, IRA folder, Meskwaki Historic Preservation Department and Museum, Tama, Iowa (hereafter MHPDM). The name "Tataposh" also appears as "Tatoposh" and "Tatapache" in source materials.

2. See Calvin W. Gower, "The CCC Indian Division: Aid for Depressed Americans, 1933–1942," *Minnesota History* 43 (Spring 1972): 3; Roger Bromert, "The Sioux and the Indian–CCC," *South Dakota History* 8 (Fall 1978): 340–56. This essay uses the preferred tribal spelling, "Meskwaki," throughout.

3. The Office of Indian Affairs became the Bureau of Indian Affairs in 1947. This essay uses "OIA" and the more colloquial "Indian Office" when referring to the agency throughout.

4. See, for example, Kevin Bruyneel, *The Third Space of Sovereignty: The Postcolonial Politics of U.S. Indigenous Relations* (Minneapolis: University of Minnesota Press, 2007); Daniel M. Cobb and Loretta Fowler, eds., *Beyond Red Power: American Indian Politics and Activism since 1900* (Santa Fe, N.M.: School for Advanced Research, 2007).

5. The histories of nineteenth-century Indian removal, treaty law, and assimilation and allotment are well-known. See Stuart Banner, *How the Indians Lost Their Land: Law and Power on the Frontier* (Cambridge, Mass.: Harvard University Press, 2008); Sidney L. Harring, *Crow Dog's Case: American Indian Sovereignty, Tribal Law, and United States Law in the Nineteenth Century* (New York: Cambridge University Press, 1994); Frederick E. Hoxie, *A Final Promise: The Campaign to Assimilate the Indians, 1880–1920* (New York: Cambridge University Press, 1989); Walter Echo-Hawk, *In the Courts of the Conqueror: The 10 Worst Indian Law Cases Ever Decided* (Golden, Colo.: Fulcrum, 2010).

6. Virginia Davis, "A Discovery of Sorts: Reexamining the Origins of the Federal Indian Housing Obligation," *Harvard Blackletter Law Journal* 18 (2002): 225. The Meriam Report was officially titled *The Problem of Indian Administration: Report of a Survey Made at the Request of Honorable Hubert Work, Secretary of the Interior, and Submitted to Him, February 21, 1928* (Baltimore: Johns Hopkins University Press, 1928).

7. Mindy J. Morgan, "Constructions and Contestations of the Authoritative Voice: Native American Communities and the Federal Writer's Project, 1935–1941," *American Indian Quarterly* (hereafter *AIQ*) 29 (Winter–Spring 2005): 57.

See also Kenneth R. Philp, *John Collier's Crusade for Indian Reform, 1920–1954* (Tucson: University of Arizona Press, 1977), 113–34; Harry A. Kersey Jr., *The Florida Seminoles and the New Deal, 1933–1942* (Boca Raton: Florida Atlantic University Press, 1989), xi–xiii.

8. Collier's personal ideology and intentions, as well as the long-term effects of the Indian Reorganization Act, are hotly debated by scholars. See, for example, Vine Deloria Jr. and Clifford M. Lytle, *The Nations Within: The Past and Future of American Indian Sovereignty* (Austin: University of Texas Press, 1984); Akim D. Reinhardt, "A Crude Replacement: The Indian New Deal, Indirect Colonialism, and Pine Ridge Reservation," *Journal of Colonialism and Colonial History* 6 (2005); Graham D. Taylor, *The New Deal and American Indian Tribalism: The Administration of the Indian Reorganization Act, 1934–1945* (Lincoln: University of Nebraska Press, 1980); Felix S. Cohen, *On the Drafting of Tribal Constitutions*, ed. David E. Wilkins (Norman: University of Oklahoma Press, 2007), xi–xxxii; Elmer R. Rusco, *A Fateful Time: The Background and Legislative History of the Indian Reorganization Act* (Reno: University of Nevada Press, 2000); Wilcomb E. Washburn, "A Fifty-Year Perspective on the Indian Reorganization Act," *American Anthropologist*, 86 (June 1984): 279–89.

9. As this article went to press, Mindy J. Morgan released an excellent essay on Native Americans during the New Deal, which includes a discussion on CCC–ID work. See Mindy J. Morgan, "'Working' from the Margins: Documenting American Indian Participation in the New Deal Era," in *Why You Can't Teach United States History without American Indians*, ed. Susan Sleeper-Smith, Juliana Barr, Jean M. O'Brien, Nancy Shoemaker, and Scott Manning Stevens (Chapel Hill: University of North Carolina Press, 2015), 181–96.

10. Gower, "CCC Indian Division," 13.

11. Deloria Jr. and Lytle, *Nations Within*, 184.

12. Jennifer McLerran, *A New Deal for Native Art: Indian Arts and Federal Policy, 1933–1943* (Tucson: University of Arizona Press, 2009), 203. See also Donald L. Parman, "The Indian and the Civilian Conservation Corps," *Pacific Historical Review* 40 (February 1971): 56.

13. Deloria quoted in Michael L. Lawson, *Dammed Indians Revisited: The Continuing History of the Pick–Sloan Plan and the Missouri River Sioux* (Pierre: South Dakota State Historical Society Press, 2009), 33.

14. Morgan, "Constructions and Contestations," 58.

15. Deloria Jr. and Lytle, *Nations Within*, 62–63.

16. McLerran, *New Deal for Native Art*, 202.

17. See Judith Daubenmier, *The Meskwaki and Anthropologists: Action Anthropology Reconsidered* (Lincoln: University of Nebraska Press, 2008), 30.

18. For further reading and debates over the relationship between Native peoples and the natural world, see Winona LaDuke, *All Our Relations: Native Struggles for Land and Life* (Cambridge, Mass.: South End Press, 1999); Linda Robyn, "Indigenous Knowledge and Technology: Creating Environmental Justice in the Twenty-First Century," *AIQ* 26 (Spring 2002): 198–220; Christopher Vecsey and Robert W. Venables, eds., *American Indian Environments: Ecological Issues in Native American History* (Syracuse, N.Y.: Syracuse University

Press, 1980); Charles R. Menzies and Caroline F. Butler, "Working in the Woods: Tsimshian Resource Workers and the Forest Industry of British Columbia," *AIQ* 25 (Summer 2001): 409—30; J. Donald Hughes, *American Indian Ecology* (El Paso: Texas Western Press, 1983); Richard White, *The Roots of Dependency: Subsistence, Environment, and Social Change among the Choctaws, Pawnees, and Navajos* (Lincoln: University of Nebraska Press, 1983); John Bierhorst, *The Way of the Earth: Native America and the Environment* (New York: HarperCollins, 1994); Richard White, "Environmentalism and Indian Peoples," in *Earth, Air, Fire, Water: Humanistic Studies of the Environment*, ed. Jill Ker Conway, Kenneth Keniston, and Leo Marx (Amherst: University of Massachusetts Press, 1999), 125—44; Shepard Krech III, *The Ecological Indian: Myth and History* (New York: W. W. Norton, 1999); Paul C. Rosier, "'Modern America Desperately Needs to Listen': The Emerging Indian in an Age of Environmental Crisis," *Journal of American History* 100 (December 2013): 711—35; William Cronon and Richard White, "Indians in the Land," *American Heritage* 37 (1986), AmericanHeritage.com; David Rich Lewis, "Native Americans and the Environment: A Survey of Twentieth-Century Issues," *AIQ* 19 (Summer 1995): 423—50.

19. On Indian removal, see Banner, *How the Indians Lost Their Land*, 256—92. On the "People of the Red Earth," see R. David Edmunds and Joseph L. Peyser, *The Fox Wars: The Mesquakie Challenge to New France* (Norman: University of Oklahoma Press, 1993), 3; and L. Edward Purcell: "The Unknown Past: Sources for History Education and the Indians of Iowa" in *The Worlds between Two Rivers: Perspectives on American Indians in Iowa*, ed. Gretchen M. Bataille, David M. Gradwohl, and Charles P. Silet (Ames: Iowa State University Press, 1978), 27.

20. Daubenmier, *Meskwaki and Anthropologists*, 31—34.

21. Johnathan Lantz Buffalo, "Oral History of the Meskwaki," in Lynn M. Alex, ed., *Wisconsin Archaeologist: From the Great Lakes to the Great Plains: Meskwaki Archaeology and Ethnohistory* 89 (January—December 2008): 5.

22. On the ways in which tribal boundaries "imposed a segregation from mainstream American society that reinforced tribal cultures and identities," see Jacki Thompson Rand, "Primary Sources: Indian Goods and the History of American Colonialism and the 19th-Century Reservation," in *Clearing a Path: Theorizing the Past in Native American Studies*, ed. Nancy Shoemaker (New York: Routledge, 2002), 136—37.

23. Daubenmier, *Meskwaki and Anthropologists*, 33.

24. Eric S. Zimmer, "Settlement Sovereignty: Land and Meskwaki Self-Governance, 1856—1937" (MA thesis, University of Iowa, 2012), 22. See also C. F. Larrabee to John Briar, July 27, 1908, Governor, Correspondence—Miscellaneous, 1902—1908, Indian Affairs; Box 3, Record Group 043, Special Collections, State Historical Society of Iowa (Des Moines) (hereafter SHSI—DM); Daubenmier, *Meskwaki and Anthropologists*, 33.

25. Donald Wanatee, "The Lion, Fleur-de-lis, the Eagle, or the Fox: A Study of Government," in *Worlds between Two Rivers*, ed. Bataille, Gradwohl, and Silet, 79. On the "confinement" of American Indian nations within the American bureaucratic and political system, see C. Joseph Genetin-Pilawa, *Crooked Paths to*

Allotment: The Fight over Federal Indian Policy after the Civil War (Chapel Hill: University of North Carolina Press, 2012), 2, 13–28.

26. Zimmer, "Settlement Sovereignty," 28–31.

27. Larry Nesper and James H. Schlender, "The Politics of Cultural Revitalization and Intertribal Resource Management: The Great Lakes Indian Fish and Wildlife Commission and the States of Wisconsin, Michigan, and Minnesota," in *Native Americans and the Environment: Perspectives on the Ecological Indian*, ed. Michael E. Harkin and David Rich Lewis (Lincoln: University of Nebraska Press, 2007), 281. For another in-depth discussion of the politics surrounding Native environmental rights, and the battles over them in the late twentieth century, see Larry Nesper, *The Walleye War: The Struggle for Ojibwe Spearfishing and Treaty Rights* (Lincoln: University of Nebraska Press, 2002).

28. Zimmer, "Settlement Sovereignty," 28–33.

29. David M. Kennedy, "What the New Deal Did," *Political Science Quarterly* 124 (2009): 252, 267; Margot Canaday, *The Straight State: Sexuality and Citizenship in Twentieth-Century America* (Princeton, N.J.: Princeton University Press, 2009), 18. Officially known as "Emergency Conservation Work," the federal government gave it the more popular moniker "Civilian Conservation Corps" in 1937. For an overview of the Civilian Conservation Corps, see also John A. Salmond, *The Civilian Conservation Corps, 1933–1942: A New Deal Case Study* (Durham, N.C.: Duke University Press, 1967).

30. Canaday, *Straight State*, 18.

31. Neil M. Maher, "A New Deal Body Politic: Landscape, Labor, and the Civilian Conservation Corps," *Environmental History* 7 (July 2002): 435.

32. On Meskwaki politics, the creation of their tribal constitution, and the IRA more generally, see Daubenmier, *Meskwaki and Anthropologists*, 37–45; Zimmer, "Settlement Sovereignty," 20–36, 44–63; and Stephen Warren, "'To Show the Public That We Were Good Indians': Origins and Meanings of the Meskwaki Powwow," *American Indian Culture and Research Journal* 33 (2009): 7–8.

33. John M. Byrd, "Educational Policies of the Federal Government toward the Sac and Fox Indians of Iowa, 1928–1937, with Resulting Changes in Indian Educational Attitude: A Study in the Process of Assimilation" (MS thesis, State University of Iowa, 1938), 23. See also Daubenmier, *Meskwaki and Anthropologists*, 35–36; Zimmer, "Settlement Sovereignty," 42–44.

34. Richard Frank Brown, "A Social History of the Mesquakie Indians, 1800–1963" (MA thesis, Iowa State University, 1964), 74.

35. Jacob Breid, "1934 Annual Report," 3, Annual Reports 051, 1931–1935, Box 113, Bureau of Indian Affairs, Sac and Fox Agency Tama, Iowa, Record Group 75, National Archives and Records Administration—Great Lakes Region (Chicago) (hereafter NARA–GLC). On other sources of Meskwaki income, and especially for a discussion on the powwow that infused much-needed cash into the tribal economy, see Warren, "To Show the Public That We Were Good Indians," 21–23.

36. Edgar R. Harlan to H. D. Bernbrock, April 30, 1932, 49C, Part 8 folder, Edgar R. Harlan Papers (hereafter ERH Papers); and H. M. Rhode, memorandum dated December 15, 1930, 49C, Part 7, ERH Papers, both in SHSI–DM.

37. Gower, "CCC Indian Division," 4.

38. Jason Scott Smith, *Building New Deal Liberalism: The Political Economy of Public Works, 1933–1956* (New York: Cambridge University Press, 2006), 1.

39. C. N. Alleger and C. A. Alleger, *Civilian Conservation Corps, Iowa District History* (Rapid City, S.D.: Johnston and Bordewyk, 1935). On WPA projects in Iowa, see Lea Rosson Delong and Gregg R. Narber, *A Catalog of New Deal Mural Projects in Iowa* (Des Moines: Iowa Humanities Board, 1982); Mary L. Meixner, "The Aims Corn Mural," *Palimpsest* 66 (1985): 14–16; Gregg R. Narber, "These Murals Were a New Deal," *Iowan* 32 (1984): 8–17; "States and Cities, Iowa," *Living New Deal*, n.d., LivingNewDeal.berkeley.edu.

40. Gower, "CCC Indian Division," 4, 12.

41. "Work for Uncle Sam Started by Tama Indians," *Tama News-Herald*, July 20, 1933; Gower, "CCC Indian Division," 5. The highest "manpower quota" allowed for a CCC–ID state was Arizona, with a budget for 5,500 workers. The next lowest after Iowa was Nevada, with eighty available positions.

42. Breid to Collier, March 8, 1934, Nelson to Collier, May 31, 1934, both Correspondence, Letters Sent, CCC–ID, April 21, 1933–December 1933 (hereafter AD 1933), Box 306, NARA–GLC. Nelson replaced Breid as the superintendent of the Tama Agency upon his retirement in early 1934.

43. Davis, "Discovery of Sorts," 228; D. E. Livesay to John Collier, February 25, 1937, and Livesay to Collier, March 17, 1937, both Indian Relief and Rehabilitation Emergency Relief Records: 1935–1937, Box 320, NARA–GLC.

44. D. C. Johnson to Harlan, June 3, 1935, 49U part 44, 1935–1937 and n.d., ERH Papers, SHSI–DM; "Indians to Get Old Age Help," *Tama News-Herald*, April 11, 1935; and Nelson to Collier, January 8, 1936, CCC–ID Correspondence, 1934–1936, Box 307, NARA–GLC.

45. Daubenmier, *Meskwaki and Anthropologists*, 30–31; and "12,000 Qts. Vegetables Canned by Indian Women," *Tama News-Herald*, October 30, 1941. Only men were allowed to participate in CCC or CCC–ID work. For an excellent analysis of the ways in which the CCC and other New Deal relief programs were designed to promote "traditional" American gender roles and, specifically, to encourage the maintenance of a nuclear family led by a heterosexual male breadwinner, see Canaday, *Straight State*, esp. 91–93, 117–25.

46. "Mesquakies Given Rights of Individuals under A.A.A. Plan," *Tama News-Herald*, April 27, 1939. On the AAA, see Briggs Depew, Price V. Fishback, and Paul W. Rhode, "New Deal or No Deal in the Cotton South: The Effect of the AAA on the Agricultural Labor Structure," *Explorations in Economic History* 50 (October 2013): 466–69.

47. "Mesquakies Make Maple Sugar for Use in Trading," *Burlington Hawkeye*, March 27, 1932.

48. Daubenmier, *Meskwaki and Anthropologists*, 31.

49. Canaday, *Straight State*, 117; Gower, "CCC Indians Division," 6.

50. Parman, "The Indian and the Civilian Conservation Corps," 45–46. See also Bromert, "The Sioux and the Indian–CCC," 345.

51. Breid to Collier, February 12, 1934; and July 3, 1933, both in AD 1933, Box 306, NARA–GLC. On salaries for regular CCC enrollees, see Canaday, *Straight State*, 118.

52. "Work for Uncle Sam Started by Tama Indians." On the size of the settlement in 1933, see Breid to Collier, May 19, 1933, AD 1933. Box 306, NARA–GLC.

53. See Bureau of Indian Affairs Midwest Regional Office, Ft. Snelling, Minnesota, in Cooperation with the Sac and Fox Tribe of the Mississippi in Iowa, "Forest Management Plan and Inventory Analysis for the Sac and Fox Tribe of Iowa," January 2009, report shared with the author by the Geographic Information Systems Office of the Meskwaki Nation (copy in the author's possession).

54. See maps of "Sac and Fox Reservation, Tama County, Iowa," in Conservation Work Program Report, April 1, 1935; and Sac and Fox Reservation, Iowa, R. W. Hellwig, Junior Forester, April 18, 1935, Box 311, both in NARA–GLC.

55. Kennedy, "What the New Deal Did," 253–54.

56. Parman, "The Indian and the Civilian Conservation Corps," 44.

57. Randolph W. Hellwig to Collier, July 13, 1942; Letter to Commissioner of Indian Affairs over Close of CCC Program at Sac and Fox Sanatorium, July 13, 1942, Box 308; Victor L. Rushfeldt to William Heritage, January 7, 1939, Correspondence, Letters Sent, 1939, Box 306, all in NARA–GLC; and Donald Wanatee (Meskwaki elder and author) in discussion with the author, June 27, 2014.

58. Hellwig to Collier, July 13, 1942; "Original Tama Indian Team Organized" and "Indian Ball Park Is Being Remodeled; To Be Ready by May 26," both *Tama News-Herald*, May 23, 1935. The annual Meskwaki Powwow was a major economic boon to the tribal economy, bringing over five thousand spectators in 1934 alone. See also "Road Maintenance at Sac and Fox Sanatorium," *Indians at Work* (hereafter *IAW*) 3 (June 15, 1936): 50; "Over 5,000 See Indian Pow Wow; Willford Speaks: Young Bear Leaves Sick Bed and Speaks on Sunday," *Tama News-Herald*, August 23, 1934; Warren, "To Show the Public We Were Good Indians," 21.

59. Bromert, "The Sioux and the Indian–CCC," 344.

60. "Weekly Group Progress Report," September 7, 1934; Fred Anderson to Collier, February 18, 1935, both in Forms 8&9 IECW, FY 1935 (hereafter IECW 1935), Box 309, NARA–GLC.

61. "Weekly Group Progress Report," April 5, 1935; and "Weekly Group Progress Report," April 26, 1935, both in IECW 1935, Box 309, NARA–GLC.

62. Nelson to William Heritage, September 29, 1938, CCC–ID Miscellaneous Correspondence, 1938–1940, Box 307, NARA–GLC.

63. Warren, "To Show the Public We Were Good Indians," 5.

64. Nelson to Gabe E. Parker, November 15, 1938, Correspondence, Letters Sent, CCC–ID 1938 (hereafter Letters 1938), Box 306, NARA–GLC.

65. "Agreement on Work Order for a Proposed Roadside Park on the Sac and Fox Reservation, Tama, Iowa," CCC–ID Project FY 1940–1941, Box 313, NARA–GLC. Two documents in this folder share this title. The first is an agreement between the tribal council and Peter Morgan, while the second is an agreement between the council and the U.S. government.

66. Nelson to D. E. Murphy, October 9, 1937, Correspondence, Letters Sent, CCC–ID 1937, Box 306, NARA–GLC.

67. Breid to Russel E. Getty, October 6, 1933, Correspondence, Letters Sent, CCC–ID April 21, 1933–December 1934 (hereafter Letters 1933–1934), Box 306, NARA–GLC.

68. Nelson to H. M. Tidwell, May 14, 1934, Letters 1933–1934, Box 306, NARA–GLC.

69. "Report, March 15, 1935" and "Report, February 15, 1935," in both Weekly Progress Reports, FY 1934–1940 and July 1941–October 1941, Box 309, NARA–GLC.

70. "Weekly Group Progress Report," October 12, 1934, IECW 1935, Box 309; and Breid to Nelson, July 3, 1933, Letters 1933–1934, Box 306, both in NARA–GLC.

71. Transcript of "Meeting 2-12-35" between Sam Slick, Young Bear, and Nelson, 749 Community Meetings: Minutes of Meetings and Related Correspondence (hereafter 749 Meetings), Box 293; and Nelson to Collier, February 23, 1935, Letters Sent, 1933–1942, Box 309, both in NARA–GLC. See also Zimmer, "Settlement Sovereignty," 41.

72. Nelson to Collier, February 23, 1935, Correspondence, Letters Sent, 1935, Box 306, NARA–GLC.

73. Transcript of "Meeting 2-12-35"; Nelson to Collier, February 23, 1935; "Report, March 15, 1935"; and "Report, February 15, 1935." See also Zimmer, "Settlement Sovereignty," 41.

74. Nelson to Collier, October 23, 1940, CCC–ID, Letters Sent, 1940, Box 306; and Heritage to Nelson, January 28, 1936, New Special Reports and Material of Unusual Importance 1935–1936, Box 307, both in NARA–GLC.

75. D. E. Murphy to Nelson, December 15, 1937; and January 17, 1936, CCC–ID Correspondence, 1933–1939, Box 307, NARA–GLC. On CCC–ID budget cuts more generally, see Parman, "The Indian and the Civilian Conservation Corps," 51–52.

76. Nelson to Norman W. Sherer, February 11, 1939, Correspondence, Letters Sent, CCC–ID 1939 (hereafter Letters 1939); and Nelson to Heritage, November 17, 1938, Letters 1938, both in Box 306; and Nelson to Collier, December 9, 1940, CCC–ID Miscellaneous Correspondence, FY 1941–1942 (hereafter Correspondence 1941–1942), Box 307, all in NARA–GLC.

77. Nelson to Collier, March 27, 1939, Letters 1939, Box 306, NARA–GLC.

78. Nelson to Heritage, January 13, 1941, Correspondence, Letters Sent, 1941, Box 306, NARA–GLC.

79. Nelson to Collier, October 30, 1941, CCC–ID Miscellaneous Correspondence, FY 1941–1942, Box 307, NARA–GLC; Lisa Dianne Lykins, "'Curing the Indian': Therapeutic Care and Acculturation at the Sac and Fox Tuberculosis Sanatorium, 1912–1942" (PhD diss., University of Kentucky, 2002), 147; Zimmer, "Settlement Sovereignty," 40–41.

80. "Sac and Fox Roadside Park Cornerstone Laying Celebration and Program to Begin at 2:00 PM, Friday, May 16, 1941," CCC–ID Project Plans, 1940–1941 (hereafter Plans 1940–1941), Box 313, NARA–GLC.

81. Nelson to Charles Evans, March 29, 1941; Nelson to Heritage, April 3, 1941; "Agreement for the Use of Tribal Lands for a Proposed Roadside Park on the Sac and Fox Reservation, Tama, Iowa," March 21, 1941, all in Plans 1940–1941, Box 313, NARA–GLC; and "Rustic Shelter House Being Built by CCC on Indian Reservation," *Tama News-Herald*, May 8, 1941.

82. Heritage to Collier, March 3, 1941, Correspondence 1941–1942, Box 307, NARA–GLC.

83. Nelson to Collier, July 24, 1941, IECW CCC–ID program, FY 1942 (hereafter IECW 1942), Box 313; Nelson to Collier, February 6, 1942; and Hellwig to Heritage, May 1, 1942, Correspondence, Letters Sent, January–September 4, 1942 (hereafter Letters JS 1942 folder), Box 306, all in NARA–GLC.

84. Nelson to Collier, November 28, 1941, IECW 1942, Box 313, NARA–GLC.

85. "Indians in the War for Freedom," *IAW* 9 (April 1942): 5.

86. Jeanne Clarke, "Indian Women Harness Old Talents to New Jobs," *IAW* 10 (n.d.): 35. Several tribal members joined the military before the war had even begun. See "Eight Sac-Fox Indians Enlist in National Guard," *Tama News-Herald*, February 13, 1941.

87. Hellwig to Collier, July 13, 1942; Parman, "The Indian and the Civilian Conservation Corps," 54.

88. Larry Lasley, personal communication with author, October 29, 2013 (copy in the author's possession).

89. The Harvard Project on American Indian Economic Development, *The State of the Native Nations: Conditions under U.S. Policies of Self-Determination* (New York: Oxford University Press, 2007), 95.

90. Wanatee in discussion with author, June 27, 2014.

91. Lewis, "Native Americans and the Environment," 439.

92. Wanatee in discussion with author, June 27, 2014; and "Buffalo Meat Distribution," flier posted at Meskwaki tribal center, June 2014.

93. "Meskwaki Food Sovereignty Initiative," Corporation for National and Community Service, n.d., 1.USA.gov. See also Brandi Janssen, "Blending Old and New on the Meskwaki Settlement," *Edible Iowa River Valley* 32 (Summer 2014): 26–27.

94. Nelson to Heritage, April 25, 1942, Letters JS 1942, Box 306, NARA–GLC.

95. Young Bear to Nelson in transcript of "Weekly Meeting, January 8, 1935," 749 Meetings, Box 293, NARA–GLC.

JENNIFER ANDREWS

The Erotic in Contemporary Native Women's Poetry in Canada

The erotic . . . "forms the bridge between the spiritual and the political." . . . It is creation of a connection between an embodied self and the world in which that self exists.
—ROBERT WARRIOR

Native women's love poetry and erotics are so invisible, so far back in the closet, that they are practically in somebody else's apartment.
—CHRYSTOS

IN "RED HOT TO THE TOUCH," Anishnaabe poet, editor, and publisher Kateri Akiwenzie-Damm argues for the need to "bring the erotic back into Indigenous arts" by depicting Aboriginal female sexuality, in particular, in a celebratory fashion (113). She eschews long-standing stereotypical depictions of Indigenous woman as passive objects of male exploitation and violence, especially as inflicted by white Western men as part of the ongoing project of colonization. Akiwenzie-Damm has collected and edited a groundbreaking collection of Indigenous erotica from writers of both sexes living in Canada, the United States, Australia, and Aotearoa (New Zealand) titled *Without Reservation: Indigenous Erotica*. She has also contributed to Drew Hayden Taylor's *Me Sexy: An Exploration of Native Sex and Sexuality*, a provocative and compelling compilation of essays and creative work on Indigenous sexualities. More recently, Playwrights Canada Press published *Two-Spirit Acts: Queer Indigenous Performances*, a trio of performance scripts that include Muriel Miguel's *Hot'n'Soft*, which first premiered in Toronto in 1991 and explicitly depicts "lesbian erotica" (xxi) by eschewing what Daniel Heath Justice has called the "sexaphobic settler regime" (208). And an essay in the just-published volume *Indigenous Poetics in Canada*, Anishnaabe poet and scholar Waaseyaa'sin Christine Sy describes the impact of many of these publications on her own work, highlighting how Akiwenzie-Damm and other Native writers of the erotic have inspired her to explore "*our* sexuality and sensuality, *our* way of writing our life force" (189). Despite this growing body of primary texts, relatively little critical attention has been paid to the popularity of Native erotica as manifested in the work of Indigenous women and especially poets within Canada.

This silence is not surprising, given that writing erotica is perceived as especially risky for Native authors who remain marginalized, regardless of their sexual orientation, within the nation-state. In "Decolonizing the Queer Native Body," Chris Finley explains that while "Natives, and lots of other folks, like sex," they "are terrified to discuss it" because it may endanger the speaker or writer by unearthing "the colonial legacies of sexual violence" (32) and their ongoing impact on tribal peoples. The structures of colonialism in Canada and the United States, as Mark Rifkin outlines, historically depended—and in many cases, still do—on the enforcement of "compulsory heterosexuality" (2011b, 5) to ensure the perpetuation of a fundamentally white, Christian, patriarchal form of nationhood, one in which any Indigenous "emotional and bodily sensation," especially those which challenge established institutions of governance, is strategically discounted or ignored (2012, 27).

Within this framework, Native women are useful for one purpose: to bear children, whose white fathers will ensure their racial integration. Conversely, Indigenous men are unacknowledged as subjects in their own right or they are feminized to induce their complicity. As Finley points out, "It is not only Native women who are (hetero)sexually controlled by white heteropatriarchy, for Native men are feminized and queered when put in the care of a white heteropatriarchal nation-state" (35). Paradoxically some of the most important recent critical interventions in the field of queer theory continue to rely on a "primitivist notion of the indigenous as the space of free and unfettered sexuality that allows the white queer citizen to remake his or her sexuality" without actually forging relationships of solidarity with Indigenous peoples when it comes to their "land struggles" (Smith, 49). For all the promise of queer theory's desire to represent marginal populations, the colonization and erasure of Indigenous peoples remains a fundamental problem. Likewise, Andrea Smith notes that in much contemporary ethnic and queer of color work, Indigenous subjects who attach themselves to a land base or insist on "nationalistic identifications" rather than that of the diasporic or Mestizo subject are perceived as "infantile" precisely because they insist on being "rooted" and thus resist straddling a multitude of borders (51). Yet there is a plethora of Native women writers in Canada whose interest in and commitment to land claims is articulated through prose that is erotically charged, combining a sophisticated vision of their speakers' desires with their relationships to a home/place.

Through close readings of selected poems from all three of Connie Fife's collections—*Beneath the Naked Sun*, *Speaking through Jagged Rock*, and *Poems for a New World*—as well as Marilyn Dumont's *green girl dreams Mountains*, this essay examines how two Indigenous women poets (one Cree and the other Cree/Métis) articulate the sexual identities of their speakers in ways that embrace the erotic without overlooking the challenges of locating themselves within multiple contexts—as Native women living in Canada, either on or off reserve, who want to celebrate their intimate connections to the natural world. By understanding and exploring the "erotic" as a category that encompasses and exceeds sexuality, deliberately creates distance from "the ideologies normalized with Euroamerican discourses of [regulatory] sexuality," and attends to "the entire matrix of bodily and emotional sensation" (Rifkin 2012, 29), these poets portray the dynamic and complex "force field[s] of lived relations" (4) in ways that rethink dominant definitions of identity and belonging. Such an argument is not altogether new, given the work of scholars like Robert Warrior, whose essay "Your Skin Is the Map: The Theoretical Challenge of Joy Harjo's Erotic Poetics" considers how Harjo's treatment of the erotic challenges "the development of Native theory" by insisting on the deep connections between "our bodies[,] . . . our intellects, and the material realities" of Indigenous life (340). For Harjo, the erotic is closely linked to images of reproduction and birthing, often in a heterosexual context. Treating the concept of the erotic as grounded in tangible, physical bodies ensures its materiality. This approach is especially helpful when comparing the work of Fife and Dumont, because it not only reveals the pragmatic and powerful impact of pairing eroticism with specific locales but also shows differing ways that such an articulation of identity asserts the vitality of these women as active sexual beings whose experiences of the erotic are deeply political. But Fife and Dumont bring another dimension to discussions of the erotic by—in contrast with Harjo—focusing on same-sex and heterosexual relationships that do not necessarily populate future generations through reproduction but pointedly articulate the necessity of honoring the land claims of those who are alive today.

To invoke nation-state demarcations in an examination of Indigenous erotic poetry may seem counterintuitive given Cherokee writer Thomas King's observation that "the line that exists between the US and Canada" is, at least for him, "an imaginary line. It's a line from someone else's imagination" (Rooke, 72). While the dictates of nation-state identities often ignore, exclude, or marginalize Native self-definition by relegating tribal communities to mere colonies, understanding and exploring the relationship between "private desires (as linked to national identity)" and their public declaration and circulation, through literary publication, becomes an important step in the process of shaping the processes of decolonization (Mayer, 1). Much of the scholarly work done on Native erotica has been American-centered, such as Deborah Miranda's "Dildos, Hummingbirds, and Driving Her Crazy: Searching for American Indian Women's Love Poetry and Erotics," which offers close readings of the erotic in Chrystos's poetry but also draws on Aboriginal writers from across North America to make its points, despite the reality that the history of Native colonization in Canada differs from that of the United States (see, e.g., Franks)[1] and that gay marriage was made legal by the Canadian federal government in 2004 and has remained so. This ruling was fundamentally different from the state-by-state legislation in the United States. Miranda hints at this point when she notes that "there is a significant difference between the creation of poetry and the embrace of the erotic.... Living the erotic (as women of colour who break stereotypes such as gender roles, sexual orientation expectations, or silence) *within your poetry* can limit your ability to earn a living or even get you killed" (142). She goes on to ask why U.S. culture continues to feel compelled to repress "the erotic in Indian literature," a question that I would frame slightly differently here, by asking why readers, publishers, scholars, and critics continue to do the same with Indigenous women writers who live north of the 49th parallel, despite seemingly more liberal national policies regarding same-sex coupling?

Of course, the production and consumption of erotica does not depend on the legalization of gay marriage. Nor is the Canadian government exempt from a long history of legally privileging "the male-headed, nuclear-family household in Canadian Indian Policy," a "strategy of assimilation" that has ensured the institution of "exploitative relations of power" between Indigenous men and women as authentically and traditionally Indian and thus fundamentally shaped land claims across the country (Rifkin 2011b, 21). Joyce Green explains that prior to 1982, the British North America Act gave the federal government "sole jurisdiction" over "Indians, and Lands reserved for Indians" (146). As a result, the federal government was able to pass and enforce the Indian Act and strip "generations of women of their status as Indians, simultaneously depriving them of the right to live in their communities, raise their children in their cultures and participate in the social, economic, and political life of their communities" (146). The patriation of the Constitution and the creation of the Charter in 1982 led to the explicit constitutional protection of Aboriginal men and women, and an amendment in 1983 secured Indigenous rights with respect to "modern land-claims settlements" (146). However, until the enactment of Bill C-31 in 1985, Native women who married non-Natives, along with their descendants, were denied status under the Indian Act.[2] The long-standing impact of this pattern of exclusion based on race and gender, much like the traumatic experiences of residential schooling for many, continues to shape the lives of Indigenous people across Canada (see, e.g., Palmater, 15–22, 101–42).[3] So while the desire (all puns intended) to move beyond the borders of the nation-state may be a critical step in the formulation of tribal self-definition, the need to garner recognition from the federal government and to negotiate land claims, ideally on a nation-to-nation basis, remains critical to the economic, political, and cultural survival of many tribes in Canada and the United States.

Writing the erotic is a powerful way to enact "a changed understanding of the relationship between *sexuality* and *sovereignty*" and to ensure that the former does not determine the latter, particularly by acknowledging the broad range of physical and emotional sensations people experience through their relationship to land (Rifkin 2011a, 174). Rifkin draws on the work of Cherokee queer scholar Qwo-Li Driskill to demonstrate the importance of thinking differently about individual and collective links to land, and especially homeland, as a connection grounded in "reciprocity" and mutual respect (2011a, 177; 2012, 73). He explains that "land is both desired and desiring ... [; it] is not a thing that can be priced and traded, [and] is [therefore] a feeling entity" (177; 73). In doing so, Rifkin suggests that the meaning of sovereignty can be fundamentally altered, "shifting from the idea of an exertion of juridical control over a dead quantum of space to the emotional interdependence and physical joining of lovers" (177; 73). Native territory cannot be readily reduced to "an inert, saleable thing" (177; 73). Given this approach, it seems appropriate—and even necessary—to remain attuned to nation-state borders when examining Natives writing the erotic, if only to consider how Aboriginal writers employ "feeling—the mesh of emotive and sensory experience" to "push against the boundaries inscribed by settlement" (2011a, 182).[4] If, as Finley has argued, "part of the decolonizing project [for Native peoples] is recovering the relationship to a land base and reimagining the ... Native body" (41), then paying attention to the connections made by Indigenous authors to particular geographic locations is an essential part of this conversation.

The poets under consideration here insist on a detailed and locatable interaction with landscapes and foreground the erotic aspects of these relationships in a way that broadens how readers may conceive of or define being "in the erotic" (Harjo, 21) far beyond the heterosexual penetration that typically characterizes the colonizing of territories. Paying attention to how the erotic is manifested in contemporary Native Canadian women's poetry is warranted as part of a wider effort to make the erotic writing of Indigenous women visible—to take it "out of the closet" or even the bedroom through a careful unpacking of poems, in this case by Connie Fife and Marilyn Dumont, who share a Cree tribal heritage but use different strategies to explore the roles of desire and love in their work. Fife reconfigures the historic tradition of rendering the female Indigenous body as a landscape to be sexually claimed by a male settler by drawing her own word map of her body, one that relies on pleasuring its cartographer with specific instructions that carefully invoke the distinct beauty of female anatomy and shared stimulation between female lovers. Her poems subvert hierarchal dominance as well as the right to dictate land ownership or the body's present and future uses. Fife ultimately renders poetry—its creation and readers' engagement with it—as a vehicle for erotic exploration and expression that is securely grounded in her Cree tribal heritage and ancestral lands. Dumont's more precarious status as a Cree/Métis woman who has spent much of her life in urban locations, physically distant from her Alberta ancestral roots, leads to the creation of erotic landscapes that reclaim her homelands through the depiction of heterosexual and lesbian encounters. Thus she revisions how readers may understand the historical denial of Métis rights in Canada as distinct while simultaneously deconstructing presumptions that heterosexuality is always already complicit in the process of colonial exploitation. Dumont goes further by depicting how a white, Christian, biblical garden might be imagined of in terms that could accommodate and celebrate both heterosexual *and* lesbian sensuality and embrace—literally and figuratively—people, plants, and animals of all persuasions. Dumont's poetry engages with the erotic by insisting on the sustained vitality of the Métis people, despite the Canadian government's hope that this population would die out or intermarry to such a degree that they would disappear altogether.

Born in Prince Albert, Saskatchewan, and raised in Fiji and England before returning to Canada, Cree lesbian poet Connie Fife concludes her first collection of poetry, *Beneath the Naked Sun*, with a biographical statement in which she asserts that "i write who i am; from my perspective as well as from the place most people would like me to stay" (91). Fife's work has not garnered much scholarly or popular attention.[5] Paradoxically, Fife's work contests the fixity—and silencing—of her voice by a "racist, homophobic society," by exploring her "own eruptions" through the erotic depictions of her body as a landscape to be traveled through and engaged with in a process of mutual pleasuring (91). In her poetry, the erotic is alive and thriving.

In her first book, Fife literalizes the concept of the "embodied self" in the aptly titled "Journey," with the poetic speaker calling on her lover to take a physical and spiritual walk over her physique with its shifts in elevation (evoked by the lower case "i" she employs throughout the collection), roaming through "crystal lake[s]" and "valleys" that lead across her "heart" to pools of water and eventually reaching another world, "the other side of darkness" accessible by only looking into "the cavity of my vulva" (38). The speaker uses a series of imperatives in this free-verse poem to guide the unidentified lover to engage all five senses in learning about the powers of the natural world and the landscape of this body in an interactive manner that anticipates and directs how the lover and the speaker can and will merge into each other: "*hear* the moon singing her lament . . . / *lie* across the smoothness of my back / listen to the stories engraved in my heart" (38; my emphasis). Not only does Fife's speaker portray how bodily and emotional sensations are deeply interwoven, but she asks readers to attend to the strategic and specific dimensions of what is a sensual lived relation between individuals and the land on which they dwell, in distinct contrast to Western colonial practices. And she does so with a deep attentiveness to her own tribal beliefs. For the Cree, as Jean Okimāsis explains, "celestial bodies" have been traditionally used to measure the passage of time (57). Each moon signifies "a certain phase in the growth of animal and plant life" over the course of a year, providing a way to compartmentalize time based on observations of the natural world as well as women's reproductive cycles (57). The result is a thirteen-month lunar calendar rather than a Westernized twelve-month calendar, the former of which is structured by the changing female body in concert with the landscape.

In "Journey," Fife employs this Cree conceptualization of time to portray what is a passionately physical love relationship, bridging the distance between theory and praxis through her poetry. The lover becomes one with the speaker by "swim[ming] in the depths of my blood / wash[ing] the wounds of your hardened insides," a commingling of fluids that heightens the multisensory experience of the poem and vividly foregrounds the significance of the lunar cycles. In keeping with traditional tribal principles, in Fife's text generic distinctions are broken down: the poem becomes a "song," and the voyage functions as an ecstatic tribute to the speaker's "beloved" (38). Fife pointedly merges her speaker's body with Cree belief systems, creating an erotic topography of mutual love and respect that celebrates this trip by initiating readers into a world of tender desire that values the shared pleasure of animate bodies above all else.

In particular, Fife's poetry is shaped by her tribe's belief that "social values" like "reciprocity apply to human—animal as well as to social relationships" because people are regarded as merely one part of a "'community of beings' within the ecological system" (Berkes, 97). But asserting and sustaining such a perspective is increasingly difficult, particularly because as Gail Guthrie Valaskakis notes, "today, more than half of North America's Native people live in urban areas" (247), a context that, at least for Fife, does not readily lend itself to a sense of mutual respect. Fife uses bodily experiences in a variety of landscapes to demonstrate both the strong emotional and physical ties that bind her speaker to her homeland and the instability that is felt when her speaker moves to an urban locale, a relocation that invariably creates internal distress and explores a larger tribal and political conflict: the challenge of being distant from one's community of origin.

The struggle to keep the body alive and experience joy, rather than the pain of longing, is a central feature of Fife's erotic writing about urban spaces in this early collection. Like Harjo and Dumont, as we will see shortly, for Fife cities may dull or even suppress the tribal erotic.[6] In "Sunsets," for example, Fife's poetic "I" portrays the disjuncture between "the home of / My people," where the speaker has a fluid relationship with the natural world, and "the city," where "daily isolation is a fact / Of life" and the rhythms of the earth's light are "[c]ontrolled by streetlights" rather than the solar and lunar cycles (58). As the title of this first book, *Beneath the Naked Sun*, reminds readers, erotic interaction with and willingness to be open to all livings things directly counters the colonial insistence on possession and control of land, animals, plants, and even the moon and the sun, a disconnect that is often most visible in cityscapes. Fife's invocation of a naked sun recalls the vulnerability of all humans whose bodies, when stripped of clothing, reveal them as possessing the same basic attributes and desires. However, the speaker of "Sunsets" makes clear that such a relationship has been violated and exploited by "the privileged whites / Who we discovered in 1492" (58). Not ready to surrender, Fife's first-person speaker employs the sensual warmth of sun touching skin to make an erotically charged political statement, concluding that "sunsets are / Only for those who live and / Die in the struggle to receive / Its warmth" but "without claiming / Ownership to its message" (58—59). Although the sunlight cannot provide sanctuary from colonial intruders, it becomes an instrument in Fife's poetic toolbox for survival in the city and a natural symbol of the power of language. By appreciating the sunset without coveting it, and cultivating a feeling of gratitude for its generosity, as this poem does, Fife employs words to preclude what might otherwise be a "[c]ertain death" for those Cree who were raised on tribal lands yet now find themselves living in cities (59). The poem embodies Fife's commitment to making the erotic central to her poetic voice, even in places that may try to deaden her resolve.

With her second collection, *Speaking through Jagged Rock*, Fife recalls and reconfigures the significance of her first book by invoking and reframing the landscape of sexual desire through the title poem, which begins, "i will take you / amongst jagged rocks / lick you smooth / beneath a naked sun" (45). Here, Fife recycles the title of her previous collection yet squarely locates her new work in the landscape of her birthplace, northern Saskatchewan, which consists of the Precambrian Shield bridging the area between the northern tundra and the southern parkland with its rocky and rugged terrain. The opening lines of the poem take on a dual significance, by invoking images of an animal nurturing her newborn in the wilderness and female lovers who find mutual stimulation and pleasure in the landscape of Fife's birth. As her speaker explains in an earlier poem from the same collection titled "i am a people," the distinctive prairie topography and the sounds it produces—

"the voice of prairie wind . . . [and] sheaves of wheat / rippling across a blue field" (18)—serve as markers of identity that are inclusively broad yet purposefully distinctive in locating the poem's setting and animating it with a sensuality that echoes that of the human body by invoking the senses of sound and touch. The poem concludes with the assertion "i am a people / we are a nation" (19), a couplet that belies white, Western distinctions between identity and community, establishing a Cree principal of responsibility based on reciprocity within the pages of this volume.

For Fife's speaker, interacting with the land is inherently sensual yet deeply political. In "speaking through jagged rock," the poetic "i" with its deliberate lowercase spelling moves from an initial scene of maternal care and/or mutual erotic stimulation to "bask[ing] / amongst tall grass" and watching "sunset / . . . dance across our breasts until / moon begins to sing" (45). In these latter moments, the speaker relishes the intimacy of contact and the experience of bodily vibrations, portraying a lived relation between human beings and the natural world that is resolutely female-centered and unwaveringly carnal in its promise to "take you" as the reader to the heights of pleasure. Through coupling the "jagged rocks" of Prince Albert National Park with, at the southern end of the protected area, fescue grasslands, an unexpected and very rare type of tall grass that has been wiped out elsewhere by urban development but is abundant in this poem, Fife's speaker narrows its likely locale and deliberately blurs the boundaries between these Cree women's bodies, the topography they interact with, and their beliefs.

Throughout "speaking through jagged rock," Fife's poetic "i" situates herself, her female ancestors, and her current lover in a dynamic and sacred relationship to a particular tribal space across time. The life cycle that her speaker tracks of an infant animal being licked clean and the subsequent transition to adult passion and erotic love affords Fife the opportunity to depict and celebrate sexual diversity from birth to death. It also literalizes the important bonds that Indigenous people—and in her case, a queer Cree writer—share with their home/place, connections that deserve recognition. Without excluding readers of both sexes, the speaker directs her energy to a collective "we" and "us" that is decidedly female, with breasts that are caressed by the rays of the sun and moon, even promising her lover that "(they will dance / a stomp song for us)" (45). By referencing the stomp songs, a call-and-response ceremonial exchange that is common to many Native North American tribes, Fife alters the presumption that such ceremonies enforce heterosexuality. Stomp songs can become a site for gender-bending as men have on occasion taken up women's roles in the ceremony and vice versa (see Gilley, 141). In this case, Fife's use of parentheses, which typically offer supplementary information, draw attention to that which is otherwise excluded:

queer love. The speaker in Fife's text goes so far as to assert that she and her companion will "become darkness" and even "re-arrange the lining / of the universe so that" Mother Earth will "know we exist" (45). The poetic "i" ultimately insists on the significance of the female mother/lover who deserves recognition and celebration. In doing so, Fife's speaker offers an animate and sensual double entendre that playfully turns the "i/eye" into a landscape that, from her viewpoint, is populated by undulating female curves and embodies the erotic. Not surprisingly, the women in this poem linger in and merge with the topography around the clock, whether pleasured once again "amongst jagged rocks" or "stroked by the tall grasses" as "the moon will dance across our breasts / while stars laugh our / memory" (46). While geographical specificity is part of Fife's poetic project, her efforts to animate tribal territory also pointedly counter the perception of land as dead "space" (Rifkin 2011a, 177; 2012, 73) by literally countering the dominant pairing of heterosexuality and sovereignty with generations of women who see and enact a different vision, relying on their senses in an orgasmic communion with the natural world, one that finds validation through rootedness.

Near the conclusion of *Speaking through Jagged Rock*, Fife's speaker describes another kind of erotic experience—involving the text, the poetic "I," and the reader—as she turns poems themselves into nocturnal landscapes of sensuality and intimacy that invite participation. In the final stanza of "this poem is yours," the speaker asserts, "when i sleep let it be in the arms of a poem" (61). If her previous poems have expressed deep love for another person, she extends this passionate embrace through the text to the reader. Fife's "i" brings the poem itself to life through a series of imperatives that identify the poem as a female nurturer whom the speaker calls on to nurture her—and even dream for her: "let her rock me against her skin / dream when i cannot" (61). The poem becomes a lover, literally and metaphorically, wooing the speaker with words, and offering an inclusive and collective vision of the erotic that allows for, and even encourages, interaction and participation. The sophistication of this poem both echoes and subverts the "infantile" relation that is often used in queer theory to describe Native peoples who attach themselves to a land base. Here, the lover/poem may provide comfort but also acts as a vehicle for erotic self-expression, epitomized by the promise that the speaker will be "singing" at sunrise (61). While there are traditional Cree songs that give thanks to the land in the early morning, Fife's poem can be read as more than a physical vocalization of gratitude for this shared relation, with the potential for song to convey the ecstasy of orgasm as a deeply felt bodily experience. Finally, the portability and flexibility of poem as paramour emphasizes the power of words and enables reproduction of a textual kind for the lesbian lovers who seek nurturance within "this poem is yours."

The tender love relationship between speaker, poem, and reader provides a model of community for those who take the time to read and share Fife's collection.

Fife's most recent book, *Poems for a New World*, focuses less explicitly on the intimate interaction between people and their immediate surroundings and more on the intersections between and among multiple examples of racism and exploitation, especially of women and children, within Canada and beyond. Yet it is no less engaged in writing the erotic precisely because Fife insists on the centrality of the body's lived relations in the world and what sense experiences reveal about these interactions. By expanding the scope of her subjects to include non-Natives, she strategically levels hierarchal distinctions between people based on skin color, sexual orientation, or socioeconomic status while paying tribute to them through an accounting of her own deeply personal responses to their individual struggles. In this book, Fife includes poems dedicated to particular individuals: Connie Jacobs, a Tsuu T'in mother who was shot along with her son Ty, when she refused to surrender her children to Social Services; Matthew Shepard, a young white man who was tortured and murdered for being gay in rural Wyoming; James Byrd Jr., tortured and murdered for being African American in Texas; and Anna-Marie Sewell, a Mig'Maq writer and fellow recipient of the Prince and Princess Edward Prize in Aboriginal Literature in 2000. But the collection reaches beyond North America by examining NATO's invasion of Yugoslavia, including its bombing of a passenger train, and makes a broader plea for the recognition of the pervasiveness of "genocide" and its fundamental violation of the "laws of creation" (51). In response to these widespread acts of global violence, Fife continues to cultivate an intimate relationship with her reader as she unpacks what she views as acts of senseless violence against vulnerable and marginalized populations, whose experiences echo her own as a Cree and lesbian woman in Canada. Her repeated insistence on the shared humanity of those whose lives she writes about is heightened by her continued return to sensual and evocative images that celebrate the tangible immediacy of lovemaking between people. As a poet who has spent considerable time grounding her work in a distinctive Cree landscape, the scope of this latest text suggests that Fife sees a globalized exploration of the erotic as an important next step that builds on her efforts to locate herself by reaching out to bond with others, beyond her Cree community.

As with her previous collections, Fife creates a bridge between her second and third books through her sustained exploration of the erotic female body and its connections to a material reality. Using the form of the "ode," a poem that can be chanted or sung in *Poems for a New World*, Fife recalls and revises her tribute to poetry in *Speaking through Jagged Rock* with a three-part blank-verse poem titled "Ode to Poetry" that affirms a further blending of the sensual and the ideological into a single lyrical form. Fife employs what has been traditionally a white, Western, male-authored poetic model of praising and glorifying a serious subject (see Abrams, 137–38) but Indigenizes and queers it. If the previous version of the poem's lyrics may have seemed slightly more maternal, with the poem rocking the speaker "against her skin" and "pulling her close," in this ode the poetic "i" is sexually self-expressive, pulling and vocalizing her way to a new day. While both poems move toward the birth of a "new morning," the last line of the original verse, "singing with the clarity of her tone," is displaced with the promise of a broader, more inclusive vocalization, one that is warmed by the sensuality of "her breath" (68). The image of the cradled infant is replaced by the erotic vitality of a lover.

In this newer version, Fife includes the location where the poem was written and the date of composition—"*san francisco, march 1999*" (68)—linking the revised poem to the city where the first lesbian rights movement in the United States began, and which continues to be known for its thriving gay and lesbian neighborhoods. San Francisco was also the first city in the United States to issue licenses to legally recognize same-sex marriages in 2004, contravening both state and federal laws. With this framework in place, Fife's "Ode to Poetry" creates a reciprocal relationship between poem, writer, and the natural world that invokes and directly repeats selected lines from "this poem is yours" but adds a significant twist. Here, the "stars carry" the woman-authored story of creation, in the form of a poem with ties to the celestial world, "earthbound" as the speaker is "warmed by" the distinctly female "breath" of the poem itself (68). The "her" of the text, as in the previous version of this poem, evokes images of both maternal and sexual love, creating a sensual bond that cultivates reciprocity with the natural world and draws on the Cree stories of the creation of Turtle Island but also insists on the legitimacy of including diverse sexualities within the speaker's multiple community affiliations. The poem thus becomes an erotic ode to the power of words and song to convey the varied ways in which meaningful emotional ties can be cultivated and sustained, whether through a mother cradling a child or a woman stimulating her female lover to orgasm. Fife also pays tribute to San Francisco as a site of potential equity for lesbian women seeking a safe space to explore their sexuality and publicly recognize their romantic partnerships, if they desire.

By the end of the collection the erogenous nature of the female body (especially when physically aroused by a female lover) and the power of the maternal bond are transformed once again into life-sustaining forces which the writer is prepared to share with her companions, friends, and family as the speaker, anticipating "the likelihood we should meet again," declares that "I have prepared a bowl of ripened poems / with which to ease our hunger" and sustain our "memories . . . [and] stories" (86). Fife's description of her collection as a bowl of fruit, ready to eat, becomes an offering to readers and lovers that can be seen as also celebrating the centrality of the ripened berry, native to Saskatchewan, to the Cree people, which they called the "misâskwatômina" or "Saskatoon berry" (Steager). Traditionally a central food source for the Cree, the Saskatoon berry's existence is increasingly threatened by urban growth; in this context, Fife's poem can be read as an effort to acknowledge its tangible contribution to the continued survival of the Cree. While that physical pull on Fife's speaker resonates throughout the text, which was written elsewhere (namely, Vancouver), the ripened fruit metaphor is further infused with sexual anticipation through the promise of the eating of berries, an act that symbolizes Fife's efforts to convey the presence of her poetic "i" "in the erotic" as a living, breathing woman who embraces intimacy with her female lover(s) and delights in teasing her readers with a testament to her vitality.

Like Fife, Marilyn Dumont, who is of Cree/Métis descent and grew up in rural Alberta, struggles with her desire to reclaim a homeland for her tribe, an especially difficult task given the historically precarious and frequently unacknowledged status of the Métis in Canada, who were not given reservation lands by the federal government to compensate for their physical displacement but instead were told to negotiate with the provinces. As a result, the only province to have negotiated any kind of a land-claim settlement with the Métis is Dumont's birthplace of Alberta. A recent landmark ruling by the Supreme Court of Canada that the Métis are indeed Indians under federal jurisdiction and deserve equal access to programs and services offered to status Aboriginals through the Constitution may further efforts to negotiate for compensation, whether in the form of money or land, but this remains unclear. *green girl dreams Mountains*, published in 2001, documents this legacy of uncertainty in the context of the nation-state from a contemporary Cree/Métis woman's perspective. Using the erotic, her texts trace her physical, sexual, and psychological return to the rural landscapes of her formative years, spent in Alberta, and portray her efforts to locate herself within the urban spaces she has subsequently called home, most prominently Vancouver.

In an early section of this second collection, Dumont includes a series of poems titled "City View" in which her first-person speaker comes to terms with visible sexual exploitation of Native and Métis peoples in Vancouver, particularly in the downtown East Side, where "the drift of urban Indians," like herself, has resulted in "a daily exchange for skin, for paper, for cloth, for power— / everything here can be bought or exchanged" (39). Like Fife, Dumont experiences discomfort and alienation from the city and its inhabitants. Socioeconomic segregation along with both overt and covert racism heightens the feelings of isolation for the poetic "I." Yet, over time, Dumont's speaker comes to value the bodily sensations and lived relations that are part of the cityscape she inhabits, discovering and embracing the sensations it evokes by turning the city itself into a lover. In the final poem of the section, she declares, "I am now Hastings and Main, . . . / I am . . . the panhandlers, the junkies, the hookers, the homeless . . . I am now more city than I thought" (48). This prose poem, with its highly confessional voice, admits surprise at the city's seductive powers, its ability to infuse her skin, but Dumont stresses that, despite its physical grounding in the "plum tree blossoms, . . . the green smog over Abbotsford, the blueberries, humidity, [and] three weeks of rain" (48), her recognition of the city as animate is not the same as the relationship she has to her home/place of Alberta. Indeed, in the section that follows, the "I" of "nothing asks me to leave" describes in detail the paradox of being in Vancouver, "my back to the land" (53), a pun that acknowledges both the "intimate animal / smells of rot and birth" that flavor the ocean air and the reality that she has "immigrate[d] to an / ocean bigger than the prairie" that cannot possibly fulfill her desires (48).

As with Fife, for Dumont's speaker the prairies are the place where the erotic comes alive. However, in contrast to Fife's work, which focuses on lesbian love, Dumont's poems range across sexual orientations, juxtaposing scenes of consensual heterosexual and lesbian desire without favoring one over another. In the title poem of her second collection, *green girl dreams Mountains*, Dumont's first-person speaker reminisces about her sexual awakening as a teenager through a series of metamorphoses that reach back in time, eventually blurring the speaker's body with the landscape that she comes to embody literally. The poem begins with the visual description of "a green girl then / round-eyed and hardly hurt" who, with the help of "a sun's blade / on Cypress mountain's greenness," recalls "that time" when "I rode horses" alongside "a boyfriend whose hair / was the colour of corn silk" (59). This description alludes to the distinctive historical union of Cree women and French fur traders, resulting in descendants with physical features that defy Native stereotypes, including blond hair.

Though the poem offers, at least initially, a fairly conventional heterosexual account of young love, the choice of location symbolically invokes a long history of Cree and Métis struggles over the federal government's attempts to claim ownership of and police the area known as Cypress Hills (now a large-scale national park that straddles the Alberta/Saskatchewan border). Dumont's speaker alludes to the establishment of a Royal Canadian Mounted Police detachment (Fort Walsh) in response to the Cypress Hills massacre in which a group of migrating Nakoda were blamed and brutally murdered by white traders for stealing horses despite having no direct involvement in the incident (see Hildebrandt and Hubner, 73–75). But Dumont, rather than dwelling directly on the political resonances of the locale she has chosen, turns to the linguistic and spiritual dimensions of the Cypress Hills, which for the French and Métis were known as "montagnes aux cypress" or Cypress Mountains (Hildebrandt and Hubner, 22). In this instance, the poetic "I" becomes one with the landscape and the animals that inhabit it, focusing on the sensuality and power of her youthful desires: "My breasts were weasels' noses / my hips narrow and firm / In those days my body / volunteered me, pulled me / onward" (59). Her newly developed curves take on the character of the weasel, an animal valued historically by hunters for its rich fur coat, known for its strength and tenacity in confrontations with other creatures, and its acute sense of smell. By making this connection to the weasel, Dumont's speaker personifies the intimate connection between the landscape and the carnal body and simultaneously critiques primitive notions of Indigenous peoples as embodying "free and unfettered sexuality" (Smith, 49), ripe for exploitation by non-Aboriginals. The poetic "I" of the text may seek stimulation and gratification but on her own (weasel) terms.

If Fife is primarily concerned with writing a queer erotic, Dumont vigorously subverts clichéd depictions of a heterosexual Native erotic in both the title poem of the collection and the text that follows. Dumont strategically juxtaposes "green girl dreams Mountains," which celebrates youthful lust with "naked wind" which follows it directly, and describes even more explicitly the speaker's desire as she lies with her lover under "a willow tree," "tasting / his lips, savouring his sweat, and feeling the heat / . . . melting to my groin / until I . . . ride him in the naked wind" (60). Playing on the nostalgic image of the "sexualized male Indian" (Bird, 69) and punning on the word "ride," Dumont's text blurs the boundaries between the natural movement of air and the freedom experienced by these lovers who find satisfaction in physical interaction with the Alberta landscape, populated by the "willow tree" as well as their own bodies (60). While compulsory heterosexuality is, in many instances, a "key part of breaking up indigenous land holdings" (Rifkin 2011b, 5), Dumont's poems resist dismissing heterosexuality altogether but instead explore how the sexual fantasies of Indigenous women include scenes of heterosexual lust and love that are explicitly tied to tribal homelands. Moreover, Dumont's poem can be read as undermining the colonial tendency to feminize and queer Native men by reclaiming and celebrating the desires of this Native woman for what may or may not be an Indigenous man in an explicitly heterosexual context. In doing so, the poem questions a key presumption of colonial narratives that are used to justify imperialist behavior—that Native women inherently desire only white men and want to be "sexually and reproductively conquered" (Finley, 36). Paradoxically, as a Cree/Métis woman, Dumont writes about her light-skinned mother and her "Indian" father who struggles daily with racism because of his visible otherness, in an earlier section of *green girl dreams Mountains*, aptly titled "Homeground"; Dumont's father is literally and figuratively "ghosted" (33–34). In this respect, the poem titled "naked wind" counters the Indigenous male self-loathing that Dumont's speaker so poignantly depicts, and explicitly attributes to colonialism in the poem titled "ghosted."

In "naked wind," Dumont's poetic "I" describes an intimate scene of erotic fantasy in which her female narrator is an active participant who seeks out a male partner to be her equal; she is no vessel of imperial dominance. But Dumont goes even further, as her poem insists on and celebrates the presence of a heteronormative Native male who can fulfill the speaker's desires by letting her mount him and "ride him" (60) while communing with the natural world. If, according to Finley, "in colonial narratives Native men must be queered as sexually unavailable object choices for Native women" (36) and Indigenous women are necessary to gratify white male desires and produce offspring, then Dumont's poem refuses to comply with these dominant narratives. Instead, it offers a vital and sensual experience of heterosexual love that favors female strength and focuses on her willingness to subvert deeply rooted clichés about race and sexual orientation.

The sophistication of the love relationship that Dumont's poetic voice traces, and the mutual respect that emerges in the poems that follow "naked wind," attest to the speaker's—and her lover's—continued vitality and growth in defiance of colonial erasure. Self-knowledge, a wealth of experience, and the passage of time provide a strong foundation for individual and shared pleasure. For instance, in the pages that follow, Dumont's poetry embraces this new stage of the erotic, in which two lovers with "one look" can "negotiate the minefields of wounds" (61), and conversely celebrates the intense physical needs that shape their interactions in poems like "scorching," which describes "my / desire" as being "hotter than the red lips" (66). Nor is desire located in or defined by a single set of sexual practices. "scorching," in particular, resists categorization as resolutely heterosexual or homosexual through its several graphically evocative sexual puns, including a "burning bush" (potentially an engorged vagina) and an "assflower" that "melts open / into its hands / imagined mouth / cupping my nectar" (66), alluding to rectal copulation and stimulation. It also explores the broader subject of sexual ageism and the power of fantasy, as the narrator describes how, "I wait / and wait / and / wait . . . for my young lover to be at my door" (67), in anticipation of his arrival, lines that could be read as ironically evoking the deep desire for an end to the waiting game that the Métis have experienced at the hands of the federal government. While the poem offers no immediate confirmation that the lover will actually appear on the speaker's doorstep or that there will be a resolution of any kind, Dumont gives value to the intense pleasure of sexual anticipation and the richness of the speaker's imagination. Here, the erotic is metaphorically politicized as the poetic "I" enacts a sustained commitment to desire (sexual) self-expression, regardless of the speaker's physical distance from her tribal roots.

The final section of Dumont's collection, titled "Among the Word Animals," foregrounds the slippage between language, bodily experiences, and the natural world and represents the riskiness of living the erotic "*within your poetry*" (Miranda, 142). In particular, the poem "I give you arbutus," which is included in Akiwenzie-Damm's *Without Reservation*, revels in the sexual energy between speaker and reader, with the first-person voice offering "you / this . . . garden" where "flowering vulvas, host- / white tulips and lipstick tube / buds [are] penetrating the shy evening" (87). Sophie Mayer, in "This Bridge of Two Backs: Making the Two-Spirit Erotics of Community," praises Dumont for her creation of a scene in which "explicitness and sacredness" collide, with "sexually suggestive blooms . . . set scandalously against the virginal pallor of Christian tulips" (21). Like Fife, Dumont was raised Roman Catholic and thus her intrusion into this sacred Christian space that has played a central role in the religious conversion and assimilation of Indigenous peoples in Canada poses a direct challenge to white, patriarchal forms of nationhood and the systematic disregard of the Métis people. In contrast to the biblical Garden of Eden, the abundance of flora in Dumont's poem sparks the imaginative cultivation of erotic desires that include but are not limited to sexual penetration of various kinds.

While Dumont's knowledge of the Cree language is limited (Andrews 2004, 146–47) and she does not use Cree words in this collection, her depiction of an alternative to Eden reflects a distinctly Cree sensibility, which embraces sexual stimulation as pleasure rather than repressing it. Such an approach reflects what Tomson Highway has described as the "dynamic" relationship between "nature and humankind" that is inherent to the Cree language and culture (39). In particular, Highway points out that "if you think of the human body as the original garden of beauty, the garden of pleasure, the garden of joy—then the English language, at one point in its history, was evicted from that body," while the Cree language does the reverse by embracing and celebrating biology (38). As Dumont's speaker in one of the final poems of the collection, called "blond syllables," explains, "those blue-eyed long-lashed sentences . . . peaches-n-cream commas and . . . little tight-assed / suffixes make me . . . swear a red fuckin' Cree streak" (95). Dumont's irreverent treatment of the English language and her desire to articulate the erotic dimensions of her Cree/Métis heritage become a tool for reenvisioning the garden as "a garden of beauty, a garden of pleasure, a garden of joy" that need not lead to punishment or exile (Highway, 39).

As part of the project of fertilizing this alternative version of the garden, Dumont's poetic speaker takes great pride in introducing other species of plants, which further complicates easy labels, whether horticultural or sexual: "I give you the sand smooth arbutus / laughing yellow vines . . . / the brush of cool fronds, light / tails trailing through dark cedars" (87). This list of species includes the rugged arbutus tree, a tall and hardy evergreen tree that is strikingly beautiful with its dark green leaves, white flowers, and red berries; it needs to be in close proximity to the ocean and thus is abundant in southern British Columbia (including Vancouver). The arbutus tree in Dumont's work, as Cara DeHaan notes, undergoes its own sensual progression; in two poems that immediately follow "I give you arbutus," the "evergreen . . . sheds coppery red bark for a young green skin" (244), remaking and renewing itself through an intimate embrace with the first-person speaker. But the poetic "I" also adds the dogwood, an equally robust shrub that thrives on the Alberta plains, "dark cedars" that were used by Aboriginal peoples in British Columbia for carving and medicinal purposes, along with vines and ferns that cover the low-lying areas, to create a rich visual space that is designed to ignite the senses and draw attention to the ground cover with its light-dappled sensuality, enticing full bodily engagement through touch, taste, and smell. Dumont's garden portrays sexual diversity through a compelling set of metaphors while mocking the rigidity of phallocentric colonial narratives. The lush "brush"/bush cover leading to the "cool hollow of the earth" (87) evokes an erotic vision of a garden that celebrates self-love and the love of others across an array of species and insists on the need to pay closer attention to the full complement of flora in this garden as an example of a different kind of ideal garden—one that embraces a "sexuality . . . without reservation" (Mayer, 21).

Dumont's poem demonstrates how writing an Indigenous erotic into the garden can be a critical strategy for grounding Native identity in specific home/lands while respecting the fact that many contemporary Aboriginal people live off the reserve and far from their birthplace, family, and tribal community. Such a situation is not unusual in an era of globalization, but as Dumont (and Fife) make clear, their communities continue to suffer from, and struggle with, the effects of a long-standing and systematic dispossession of their homelands by the nation-state, a situation that is especially true for the Métis. By invoking flora from both her birthplace (Alberta) and her city of residence (Vancouver) as sites of inspiration while writing these poems, Dumont's poetic "I" highlights how this movement between differing sites of identification needs to be understood as strengthening rather than undermining the centrality of home for the speaker; her sensual garden space marries the two and is strategically tethered to the geographical locales that have defined her, regardless of their status according to the nation-state.

Using the erotic to position oneself geographically, culturally, and politically is a risky strategy for Native women poets in Canada, one that often results in critical and commercial marginalization. The most overtly political poems of Dumont's first collection, *A Really Good Brown Girl*, garnered academic praise and subsequently have become part of the Canadian literary canon, appearing regularly on university syllabi, but *green grass dreams Mountains* has not received the same attention, arguably because of its erotic content and its small-press publisher. Fife's poetry collections have been published by three different small presses, all with limited financial resources in an increasingly competitive literary market, a reality that illustrates the precariousness of writing the erotic. Despite this, Fife and Dumont continue to animate their poetry through sexuality, strategically blurring the boundaries between human beings, animals, land, and plants to embrace desire in a wide variety of forms. Informed by Cree and Métis traditions, they see sensuality as an integral part of their identities as Indigenous women, and as a critical political tool in their efforts to claim a home/land within the nation-state. In Fife's case, her birthplace of Prince Albert is now designated an urban Cree reserve under a unique framework agreement, signed in 2000, between the federal and provincial governments and the Federation of Saskatchewan Indian Nations. Yet definitions of sovereignty remain a crucial subject of debate for the parties involved in ensuring that this "Framework for Governance" can and does lead to eventual consensus on how to proceed in negotiating "bilateral and tripartite governance agreements" (Arnot, 9). For Dumont, the challenges of her people remain even more complex by virtue of their erasure from the landscape and lack of recognition within the Canadian nation-state until very recently. Rifkin's call to rethink the "relationship between *sexuality* and *sovereignty*" (2011a, 174) in the context of these poets and their works becomes a complex and multilayered project that requires attentiveness to geographic location and to distinct ways in which each writes the erotic to erode dominant stereotypes about Indigenous peoples and to insist on their vitality and sensuality as manifested through a variety of sexual orientations. Most important, Fife and Dumont create a poetics that is grounded in the erotic body and its reciprocal relationship to the natural world, drawing readers into texts that enact the imaginative leap of faith needed to embrace a different kind of sovereignty—based on a collective respect for and embrace of sexual diversity and a willingness to celebrate desire without losing sight of the need for a land to call home.

JENNIFER ANDREWS is professor and chair of the Department of English at the University of New Brunswick. She is author of *In the Belly of a Laughing God: Humour and Irony in Native Women's Poetry* and coauthor of *Border Crossings: Thomas King's Cultural Inversions*.

Notes

1. See Cook and Lindau; Dickason; Asch; Newhouse, Voyageur, and Beavon, among others, for helpful introductions to Native–Canadian relations in a historical context, some of which include a comparative American perspective.

2. See "5. The Grandchild" in Monkman's *Justice of the Peace* (85), which describes how the introduction of Bill C-31 does not change the exclusion of the children of Natives who married non-Natives and were born before 1985.

3. See Suzack, Huhndorf, Perrault, and Barman; Green; Hoy; Brant; Valaskakis; Anderson; and LaRocque—among others—for useful studies of the links between Canadian Native history, literature, feminism, and activism.

4. While Rifkin's *Erotics* explores, through an "erotics of sovereignty," "modes of Indigenous selfhood" that challenge or exceed federal governments' efforts to employ "settler-imposed frameworks" (10) regarding, for instance, land claims, he stresses that "rather than suggesting the irrelevance of what might be termed nationalist aims or simply refusing any engagement with the terms of settler recognition, which as I have suggested profoundly affect Native realities and experiences and thus cannot simply be dismissed as exterior to contemporary Indigenous identity, these texts mediate the claim on reality exerted by settler institutions" (39). In other words, Rifkin, like myself, offers close readings of texts to probe how the erotic subverts and rethinks the limits of this imposed reality in an effort to imaginatively and pragmatically alter how readers understand tribal identities beyond government-imposed definitions.

5. Fife's work may have been neglected for several reasons, including the queer sexual politics of her writing, which is closely linked to her Cree identity, and the difficulty of accessing her poetry collections, which were published by three small presses across Canada (Broken Jaw in Fredericton, Ronsdale in Vancouver, Sister Vision in Toronto) (the efforts of small presses to survive financially have often meant limited print runs, which creates challenges when trying to locate and order Fife's books). Likewise, while Dumont's first collection, *A Really Good Brown Girl*, published by Brick Books, a larger and nationally established poetry publisher, has remained on course syllabi and received a great deal of critical attention, her subsequent books by smaller regional presses (for instance, *green girls dream Mountains*, published by Oolichan, a First Nations press in British Columbia) are much harder to locate.

6. See Warrior for a discussion of how Harjo employs the erotic to address her ambivalence about urban spaces in her poetry (348).

Bibliography

Abrams, M. H. 1993. *A Glossary of Literary Terms*. 6th ed. Fort Worth, Tex.: Harcourt Brace.
Akiwenzie-Damm, Kateri, ed. 2003. *Without Reservation: Indigenous Erotica*. Cape Croker, Can.: Kegedonce.
———. 2008. "Red Hot to the Touch: WRi[gh]ting Indigenous Erotica." In *Me Sexy: An Exploration of Native Sex and Sexuality,* ed. Drew Hayden Taylor, 109–23. Vancouver: Douglas and McIntyre.
Anderson, Kim. 2000. *A Recognition of Being: Reconstructing Native Womanhood*. Toronto: Second Story.
Andrews, Jennifer. 2004. "'Among the Word Animals': A Conversation with Marilyn Dumont." *Studies in Canadian Literature* 29, no. 1: 146–60.
Arnot, David M. 2007. *Treaty Implementation: Fulfilling the Covenant*. Saskatoon, Can.: Office of the Treaty Commissioner.
Asch, Michael, ed. 1997. *Aboriginal and Treaty Rights in Canada: Essays on Law, Equality, and Respect for Difference*. Vancouver: University of British Columbia Press.
Berkes, Fikret. 2008. *Sacred Ecology*. 2nd ed. New York: Routledge.
Bird, S. Elizabeth. 2001. "Savage Desires: The Gendered Construction of the American Indian in Popular Culture." In *Selling the Indian: Commercializing and Appropriating Indian Cultures*, ed. Carter Jones Meyer and Diana Royer, 62–98. Tucson: University of Arizona Press.
Brant, Beth. 1994. *Writing as Witness: Essays and Talk*. Toronto: Women's Press.
Cook, Curtis, and Juan D. Lindau, eds. 2000. *Aboriginal Rights and Self-Government: The Canadian and Mexican Experience in North American Perspective*. Montreal and Kingston, Can.: McGill–Queen's University Press.
DeHaan, Cara. 2009. "'Exorcising a lot of shame': Transformation and Affective Experience in Marilyn Dumont's *green girls dream Mountains*." *Studies in Canadian Literature* 34, no. 1: 227–47.
Dickason, Olive Patricia. 1997. *Canada's First Nations: A History of Founding Peoples from Earliest Times*. 2nd ed. Toronto: Oxford University Press.
Dumont, Marilyn. 1996. *A Really Good Brown Girl*. London, Can.: Brick Books.
———. 2001. *green girls dreams Mountains*. Lantzville, Can.: Oolichan.
Fife, Connie. 1992. *Beneath the Naked Sun: Poems*. Toronto: Sister Vision.
———. 1999. *Speaking through Jagged Rock*. Fredericton, Can.: Broken Jaw.
———. 2001. *Poems for a New World*. Vancouver: Ronsdale.
Finley, Chris. 2011. "Decolonizing the Queer Native Body (and Recovering the Native Bull-Dyke): Bringing 'Sexy Back' and Out of the Native Studies' Closet." In *Queer Indigenous Studies: Critical Interventions in Theory, Politics, and Literature*, ed. Qwo-Li Driskill et al., 31–42. Tucson: University of Arizona Press.
Franks, C. E. S. 2000. "Indian Policy: Canada and the United States Compared." In *Aboriginal Rights and Self-Government: The Canadian and Mexican Experience in North American Perspective*, ed. Curtis Cook and Juan D. Lindau, 222–63. Montreal and Kingston, Can.: McGill–Queen's University Press.

Gilley, Brian Joseph. 2006. *Becoming Two-Spirit: Gay Identity and Social Acceptance in Indian Country.* Lincoln: University of Nebraska Press.

Green, Joyce. 2007. "Balancing Strategies: Aboriginal Women and Constitutional Rights in Canada." In *Making Space for Indigenous Feminism*, ed. Joyce Green, 140–59. Black Point, Can.: Fernwood.

Harjo, Joy. 1992. "The Spectrum of Other Languages: An Interview with Joy Harjo." *Tamaqua* 3, no. 1: 11–23.

Highway, Tomson. 2008. "Why Cree is the Sexiest of All Languages." In *Me Sexy: An Exploration of Native Sex and Sexuality*, ed. Drew Hayden Taylor, 33–40. Vancouver: Douglas and McIntyre.

Hildebrandt, Walter, and Brian Hubner. 2007. *The Cypress Hills: An Island by Itself.* Saskatoon, Can.: Purich.

Hoy, Helen. 2001. *How Should I Read These? Native Women Writers in Canada.* Toronto: University of Toronto Press.

Justice, Daniel Heath. 2010. "Notes toward a Theory of Anomaly." *GLQ: The Journal of Lesbian and Gay Studies* 16, nos. 1–2: 207–42.

LaRocque, Emma. 2010. *When the Other Is Me: Native Resistance Discourse, 1850–1990.* Winnipeg: University of Manitoba Press.

Mayer, Sophie. 2008. "This Bridge of Two Backs: Making the Two-Spirit Erotics of Community." *Studies in American Indian Literatures* 20, no. 1: 1–26.

Miranda, Deborah A. 2002. "Dildos, Hummingbirds, and Driving Her Crazy: Searching for American Indian Women's Poetry and Erotics." *Frontiers* 23, no. 2: 135–49.

Monkman, Kent. 2013. *Justice of the Peace.* In *Two Spirit Acts: Queer Indigenous Performances*, ed. Jean O'Hara, 71–89. Toronto: Playwrights Canada.

Newhouse, David, Cora J. Voyageur, and Dan Beavon, eds. 2005. *Hidden in Plain Sight: Contributions of Aboriginal Peoples to Canadian Identity and Community.* Toronto: University of Toronto Press.

Okimāsis, Jean. 2004. *Cree: Language of the Plains.* Regina: Canadians Plains Research Center.

Palmater, Pamela D. 2011. *Beyond Blood: Rethinking Indigenous Identity.* Saskatoon, Can.: Purich.

Rifkin, Mark. 2011a. "The Erotics of Sovereignty." In *Queer Indigenous Studies: Critical Interventions in Theory, Politics, and Literature*, ed. Qwo-Li Driskill et al., 172–89. Tucson: University of Arizona Press.

———. 2011b. *When Did Indians Become Straight? Kinship, the History of Sexuality, and Native Sovereignty.* New York: Oxford University Press.

———. 2012. *The Erotics of Sovereignty: Queer Native Writing in an Era of Self-Determination.* Minneapolis: University of Minnesota Press.

Rooke, Constance. 1990. "Interview with Tom King." *World Literature Written in English* 30, no. 2: 62–76.

Smith, Andrea. 2011. "Queer Theory and Native Studies: The Heteronormativity of Settler Colonialism." In *Queer Indigenous Studies: Critical Interventions in Theory, Politics, and Literature*, ed. Qwo-Li Driskill et al., 43–65. Tucson: University of Arizona Press.

Steager, Tabitha. n.d. "Saskatoon Berry." *Slow Food Canada.* SlowFood.ca.

Suzack, Cheryl, Shari M. Huhndorf, Jeanne Perrault, and Jean Barman, eds. 2010. *Indigenous Women and Feminism: Politics, Activism, Culture*. Vancouver: University of British Columbia Press.

Sy, Waaseyaa'sin Christine. 2014. "Through Iskigamizigan (The Sugar Bush): A Poetics of Decolonization." In *Indigenous Poetics in Canada*, ed. Neal McLeod, 183–202. Waterloo, Can.: Wilfred Laurier University Press.

Taylor, Drew Hayden. 2008. *Me Sexy: An Exploration of Native Sex and Sexuality*. Vancouver: Douglas and McIntyre.

Valaskakis, Gail Guthrie. 2005. *Indian Country: Essays on Contemporary Native Culture*. Waterloo, Can.: Wilfred Laurier University Press.

Warrior, Robert. 2008. "Your Skin Is the Map: The Theoretical Challenge of Joy Harjo's Erotic Poetics." In *Reasoning Together: The Native Critics Collective*, ed. Craig Womack et al., 340–52. Norman: University of Oklahoma Press.

Reviews → BOOKS

JILL DOERFLER

Métis: Race, Recognition, and the Struggle for Indigenous Peoplehood
University of British Columbia Press, 2014
by Chris Andersen

IN *MÉTIS: RACE, RECOGNITION, AND THE STRUGGLE FOR INDIGENOUS PEOPLEHOOD*, Andersen examines the misrecognition and racialization of the Métis. Who are the Métis? In my experience, many Americans (Native and non-Native) have no idea that the Métis even exist and/or are confused about who they are. I study Anishinaabe identity and racialization and did not have a firm grasp on Métis identity. I have read some scholarship on the development of the Métis at both Red River and Sault Ste. Marie that generally described them as people of mixed ancestry who formed a new and distinctive culture. I found this scholarship a bit perplexing as many peoples have some mixed ancestry and maintain a variety of distinct identities (i.e., there are many people who have mixed ancestry who are not Métis). As it turns out, I am not alone. Andersen explains that most Canadians think that "Métis" means mixed or mixed-race as a result of a wide range of systems that have validated and reproduced this idea. Métis is often thought of as a racial category.

In contrast, Andersen explores Métis in terms of political, peoplehood-based relationships, highlighting that this is a major shift in both scholarship and popularly held beliefs. He notes that the mere fact of the mixed ancestry of a people does not make them Métis, noting, "From my perspective, whether or not an Indigenous individual or community self-defines as Métis today, and whether or not the Indigenous community is 'older' than Red River, if the individual or group lacks a connection to the historical core in the Red River region, it is not Métis" (6). Andersen effectively contrasts the racialized definition of Métis with a nationhood-based positioning, placing Métis in connection to a "national core." Andersen effectively explores the complex tensions between racialized and national discourses about Métis.

There are several repercussions of the racialization of Métis identity. Andersen points out that if Métis are mixed then First Nations and Inuit must not be "mixed"—otherwise, to be mixed is not distinctive. Furthermore, if Métis are mixed and First Nations and Inuit are not, then Métis must be less Indigenous. Consequently, the racialization of Métis identity has effects beyond the Métis. Andersen discusses the ways in which an emphasis on biological origins results in the misrecognition of political status. Andersen employs an events-based narrative as the basis for a nationalist Métis identity to highlight the ways in which events facilitated and honed collective self-understandings of Métis identity.

He tackles the challenging issues surrounding the ways in which Statistics Canada and the Canadian courts have, in many cases, both legitimated and replicated problematic and dangerous racialization of Métis. Andersen does a superb job of engaging with the scholarship of the field, allowing the reader to gain a clear understanding of its historical trajectory and where Andersen's work stands in comparison. He ends with a series of suggestions for the ways in which both the census and the courts can better recognize and support Métis peoplehood. In addition, he calls for scholars to write about Métis in non-racialized ways and delineates five strategies for doing so. *Métis* is an important contribution and I expect that it will spur lively discussions, productive critiques, and shift the scholarship in the field.

JILL DOERFLER (White Earth Anishinaabe) is associate professor and department head of American Indian studies at the University of Minnesota—Duluth. She is coauthor of *The Constitution of the White Earth Nation: Ratification of a Native Democratic Constitution* and *Those Who Belong: Identity, Family, Blood, and Citizenship among the White Earth Anishinaabeg.*

STEVEN WILLIAMS

The Death and Afterlife of the North American Martyrs
Harvard University Press, 2013
by Emma Anderson

EMMA ANDERSON'S *The Death and Afterlife of the North American Martyrs* is an impressively researched and well-crafted intersectional analysis of the deaths and legacies of the eight colonial Jesuits collectively known as the "North America martyrs." These eight Jesuits were killed in Huronia during the turbulent 1640s by factions of the Wendat and Iroquois of whom they were attempting to forcibly convert to Catholicism. Previous hagiographic literature has primarily traced the martyrs' attempts to convert Native peoples of North America through descriptions of their suffering and deaths in what Anderson describes as "crescendos" to narratives of martyrdom. In contrast, her text shifts the focus by beginning with the martyrs' deaths as the point of departure for understanding their "afterlives." Rather than focus solely on Anglo-Christian perspectives that have framed Native North Americans as simply antagonists in narratives of Jesuit martyrdom, Anderson analyzes the narrative afterlives of the martyrs as "hybrid events" requiring recognition of the diversity of roles and perspectives of Native participants.

Anderson explores how multivalent meanings, historical memories, and affectual experiences of martyrdom have lived on in narratives of colonialism, nationalism, religion, spirituality, and resistance. This analysis illuminates the contrasting and often adaptive coming together of Native and Christian concepts such as the meaning of "good death," sacrifice, suffering, victimhood, superiority, and survivance (among others) that converge in individual and collective understandings of the martyrs. Anderson's analysis thus importantly highlights the circumstances of Native North Americans' erasure from historical narratives of martyrdom and the way in which those erasures continue to perpetuate a legacy of colonization for contemporary Native peoples.

Anderson's text is well worth reading for scholars in religious studies, Native Indigenous studies, American studies, transnational and border studies, and history. Her particular interest in conveying the visceral qualities of martyrdom art, literature, and artifacts and how "witnessing" these artifacts has led individuals to "imaginatively" engage the martyrs, importantly contributes to a deeper understanding of why the North American martyrs have left such lasting yet complex legacies.

For scholars in Native and Indigenous studies, I highlight just three of the many contributions that may be of particular interest. Chapter 1, "A Spectacle of Men and Angels," narrates the deaths of the eight North American martyrs through an "aboriginal context." This approach brings to light the ways in which Wendat and Iroquois, in the face of tremendous social upheavals, reasserted and often adapted traditional conceptions of soul return and sacrifice in postwar practices of ritual torture and adoption. Attention to the aboriginal context disrupts hagiographic narratives that frame the martyrs' deaths as religious persecution, therein revealing the diversity and complexity of Native actions and responses to the Jesuits.

Chapter 4, "For Canada and God," notably analyzes the ambivalent representations of Native peoples by Anglo-Canadians in two nationalistic cult commemorations of the martyrs' deaths held in 1949 at the Midlands Martyrs' Shrine. These commemorations recast Native actors as "descendants of the slayers" while narrating apparent conversions as the "triumph of Christianity." Anderson compares these productions with the disinterment of Wendat remains originally buried at Ossossané in 1636 to demonstrate that these tropes rendered Native actors/peoples a "silent presence." This erasure of Native histories has led to conflicting conceptions of the "sacred" at the sites and the unequal treatment of Native and non-Native remains in the pre-NAGPRA era.

Chapter 5, "Bones of Contention," analyzes the NAGPRA-era repatriation and reburial of 681 Wendat skeletons at Ossossané in 1999. Anderson illuminates significant shifts in cultural and religious power that occurred through repatriation as Native peoples attempted to reconnect with ancestors through the context of the Feast of the Dead ritual of reburial. Repatriation reinscribed Ossossané as a site of Native survival and resistance to martyr histories that had previously led to the erasure of diverse Native responses to the martyrs. These responses ranged from Catholic conversion to returns to "traditional" Native concepts that rejected conversion. These erasures, in turn, led to the unequal treatment of Native remains both past and present. Adding critically to this understanding, Anderson highlights the diversity of individual and collective ceremonies "experienced" by participants during repatriation and the Feast of the Dead as well as the discord that emerged between Catholic and "traditional" participants over the appropriateness of the inclusion of Catholic prayer and relics. Anderson examines the contemporary Feast of the Dead to consider both the legacy of the ancestors at Ossossané and a "sobering awareness" by the ceremonies' Native participants of the lasting divisions caused by Native encounters with Christianity that also connected contemporary Natives to their ancestors.

STEVEN WILLIAMS is a Mellon postdoctoral fellow and visiting professor in comparative American studies/Native American and Indigenous studies at Oberlin College.

ERICA NEEGANAGWEDGIN

The Students of Sherman Indian School:
   Education and Native Identity since 1892
University of Oklahoma Press, 2014
by Diana Meyers Bahr

DIANA MEYERS BAHR'S RECENT BOOK, *The Students of Sherman Indian School: Education and Native Identity since 1892*, examines the history and experiences of students who attended the federal boarding school. Opened in 1892, the school was one of the many federal boarding schools throughout the United States. Bahr points out that this was a time of assimilation into mainstream society, and the school's goal was to assimilate Native people into the now-dominant white Euro-American culture. The notion of "civilizing" as a deliberate process is a central theme throughout the work.

Bahr provides some analysis of the objective of the Office of Indian Education Programs. For example, the government's policy of assaulting identity by forcing students to learn English very quickly is a major theme that permeates this work. However, Bahr's work also provides strong accounts of Hopi children's resistance to losing their Native language and identity. While some learned English quickly, they also were determined to maintain their own language and become bilingual. This speaks to the ways in which the children adapted to the situation in which they found themselves and made it work.

One important part of Bahr's work is her reminder that the "education" of Indigenous peoples did not begin with colonial schools. Rather, she reminds readers that Indigenous education and the teaching of Indigenous worldviews started within families and clans. Native peoples, no matter where they are, have their own knowledge systems, which operate both formally and informally. Bahr's work reinforces this very critical point.

Bahr discusses what is referred to as a "middle course," which means that the students of Sherman Indian School were not passive pushovers, but that they made decisions and took actions that allowed them to cope with the confrontation or tensions between white and Native cultures. Students negotiated these issues based on the situation and tried their best to self-determine and redefine themselves from their own perspectives.

This work goes beyond the historical experiences and imposed government policies of the boarding school to look at the broader context of Native education and the role of various governments and actors in education reform for Native peoples nationally. For example, the Native American Languages Act of 1990 was implemented with the goal of the preservation of Native languages. This reinforced the notion of cultural continuity and self-determination, which was a stark contrast to the civilizing mission of boarding schools throughout the United States, which Bahr addresses. However, I would have liked to see more discussion on the role of Indigenous peoples in the implementation of this policy on language preservation. This would further strengthen Bahr's already important work. Bahr's book also addresses the inequities, disparities, and realities that continue to exist for Native people and their education today.

While the Sherman Indian School still exists, its mission has changed from forcing government policies of *civilization* to cultural continuity. Strong themes of disparity remain salient, however, and employees of the school have lost their jobs as a result of funding cuts. Nonetheless, the stories and accounts this work provides demonstrate the spirit of the students and their families who were faced with adversity, their narratives past and present, their remarkable determination as original people on their lands, and their zest for learning and self-determination.

Bahr provides an excellent historical account of white—Euro domination and assimilation policies that were forced on Indigenous people. This was done using education, Christianity, language, and the push toward the dominant European philosophies and outlook on life, and its purpose was to eradicate Native cultures and peoples. Some of the most engaging aspects of Bahr's work include the voices, experiences, words, and accounts from students themselves.

This book is an important addition to the stories of boarding/residential schools in North America. It provides an excellent historical examination of government-imposed boarding schools and of the policies that underlie the broader context of these institutions. The illustrations the author provides tell their own stories.

This work is engaging and compelling, and Bahr's analysis is rich. This book is a wonderful contribution to the fields of education, Native education, history, and Indigenous studies and would interest anyone who studies the history of Euro—white and Native relationships throughout North America. It provides an important contribution to existing stories and understanding of the boarding school policies and experiences.

ERICA NEEGANAGWEDGIN is assistant professor of Indigenous studies at Athabasca University.

DAN TAULAPAPA McMULLIN

Robert Davidson: Abstract Impulse
University of Washington Press, 2014
by Barbara Brotherton, Sheila Farr,
    and John Haworth

WHEN HAIDA ARTIST ROBERT DAVIDSON carved and installed his first totem pole in his home village Massett in Haida Gwaii in 1960, it was the first time a new totem pole had been erected there in nearly a century—in fact, until it was erected there were no other remaining poles there. As Davidson recalls, "One time when I came back to visit after leaving Massett, there was a circle of elders all sitting in a room. It felt really heavy; there was a sadness because everything was taken away. You know there was no songs, no dances, no art and that's when I had the idea of carving a totem pole for the village because I wanted these elders to celebrate one more time in the way they knew how." From this resolve he became the key artistic figure in a community working to bring Haida art and culture back to the present.

Robert Davidson: Abstract Impulse is the book accompanying his recent solo exhibition at the Seattle Art Museum (November 2013–February 2014) and the Smithsonian's National Museum of the American Indian, New York (April–September 2014), with essays by curator Barbara Brotherton, writer Sheila Farr, and John Haworth, director of the New York branch of the NMAI. Brotherton has known Davidson since 1977 and illustrates his journey as a Native American artist in the revival of Northwest Indigenous culture as a contemporary practitioner who both investigates Haida forms and creates new work. As she puts it, "Davidson disengages and reintegrates simultaneously, making the imagery his own."

Farr's essay looks at the history of American primitivism and the twentieth-century history of the appropriation of Northwest art and other Indigenous arts, setting the postcolonial scene in which Native artists like Davidson began working mainly after the middle of the twentieth century. Haworth's essay looks at the position of Robert Davidson today, as a respected elder of his community, a leader in the Indigenous art movement, and a great North American artist.

The book catalog *Robert Davidson: Abstract Impulse* is beautifully illustrated with paintings that are abstract in this historical context of contemporary painting, while suggesting the larger Indigenous narratives of which these paintings are a part. Although the book would have been strengthened by more Indigenous input in its commentary, the visual journey through its pages is inspiring.

DAN TAULAPAPA McMULLIN is a painter and poet from the U.S. territory of American Samoa, with a studio practice based in New York. He recently published a book of poems called *Coconut Milk*. More on his work can be seen at http://www.taulapapa.com/.

M. ARÁNZAZU ROBLES SANTANA

Feminismos desde Abya Yala:
  Ideas y proposiciones de las mujeres
  de 607 pueblos en Nuestra América
Ediciones desde abajo, Colombia septiembre 2012
by Francesca Gargallo Celentani
(review in Spanish)

EN *FEMINISMOS DESDE ABYA YALA*, la filósofa feminista e historiadora de las ideas, Francesca Gargallo Celentani, busca explorar las epistemologías, saberes, debates y propuestas de las mujeres Indígenas de los pueblos originarios de Nuestra América (término que nos refiere al ensayo del mismo nombre que el poeta cubano José Martí escribió en 1891 y que nos acerca a la diversidad cultural de América, ya que el término "latino" deja fuera a las poblaciones indígenas. Es un concepto no hegemónico y decolonizador que se aleja de la América dominada por la cultura y el poder occidental).

Se trata de un texto filosófico que ha nacido en el marco del trabajo de campo realizado por la autora desde México hasta Chile, con el fin de examinar, comprender y conocer los feminismos e ideas que están emergiendo de los diferentes saberes de las mujeres en *Abya Yala*, los cuales no tienen ninguna relación con el clásico ideario feminista occidental y académico.

Lejos de seguir una metodología filosófica clásica (la cual sí aparece como telón de fondo y envuelve el marco teórico), Francesca Gargallo analiza sus epistemologías directamente desde sus voces, desde las voces de las mujeres indígenas, lo que requiere una investigación horizontal, de campo y participativa, la cual se alinea más en las metodologías antropológicas que la puramente filosófica. El resultado es una "recopilación de diálogos e ideas" (2014: 9) a partir de las muchas conversaciones llevadas a cabo, e incluso a través de cartas. El resultado es un libro bien entretejido que intenta reflejar fielmente sus ideas y realidades desde las distintas voces, las cuales son producto de sus propias epistemologías y diferentes pertenencias.

El trabajo ha sido doble y en una doble dirección -valga la redundancia-. La primera apunta a un trabajo de conciencia, ya que la autora ha tenido que despojarse de todas sus raíces culturales fundadas en un sistema capitalista y racista, y distanciarse por un lado de los patrones académicos en los que ha sido formada -y del que forma parte-, así como de los privilegios que como ella misma dice "el sistema racista me ha reservado desde la infancia. Están tan interiorizados y normalizados que no me percato de ellos, y por ende, me abrogo el derecho de no reconocerlos, a menos que alguien me los señale" (2012: 15).

La segunda dirección se construye en el camino andado, en el trabajo de campo, en esa búsqueda de las distintas expresiones y saberes desde la realidad de ellas, de las mujeres indígenas, y solamente desde ellas.

Diversos pueblos originarios visitados como Totonicapán (Guatemala), Intibucá (Honduras), Bambú (Costa Rica), Kuna Yala (Panamá), Huancavelica (Perú), y muchos más, donde las mujeres, las relaciones de género y sus comportamientos no son homogéneos, lo que da lugar a una complejidad de pensamientos, formas de acción y de lucha divergentes que se plasman en los resultados de la investigación.

En el primer capítulo, la autora a partir de una reflexión con distintas fuentes teóricas, así como a través del diálogo con las mujeres, nos sitúa en la realidad del pensamiento y epistemología que nace y se teje en las mujeres indígenas desde su propio cuerpo, historia e identidad. La pregunta de por qué el Feminismo les ha excluido de su agenda, le lleva a cuestionar los preceptos asimilados en la sociedad de la "modernidad". En ese sentido, el debate individualismo-comunitarismo queda reflejado en las páginas del libro, donde se perciben las posiciones contrarias al sujeto femenino emancipado, liberal y autónomo que persigue el feminismo occidental, ese feminismo hegemónico que ha sido y es definido desde parámetros eurocéntricos y occidentalizados en pro de una libertad individual que queda muy lejos de la lucha por los derechos que las mujeres indígenas de Abya Yala buscan.

El segundo capítulo resalta cómo el feminismo académico está filtrado por la producción hegemónica del saber, donde no son incluidos los saberes ni las líneas de pensamiento indígenas. Así mismo, nos aproxima a las formas en las que las mujeres enfrentan las actitudes machistas, dando cuenta de cómo son objeto de injusticias en múltiples formas. La autora identifica cuatro tipos de feminismo: (1) aquellos que trabajan a favor de una buena vida a nivel comunitario, pero nos se llaman feministas porque temen que el término sea cuestionado por los dirigentes masculinos y que las demás mujeres se sientan incómodas. (2) Mujeres indígenas que se niegan a llamarse feministas porque cuestionan la mirada de las feministas blancas y urbanas. (3) Mujeres indígenas que reflexionan sobre los puntos de contacto entre su trabajo en la defensa de los derechos de las mujeres en su comunidad y el trabajo de las feministas blancas y urbanas. Se reivindican feministas o "iguales" a feministas. (4) Mujeres indígenas que se afirman abiertamente feministas desde un pensamiento autónomo.

El tercer capítulo está dedicado a los llamados Feminismos Comunitarios, donde sus integrantes, principalmente las Aymaras bolivianas de Comunidad Mujeres Creando Comunidad, representadas por Julieta Paredes, y las Xinkas de la Asociación de Mujeres Indígenas de Santa María de Xalapán Jalapa de Guatemala, representadas por Lorena Cabnal, ven el Feminismo no como una categoría occidental a combatir, sino como una herramienta teórica que les ha dado la posibilidad de pensarse como mujeres capacitadas, y estructurar un pensamiento y acción destinado a cuestionar y romper con los patrones patriarcales, heteronormativos y heterosexuales establecidos; no sólo los heredados del colonialismo, sino también los que perduran desde tiempos anteriores a la colonia, destapando así un patriarcado ancestral. Ambos patriarcados dan lugar a lo que han denominado el Entronque Patriarcal como la consecuencia de estos dos sistemas de poder de dominación sobre el cuerpo de las mujeres. Éste es sólo uno de los postulados de su pensamiento-acción para despatriarcalizar la cosmovisión y fundamentos de poder que les limitan como mujeres en sus Comunidades. Finalmente se analizan los ecofeminismos como otras experiencias de feminismos comunitarios.

En el cuarto y último capítulo, a través de un intenso debate con mujeres Mayas, Zapotecas, Misquitas, Kichwas, Nasas y muchas otras de distintos grupos indígenas, Francesca Gargallo recoge sus pensamientos sobre el feminismo, racismo, sexismo, políticas del cuerpo y colonialismo. La gran mayoría de ellas están de acuerdo en cómo el Estado ha negado la historia de los pueblos indígenas, teniendo como resultado la naturalización del racismo y sexismo para con sus pueblos, revirtiendo potencialmente sobre el cuerpo de las mujeres.

En suma, este libro cartografía las circunstancias y singularidades de la lucha de las mujeres Indígenas en *Abya Yala* y nos da a conocer sus ideas fuera de construcciones y definiciones externas. Su lectura es imprescindible para académicas/os y estudiantes interesados en conocer y reconocer la existencia de pensamientos ¿feministas? no hegemónicos.

M. ARÁNZAZU ROBLES SANTANA es doctoranda al Instituto Universitario de Estudios de las Mujeres de la Universidad de La Laguna, Tenerife, España. Es una compiladora y editora del libro *Género y conocimiento en un mundo global: Tejiendo redes*.

Notas

Este trabajo está sustentado por el Ministerio de Economía y Competitividad del Gobierno de España dentro del Proyecto FFI2011-24120 "Ciudadanía, Justicia y Género: Feminización de las Migraciones y Derechos Humanos."

1. Abya Yala es una expresión del Pueblo Indígena Kuna del Panamá que designa el territorio americano. Esta expresión nos permite reconocer América desde sus raíces indígenas y no desde una perspectiva histórica que nombra e identifica al continente a partir de la colonización europea.

M. ARÁNZAZU ROBLES SANTANA

Feminismos desde Abya Yala: Ideas y proposiciones de las mujeres de 607 pueblos en Nuestra América (Feminisms from Abya Yala: Women's Ideas and Propositions of 607 Peoples in Our America)
Ediciones desde abajo, Colombia septiembre 2012.
Online version 2014, http://francescagargallo.files.wordpress.com/2014/01/francesca-gargallo-feminismos-desde-abya-yala-ene20141.pdf
by Francesca Gargallo Celentani
(review in English)

IN *FEMINISMOS DESDE ABYA YALA*, the feminist philosopher and historian of ideas Francesca Gargallo Celentani seeks to explore the epistemologies, *saberes* (knowledges), and thoughts of the Indigenous women of the Pueblos *originarios* (First Nations) in Nuestra América (a concept that embraces the cultural diversity of America, since the Latin term leaves out the Indigenous populations; it is a decolonizing and not hegemonic concept that refers to an America independent from occidental power and domination, referencing José Marti's 1891 essay).

It is a philosophical text that was born in the context of her fieldwork that spans from Mexico to the tip of Chile with the aim to examine and understand feminisms and ideas that are emerging from the different women's knowledge in Abya Yala,[1] which are not connected with the occidental and academic feminism ideology.

Far from following a classical philosophical methodology—which appears as a backdrop and as a theoretical framework—Gargallo Celentani analyzes these epistemologies directly from the voices of the Indigenous women. This procedure requires a participatory and horizontal approach to research, which is more closely aligned to anthropological methodologies rather than purely philosophical ones. The result is a "collection of dialogues and ideas" (2014: 9) based on many conversations that took place, including through the exchange of letters, between women from different communities along Abya Yala. The outcome is an interwoven book that tries to reflect the ideas and realities from these different voices, which are a product of their own epistemologies and different belongings.

The book provides clarity about respectful dialogue with Indigenous women from different communities (Zapotecs, Kichwas, Chocholtecas, Bribris, Gnöbes, and Mapuches, among others). Because of this, in the book we cannot see a classic interview itself; we are able to read the reflections and viewpoints that the women give to the author related to such issues as discrimination, racism, power, gender topics, and others that are entirely explained through their words.

Consequently this study is double-pronged: the first half stages a critique of feminist consciousness, as the author is critically self-reflexive about her own cultural roots in relation to capitalist and racist systems. She explains why academic standards force distance from our origins and the objectivity required of the intellectual. These privileges and contradictions, she says, mark how "the racist system has produced my subjectivity since childhood. They are [privileges] so internalized and normalized that I am unaware of them, and therefore I abrogate the right not to recognize them, unless someone could point them out" (2012: 15). It is an interesting reflection that prompts academics to think critically and reflect on these racist patterns that we have internalized and may in part reproduce.

The second prong of her analysis is a critique of the road traveled in the field itself, which includes taking seriously Indigenous women's realities, expressions, and knowledge forms. The fieldwork literally walks us through the territories of all the people of Abya Yala. Gargallo Celentani visited Indigenous such communities as Totonicapán (Guatemala), Intibucá (Honduras), Bambú (Costa Rica), Kuna Yala (Panamá), Huancavelica (Perú), and many more. As a result, the scholarship represents Indigenous thought as complex and contested even within the same ethnic group. Struggles are reflected in the results of the investigation.

In the first chapter the author, from a self-reflection through a extensive theoretical framework and from the dialogue with the Indigenous women, brings us closer to the thoughts and epistemology that are born from and intertwine their thoughts, from their bodies, history, and identity. Focusing on the debate linked to white Western feminism and the ways it produces hegemonic knowledge where Indigenous women are not represented, the discussion of individualism—communitarianism and the construction of modernity is explained in relationship to Indigenous women, where we can prove that the fights of Western and hegemonic feminism are totally disconnected from Indigenous women's realities and struggles.

The second chapter highlights the ways in which hegemonic knowledge production filters academic feminism, where *saberes* and Indigenous thoughts are not included. Further, the author discusses the diverse ways that Native women in their communities fight against machismo and androcentric behaviors as a daily practice, and accounts for how they face different injustices in multiple settings (the family, community, nation-state, etc.). Gargallo Celentani identifies four types of feminists in this chapter: (1) those who work for a better life in the community but do not want to identify with the feminism label; (2) those who think that the concept of feminism represents white and urban women exclusively; (3) those who articulate a sense of comfort with the white feminist label to fight against sexist attitudes in society; and (4) those who call themselves feminist but from an autonomous thought, and they use the concept as a tool and method to deconstruct and decolonize gender roles in their communities. Different kinds of feminism are adapted to the roots of Indigenous thought, creating a historic and rightful distance and suspicion of hegemonic and traditional feminisms.

The third chapter is dedicated to the "Feminismos Comunitarios" (Communitarian Feminisms), first articulated in Bolivia by Julieta Paredes, a member of the Bolivian Aymara community called Women Creating Community, and the Xinka Lorena Cabnal of the Association of Indigenous Xinka Women of Santa María de Xalapán (Jalapa, Guatemala). The Feminismos Comunitarios are interested in breaking patriarchal patterns and heteronormative and heterosexual behaviors. Individuals like Julieta Paredes and Lorena Cabnal argue that not only is the legacy of colonialism at issue, but that there is also an ancient patriarchy in their communities. Both patriarchies (contemporary and ancient) are outcomes of what is called *entronque patriarcal* (patriarchal junction)—the result of these two systems of patriarchal power. This is just one key aspect to unseat patriarchal ancestral worldviews and power, which limits women in their own Xinka and Aymara communities. Lastly, the chapter also examines communitary ecofeminisms as other experiences of Feminismos Comunitarios.

The fourth and final chapter reflects on extensive discussions with Indigenous Mayas, Zapotecas, Misquitas, Kichwas, Zapotecas, and Nasas, among others, about feminism, racism, sexism, politics of the body, and colonialisms. Most women argue that the state is in denial about the existence of their histories as embedded racism in global societies, and that racism is naturalized as normal.

Overall, Francesca Gargallo Celentani makes clear that Indigenous women's knowledge formations are central to and necessary for her conclusions. The book is a good resource for scholars and students interested in a general overview of Indigenous women and their encounters with feminism in the Americas.

M. ARÁNZAZU ROBLES SANTANA is a PhD candidate in the University Institute of Women Studies at the University of La Laguna, Tenerife, Spain. She is coeditor of the book *Género y conocimiento en un mundo global: Tejiendo redes*.

Notes

This work has been supported by the Research Program FFI2011-24120, "Justice, Citizenship, and Gender: Feminization of Migration and Human Rights," from the Minister of Economy and Competitiveness of the Spanish Government.

1. Abya Yala is an Indigenous expression of the Kunas peoples of Panama that designates the whole American territory. This expression allows us to envision the American continent from the vision of Indigenous peoples and not from a Euro-centered point of view.

C. JOSEPH GENETIN-PILAWA

*Remembering the Modoc War: Redemptive Violence
  and the Making of American Innocence*
University of North Carolina Press, 2014
by Boyd Cothran

IN A CAREFULLY CHOREOGRAPHED CEREMONY, the U.S. Army hanged four Modoc headmen including Captain Jack, on Friday, October 3, 1873. The men had been convicted of murdering U.S. peace commissioners General Edward R. S. Canby and the Reverend Eleazer Thomas. While this public event marked the official end of the Modoc War (1872–1873), in his new book *Remembering the Modoc War* historian Boyd Cothran argues that the grisly trade in execution mementos that followed—lengths of the hangman's ropes, cabinet cards with the prisoner's portraits, locks of the dead men's hair—symbolized the beginning of a new contest over its meaning and memory. This contest, however, expanded into diffuse and long-lasting "marketplaces of remembering," including newspaper accounts, reenactments, traveling Wild West shows, memorial celebrations, and more. The process of historical knowledge production the author describes, created a framework in which Euro-Americans have and continue to justify their territorial acquisitions, conquest, violence, and colonialism as inevitable. Cothran contends "that individuals have shaped historical remembrances of the conflict, transforming an episode of Reconstruction-era violence and ethnic-cleansing into a redemptive narrative of American innocence as they sought to negotiate these marketplaces" (14–15).

Remembering the Modoc War moves beyond the problematic narratives of triumphalist military history and instead offers a nuanced, well-researched, sharply argued, far-reaching cultural history of Gilded Age settler colonialism in the American West that stretches to the present. Cothran engages with the history and historiography of the war itself, and in doing so critiques the scholarly discourse of memory studies. He asserts that much of the literature has transformed the "act of remembering . . . from a performative representation of the past to an interpretive object, and the analytical thrust is toward reading the object rather than understanding the lives of those who produced it." Memory, the author notes, "is a noun, it is a thing; remembering is a verb . . . a kind of labor in the production of a version of the past" (23). With that critique in place, Cothran demonstrates how the circulation of historical remembrances of the Modoc War wove together the conflict and ideas about Native–settler violence in such a way that privileged Indian criminality and American innocence.

The book unfolds chronologically and thematically across three parts, focusing first on the initial newspaper coverage of the war. Reporters, Cothran argued, initially tied the conflict to partisan politics of the Reconstruction era but after the death of General Canby shifted the framework to one of American victimhood and Indigenous criminality. Here the author offers not only analysis of the newspaper stories but also intriguing close textual readings of the engravings that illustrated the innocence trope for Americans across the continent. The second part focuses on the life of Toby Riddle, a Modoc translator whose stage name in the 1870s became Winema, "the Pocahontas of the Lava Beds," as she traveled the country and performed as part of the Alfred Meacham Lecture Company. By examining her forgotten career, Cothran is able to show how some Native women (and men) "used existing narratives of violence and gendered tropes of civilization and savagery" to earn national celebrity, participate in the emerging entertainment industry as performers, and even receive federal pensions, as Riddle ultimately did (83). The final part focuses on the ways early twentieth-century Americans commemorated the Modoc War. Tourism boosters and land promoters represented the war as a turning point in the region's history, the first step in a movement from savagery to civilization and an ushering in of modernity. To the Modoc it was a moment of suppression and violent subjugation. Each part of the book ends with a coda in which the author offers personal anecdotes that bring the story up to the present.

Cothran ends his study with a stunning indictment of liberal multiculturalism in the late twentieth century. Through an examination of efforts to create an "Indian-inclusive" memorial in the Klamath Basin, he argues that multiculturalism in recent years has perpetuated the persistent conception of American innocence while masquerading as a mechanism for racial reconciliation. Overall, *Remembering the Modoc War* is a welcome contribution to the fields of Native American and Indigenous studies, settler colonial studies, memory studies, the American West, and nineteenth-century U.S. history. Accessible to a wide audience, including undergraduates as well as graduates and practicing scholars, this book serves as an excellent example of the best new work in these fields. It deserves a wide reading.

C. JOSEPH GENETIN-PILAWA is assistant professor of history at George Mason University. He is the author of *Crooked Paths to Allotment: The Fight over Federal Indian Policy after the Civil War* and coeditor of *Beyond Two Worlds: Critical Conversations on Language and Power in Native North America*.

LORENZO VERACINI

Red Skin, White Masks:
   Rejecting the Colonial Politics of Recognition
University of Minnesota Press, 2014
by Glen Sean Coulthard

COULTHARD'S FUNDAMENTAL INSIGHT is that we urgently need a new theory and practice of settler decolonization. What we have is profoundly insufficient, and while everyone knows that dysfunctional indigenous communities need something, Coulthard's merit is to be absolutely clear about what is required: decolonized futures arising from a revolutionary rupture. This is not a proposition without consequence, because for thinking the intimate relationship linking decolonization and revolution there's nothing better than returning to Frantz Fanon. This is indeed not a book without consequence, and Coulthard delivers a veritable decolonizing manifesto. *Red Skin, White Masks* begins with a systematic criticism of what we have, the liberal "politics of recognition" and their normalizing universalism premised on one-way processes of inclusion within Western liberal epistemes, processes that in many fundamental respects look very much like old-style assimilation processes, and ends with what we need to accomplish: a capacity for indigenous self-affirmation that will ultimately enable "Indigenous resurgences" (unlike Coulthard, but in a very Coulthardian move that also rejects the politics of recognition, I recommend using "indigenous" in its lowercased form: as indigenous claims are premised on specific relationships to place, there is more decolonizing strength in the adjective that in the noun—nouns, after all, are eminently moveable). And for thinking the self-affirmation of colonized subjectivities there is nothing better than returning to Fanon.

Red Skin, White Masks is too important an intervention to be summarized in 750 words, and readers should not be content with a descriptive outline of its constituent parts. Rather than attempting a summary of the ways in which Coulthard arrives at his conclusions, in the following remarks I aim to engage with its achievement.

I referred above to "what we need to achieve." It is in this formulation that lies my (partial) disagreement with Coulthard's theory of settler decolonization. I am a settler and I know I am on indigenous land even when I am home, but I think there's still a "we" in a decolonizing future. If Coulthard's insight is that indigenous "resurgences" are necessarily premised on the self-affirmation of indigenous subjectivities, and that this self-affirmation must be independent of settler recognition, my suggestion is that under settler colonialism it is the settler that is affected by profound psychopathologies. This latter notion is not aimed at displacing Coulthard's focus on indigenous self-affirmation, but should parallel it. Policy has traditionally focused in settler polities on changing indigenous communities, their behavior, and their relationship with surrounding social milieus or with settler institutional settings. It is time we begin thinking about ways to change the settler and his way of being (I use "his" advisedly: as settler colonial regimes are especially about the reproduction of one sociopolitical body in the place of another, they are inevitably profoundly gendered). Reverting the focus of settler policy is needed as much as indigenous resurgence.

Similarly, the "we" contained in "what we need to achieve" questions Coulthard's vision of indigenous–settler relationships. Under settler colonialism the settler demand has consistently been for the indigenous "problem," or for the indigenous person, to disappear. In fundamental ways, the settler imagination of unproblematic futures has always aimed at the ultimate discontinuation of indigenous–settler relationships. Coulthard's neglect of the settler beyond welcoming them as potential "allies" looks very much like that discontinuation. Decolonized futures should be futures where the indigenous–settler relationship remains meaningful and ongoing. In other words, if indigenous communities need "resurgences," and they do, settlers need therapy (for this, one may even return to Fanon, after all he was a gifted psychiatrist). I am not saying something particularly new. No usurper copes well with a reminder of his ultimate illegitimacy and foreclosure is not a viable or sustainable option—everyone knows that what is foreclosed sooner or later comes back to haunt.

The decolonization of settler colonialism as a mode of domination should proceed, I believe, on parallel tracks. These tracks must remain accountable to each other, of course, but progress in one of them is ultimately predicated on its counterpart. After all, settler colonialism as a mode of domination envisages a specific relation (as it is premised on a "logic of elimination," and at times on physical elimination, a profoundly insalubrious one), and relations are by definition sustained by dynamic entities. Again, I am not saying something particularly new. Fanon summarized this constitutive dialectic by famously remarking that "it is the settler who has brought the native into existence and who perpetuates his existence." We need settler colonial studies as much as we need critical indigenous studies.

LORENZO VERACINI is associate professor in history at the Swinburne University of Technology in Melbourne. He has authored *Israel and Settler Society*, *Settler Colonialism: A Theoretical Overview*, and *The Settler Colonial Present* and is managing editor of *Settler Colonial Studies*.

CURTIS F. FOXLEY

*Fort Marion Prisoners and the Trauma
   of Native Education*
University of Nebraska Press, 2014
by Diane Glancy

PRIMARILY CONSTRUCTED OUT OF PREVIOUSLY PUBLISHED ESSAYS, Glancy's *Fort Marion Prisoners and the Trauma of Native Education* is best described as a creative, spiritual amalgam of the experiences of the Fort Marion prisoners of the 1870s and the author's personal journey of researching, writing, and reflecting on those experiences. Jumping back and forth from the nineteenth-century Florida prison to her own composition process and reflections, Glancy crafts a text that comes across as disjointed yet powerful. Adding to this reader's confusion and the text's spiritual tone, Glancy blends her literary text, which at times consists of dialogue, first-person and third-person narrative, with the text of primary resources such as letters and records. Truly, Glancy's text is "An interaction. An interpretation. An interlocutor" (60).

When Glancy does not present the reader with her travels, her reflections, and her own educational experiences, she brings to life the Arapaho, Caddo, Cheyenne, Comanche, and Kiowa prisoners of Fort Marion. Defeated by the U.S. Calvary in the 1870s, these men, women, and children were transported from Fort Sill, located in modern-day Oklahoma, to Fort Marion in St. Augustine, Florida. There, under the direction of Captain Richard Henry Pratt (later of Carlisle Boarding School fame), these captives were taught English, the Bible, and other staples of nineteenth-century Anglo "civilization." Fort Marion served as an experimental precursor to the implementation of Native American boarding schools, which shaped, even terrorized, the lives of many Native Americans during the late nineteenth and much of the twentieth century.

Throughout her text, Glancy emphasizes the importance of two key aspects of the Fort Marion experience: ledger books and the ocean. Placed in the captives' hands by Captain Pratt with instructions to draw, ledger books served as an outlet of expression for the Native prisoners and as artistic goods that prisoners sold to curious tourists. Glancy beautifully describes the power the ledger books and colored pencils had when she pens, "He made marks with the drawing sticks. He floated through the air. The drawing sticks were his wings. They were magic sticks. A horse came from the stick" (36). While the ledger books were certainly important to their contemporaries for expressive, therapeutic, and commercial reasons, today they are the primary window into the minds and hearts of the Marion captives. Along with reprinting several of these ledger drawings, Glancy brings the reader to the point of their creation, artistically describing what captives, such as Bear's Heart, thought about while drawing. Along with the ledger books, Glancy also emphasizes the ocean, which is situated alongside Fort Marion. Being from the Great Plains, many of the prisoners were unfamiliar with such a large body of water and the mysterious creatures it contained. As she proceeds through her text, Glancy demonstrates how the prisoners conceptualized the sea and how it fit into their changing worldviews.

While Glancy's text certainly is moving, followers of her work published in *Florida Review* and *Yellow River Review* will find little new material here. Due to Glancy's creative mixture of history, personal experiences, expression, narrative, and evocative spirit, this text is perhaps best for those interested in Native studies and literature, as opposed to history. Still, the brief nature of the text (totaling 136 pages) does make it a quick read for all those interested in Fort Marion, Native education, and a heart-wrenching story.

CURTIS F. FOXLEY is a master's student in history at the University of Oklahoma.

GREGORY ROSENTHAL

*A Nation Rising: Hawaiian Movements
for Life, Land, and Sovereignty*
Duke University Press, 2014
edited by Noelani Goodyear-Kaʻōpua, Ikaika Hussey,
and Erin Kahunawaikaʻala Wright

HAUNANI-KAY TRASK'S *FROM A NATIVE DAUGHTER* may have been published twenty years ago, but it is still the go-to volume for academics and activists interested in Kānaka Maoli (Native Hawaiian) resistance to U.S. colonialism. A new volume, *A Nation Rising*, offers a timely update. Organized in three parts—"Life," "Land," and "Sovereignty"—this book features sixteen chapters and six "portraits" on various aspects of the contemporary Hawaiian movement. An introductory essay by Noelani Goodyear-Kaʻōpua sets the stakes for the volume, arguing that "a diversity of positions and perspectives is a mark of a healthy nation," and that *ea* (life, breath, sovereignty) is an Indigenous political concept that unifies *ka lāhui Hawaiʻi* (the nation) in its manifold struggles and distinguishes Native Hawaiian aspirations from Western definitions of sovereignty.

The book represents a milestone in public discourse and scholarship on Kānaka Maoli resistance. It is also an achievement of great merit for its diverse assemblage of twenty-eight writers and editors, each representing a distinct voice and perspective. The editors have intentionally included works by both academics and on-the-ground activists, and many contributors fall somewhere in between. No other book has so well captured the diverse threads that constitute the Hawaiian sovereignty movement.

Three themes stand out as the book's major contributions. The first is class, represented by six "portraits" offering short biographical essays of Indigenous working-class people on the front lines of resistance to dispossession, militarization, and settler colonialism. Goodyear-Kaʻōpua acknowledges in her introduction that "an Indigenous movement without a class analysis can be vapid in terms of its ability to produce meaningful change" (12). Essays by Anna Keala Kelly and Puhipau show that the most marginalized Hawaiians (including those without employment or shelter) experience colonialism differently than do Hawaiian "leaders." Kelly forcefully argues against the elite "Hawaiian intelligentsia," those with "doctorates and law degrees" who speak out about sovereignty while "actual physical resistance . . . is left to the most vulnerable Hawaiians, the most impoverished, those who have no choice but to hold their ground" (46). Essays by Kalamaokaʻāina Niheu on the reclamation of Mākua Beach by "houseless people" as a *puʻuhonua* (sanctuary) from militarization, and Leʻa Malia Kanehe on the biocolonial enclosure of Hawaiian plants, animals, and genes as private property, also contribute to this theme.

Debates over terms such as *Indigeneity*, *colonialism*, and *occupation* constitute the second major contribution of this volume. Kūhiō Vogeler and J. Kēhaulani Kauanui each articulate the stakes of defining Hawaiians either as an occupied "independent state" or as colonized "Indigenous peoples." Kauanui argues that Kānaka Maoli should resist domestic dependent nation ("nation within a nation") status as represented by the so-called Akaka Bill. Vogeler's "occupation theory" marks Kānaka Maoli as citizens of an overthrown state rather than as Indigenous subjects. These distinctions matter because they potentially lead to strikingly different legal standing for Native subjects in federal and international law.

A third major contribution concerns debates over economic growth versus environmental protection. Davianna Pōmaikaʻi McGregor and Noa Emmett Aluli's essay on resistance to geothermal energy and Leon Noʻeau Peralto's portrait of Mauna a Wākea establish the sacredness of fire on the Island of Hawaiʻi and amplify the role of genealogy and religion as bases for Kānaka Maoli environmentalism. D. Kapuaʻala Sproat and Pauahi Hoʻokano discuss similar themes as they relate to water rights. Journalist Joan Conrow rounds out this theme with a narrative of the long history of Kānaka Maoli resistance to development on Kauaʻi Island.

This volume also points to areas for future research. Davianna Pōmaikaʻi McGregor and Ibrahim Aoudé, Kekailoa Perry, and Noenoe K. Silva all celebrate the central role of activism at the University of Hawaiʻi, showing how students and faculty exert power and influence both on and off campus. Future scholarship might explore the conflicts that sometimes arise between academics and on-the-ground activists. Ty P. Kāwika Tengan's examination of gender, nation, and memory is exemplary and also points to the need for more research at the intersections of gender, sexuality, and health, especially in relationship to racism and militarization. Another area of future research is the role of diasporic off-island Hawaiians in the anticolonial movement.

While *A Nation Rising* is admittedly not "a comprehensive accounting" of "the contemporary Hawaiian movement" (2), editors Noelani Goodyear-Kaʻōpua, Ikaika Hussey, and Erin Kahunawaikaʻala Wright have yet successfully assembled an intriguing, rich, and nuanced collection of diverse narratives. Duke University Press is also to be commended for their commitment to "Narrating Native Histories," a series that publishes many books by Kānaka Maoli scholars. Academics and activists interested in the theory and practice of national liberation struggles will find much to think about in *A Nation Rising*. Instructors, too, may wish to add *A Nation Rising* to their syllabi to encourage students to recognize that the *moʻolelo* (story) of anti-colonial struggle in Hawaiʻi is far from over.

GREGORY ROSENTHAL is assistant professor of public history at Roanoke College.

JESSICA CAREY-WEBB

Native and National in Brazil:
  Indigeneity after Independence
University of North Carolina Press, 2013
by Tracy Devine Guzmán

TRACY DEVINE GUZMÁN frames her 2013 publication, *Native and National in Brazil: Indigeneity after Independence*, with a description of the popular television personality Xuxa and one of her more famous clips, "Vamos brincar de índio" ("Let's play Indian"). In a performance that helps the reader situate tensions explored throughout the book of where Indigenous people fit within Brazilian culture and politics, the blonde Brazilian bombshell/entertainer's "brincar de índio" has Xavante Indians stand in the middle of a crowded stage, disengaged from an over-the-top performance "celebrating" the Indian. These Indians, according to Xuxa, are "living nature" (2), forming an important part of Brazilian culture, central to the popular imaginary as a primitive living past. While Xuxa proclaims the importance of the Indian, the Xavante on stage stand to the side, noticeably uncomfortable and out of place—politically and socially marginalized—drawn out from the jungle to demonstrate their difference.

Xuxa's appropriation and misrepresentation of the Xavante in "playing Indian" serves as a jumping-off point in Devine Guzmán's study of cultural and political production surrounding Indigeneity in Brazil from the mid-nineteenth century until the present day. This anecdote not only highlights the tenuous position of the Indigenous population but works as a thread throughout the book—how dominant Brazilian society has used Indigeneity as a popular trope while ignoring Indians as citizens or even human beings. Within this larger thread is the question of Indigenous authenticity—how Indigenous peoples can self-identify in an increasingly modernized world that calls for a certain performance of Indigeneity itself.

Through five chapters, Devine Guzmán skillfully demonstrates the importance of a cultural studies approach that privileges not only literature but film, history, maps, popular culture, and a multitude of cultural iterations revolving around Indigeneity.

Chapter 1 explores "inclusion through exclusion"—the move toward a measured incorporation of Indigenous populations by the Brazilian government through the creation of various organizations such as the Serviço de Proteção aos Índios (SPI), later becoming the Fundação Nacional do Índio (FUNAI). Beyond critiquing these governmental measures, Devine Guzmán works to complicate the idea of Indigeneity across multiple contexts—citing sources as varied as David Stoll and Paulo Freire, and ultimately critiquing appropriating Indigeneity for an academic audience as well. This shows a refreshing sense of self-awareness that is apparent throughout the book.

Chapter 2 centers on popular romantic representations of a somewhat "noble savage," examining the well-studied *Il Guarany* and *Iracema*. Devine Guzmán argues that these incredibly popular emblems of "operatic and literary Indianism" worked to destroy Indigenous lives through an increased belief in a "benevolent colonialism" during a critical moment in which whitening processes were becoming an established part of policy designed to eliminate the Other through miscegenation and extended periods of violence against the Indigenous population (67).

Devine Guzmán's argument becomes most compelling in chapters 3 and 4, where she explores international designs on the Amazon rain forests' resources and the Indian as one of the fundamental pillars of Brazilian national identity. By beginning chapter 3 with a now famously fake map of a U.S. plan to take over the Amazon rain forest, Devine Guzmán expands on policies laid out in chapter 1, and spatially frames how education was used as a tool to harness Indigenous labor in an increasingly industrialized and internationally exploited Amazonia.

Chapter 4, perhaps the most intriguing, examines "O caso Diacuí," in which the growing gap between ideals about Indigeneity and actual political practice came to a head when a rubber-tapper made national headlines for his marriage to a Xavante woman. During the 1950s when this case came about, the Indigenous population were still considered wards of the state, making a marriage between a Brazilian and Indian technically illegal. While intense public scrutiny of this dramatic love story played out, years of cultural production and political repression were brought to a national stage.

Chapter 5 analyzes the Indigenous movement of the new millennium, offering a survey of Brazilian Indigenous activist and intellectual production. Despite best efforts and crucial critical self-awareness, there is still a lack of Indigenous voice in the book, a lack of feel for an Indigenous community or what life is like as an Indigenous person in Brazil. This is overtly acknowledged by Devine Guzmán and in fact serves to further illustrate her argument of a hegemonic political discourse about Indigeneity that lacks a Native Brazilian voice. Also missing from this discourse is a more direct mention of the third pillar of Brazilian racial makeup—blackness. While black Brazilians are alluded to in chapters 1 and 5, it seems that a more clear comparison—if only in passing—could serve to demonstrate the exceptionality of the Indigenous case in Brazil.

Devine Guzmán's engaging and reflective book reads easily and situates itself in a growing discussion that attempts to move beyond extractive academic practices and toward a more inclusive representation that depends on collaboration between Indigenous and non-Indigenous activists and academics.

JESSICA CAREY-WEBB is a PhD student in the Department of Spanish and Portuguese at the University of Texas, Austin. Her research focuses on empire and exploration of the Amazon region.

HEIDI KIIWETINEPINESIIK STARK

*Elder Brother and the Law of the People:
   Contemporary Kinship and Cowessess First Nation*
University of Manitoba Press, 2013
by Robert Alexander Innes

WHILE QUESTIONS OF INDIGENOUS NATIONHOOD, governance, and citizenship remain central to the field, Native studies' aversion to the exploration of kinship—due to its close association with anthropology that produced evolutionary and cultural relativist theories and abstract taxonomies holding little relevance to Native studies scholars or Native communities—has precluded a potentially rich consideration of kinship's role in the maintenance and affirmation of individual and collective identity. Robert Alexander Innes, in *Elder Brother and the Law of the People: Contemporary Kinship and Cowessess First Nation*, brilliantly takes up this question to understand Cowessess responses to their relatives who had been displaced by colonialism. Defying perceptions that Indigenous peoples have internalized colonial, state-imposed notions of Indianness, Innes's work shows how Cowessess undermined the imposition of Canada's Indian Act and its legal definition of "Indian" by acknowledging kinship relations to band members who either had not been federally recognized as Indians prior to 1985 or were urban members disconnected from the reserve.

This maintenance of kinship, Innes reveals, follows Cowessess law contained in Elder Brother stories. In chapter 1, he argues that the Law of the People contained within these stories has been kept alive through the social practices of Cowessess band members that pre-dates the reserve and persists today. In the second chapter, Innes demonstrates that band membership was historically fluid, flexible, and inclusive, by providing a history of the four groups that constitute Cowessess (the Plains Cree, Saulteaux, Assiniboine, and Métis) and the emergence of the Iron Alliance. Similarities between these groups, he contends, have not been afforded proper recognition, as cultural and social differences have been regularly emphasized in Indigenous histories at the expense of attention to long-term practices of intermarriage, alliances, and cultural exchanges between these groups.

Chapter 3 extends this critique with a focus on the term "tribe," which has been used to categorize and delineate Indigenous history. Innes argues that constructing Indigenous histories along tribal lines fails to account for the role of bands as the primary social and political units eschewing how Indigenous nations both organized themselves historically and are viewed today.

As one example, Innes argues that academic framings of Métis as fundamentally distinct from First Nations have further perpetuated a focus on tribal distinctions that eclipses relatedness. Innes shows how scholarly obsession with categorizing Indigenous peoples has favored a narrative of hybridity, with the consequence of blinding scholars from seeing the rich multicultural mosaic that makes up many Indigenous communities.

The fourth chapter delves into a history of Cowessess to demonstrate the degree to which scholars have misrepresented ethnic identities of Indigenous peoples on the prairies. Cultural boundaries drawn between Indigenous groups, Innes asserts, is largely a fiction that has served some scholars and government officials but has had little relevance to the actual lives of the peoples under examination. Kinship traditions allowed the band to maintain their multicultural composition well into the twentieth century. This is demonstrated in chapter 5, which draws on interviews with Cowessess members to outline how kinship obligations have both been changed by outside forces and contemporary realities, and also persisted as critical mechanisms guiding social interactions and determining membership and belonging. Innes extends his analysis of Cowessess membership and belonging in chapter 6 by challenging dominant media discourses surrounding Indigenous responses to Bill C-31 changes to the Indian Act. Innes lays out how mistrust in the Canadian government—rooted in failed treaty implementation and assimilation policies, and fueled by 1969 attempts to terminate federal responsibilities to Indians via the White Paper—spurred First Nations leaders to oppose any changes to the Indian Act, including amendments that sought to correct discriminatory elements. He notes, "In contrast to the position of most First Nations leaders, Cowessess band members had a relatively high tolerance for band members who regained their Indian status through Bill C-31" (142).

In chapter 7, Innes looks to Cowessess' successful negotiation of the 1996 Treaty Land Entitlement (TLE) agreement, part of the comprehensive land claims process, as additional evidence of the persistence of kinship values as a central unifying factor. Here, questions remain regarding whether kinship values would assist in the achievement of this agreement or if engagement in the TLE process would potentially compel Cowessess to invigorate long-standing kinship practices to ensure that a larger claim could be put forward, resulting in the expansion of Cowessess' land base. Nonetheless, Innes's work shows the TLE process helped strengthen kinship ties and expand notions of belonging.

This book makes significant contributions to the fields of Indigenous studies, history, anthropology, and political science, to name a few. Ultimately, each chapter skillfully weaves together a powerful narrative of kinship, membership, and belonging as practices of Indigeneity, resistance, and resurgence.

HEIDI KIIWETINEPINESIIK STARK (Turtle Mountain Ojibwe) is assistant professor of Indigenous politics in the Department of Political Science at the University of Victoria. She is coeditor of *Centering Anishinaabeg Studies: Understanding the World through Stories* with Jill Doerfler and Niigaanwewidam Sinclair and coauthor of the third edition of *American Indian Politics and the American Political System* with David E. Wilkins.

JESSICA LESLIE ARNETT

*Yupik Transitions: Change and Survival
at Bering Strait, 1900–1960*
University of Alaska Press, 2013
by Igor Krupnik and Michael Chlenov

YUPIK TRANSITIONS: CHANGE AND SURVIVAL AT BERING STRAIT, 1900-1960 is a detailed ethnohistory of the Yupik people in Asia and the culmination of over thirty years of fieldwork and archival research that began in 1971. Using oral histories and archeological and documentary evidence from Russia and the United States while drawing on a substantial bibliography of secondary sources, ethnographers Igor Krupnik and Michael Chlenov have written a comprehensive historical account of Yupik social institutions. They seek, according to the prologue written in 1987, to perform a social reconstruction of the system that "allowed the Yupik to endure the centuries of changes, from the arrival of the Russian Cossacks in 1648 through the promise of Soviet communism that was never fulfilled" (xxii).

Two-thirds of the book focuses on establishing a model for the Yupik social system as Kropnik and Chlenov contend it existed from the late nineteenth century to the Soviet era. The first six chapters detail the development and function of what the authors refer to as "contact-traditional society" and describe the social structure of Yupik patrilineal tribes, family, kinship, territory, migrations, and labor relationships that centered on the village. Chapter 7 explores the "lifetime" of the "contact-traditional" model by tracing elements of Yupik society as related in Yupik oral histories through centuries of archeological evidence and European travel logs. Finally, chapters 8–10 address successive stages of the Soviet administration characterized by communist indoctrination, the collective farm era, forced Yupik relocations, and the "Great Reform" that the authors argue irrevocably shattered Yupik society by 1960.

While Kropnik and Chlenov claim to approach their study through themes of change, transition, resistance, and resilience, there are many instances in their framing and analysis that would give any scholar of Indigenous studies great pause. The authors display a troubling tendency to dismiss Indigenous knowledge and Yupik oral histories, which they frequently refer to as "memories" or "lore" (1, 45, 49, 50, 189, 210, 219). The opening lines of the first chapter state that oral histories as a form of knowledge are "fragile" and "unsecured" and therefore unreliable in comparison to those "put on paper or preserved on tape" (1). Elsewhere, they argue that employing "lore for past social reconstruction is often problematic, as it is rarely an authentic projection of the social and cultural institutions of the time" (210).

Though endeavoring to foreground Yupik strategic adaptation and resistance to Soviet colonialism, the historical narrative that emerges is saturated in the language of inevitable decline, extinction, and disappearance (xxvi, 61, 149, 225, 242, 258, 265, 293). Thus the model of Yupik "contact-traditional society" serves as an essentialized and static ideal against which any deviation is perceived as the demise of the Yupik social system. Unfortunately, this framing drowns out the dynamic and flexible nature of Yupik society and leaves readers with the impression that not only are the Yupik incapable of change in the absence of an outside catalyst, but also that Yupik society is outside the realm of "modernity." This is strikingly apparent in their study of the intensification of Soviet "modernization" (263) as the authors fail to recognize Yupik influence on the nature of these encounters, even claiming that these changes and transitions "took place completely imperceptibly to the people themselves, who did not view their society in terms of social anthropology" (259).

Additionally, the density of ethnographic description leaves little room for meaningful analysis, particularly in the context of settler colonialism and empire, constituting a tremendous opportunity the authors have regrettably missed. Numerous examples of Yupik people creatively leveraging their location at the heart of U.S. and Russian imperial borderlands surface in the text, though with little to no consideration for how these moments represent the strategic negotiation of empire by Indigenous people—an analysis that would contradict the overwhelming tone of declension that characterizes the book (8, 9, 12, 45, 96, 208, 237).

The Yupik of Asia endured the sustained encroachment of Europeans and the Soviet state, and scholarship that accounts for their response to the pressures of empire is long overdue. Kropnik and Chlenov devoted nearly four decades of fieldwork and research in an effort to address this historiographical absence. However, while *Yupik Transitions* aims to demonstrate the resilience of Indigenous people against the violence of colonialism, it is unfortunately undermined by its own framing, and the themes of change and transition remain encased in increasingly obsolete colonial binaries that reinforce stereotypical tropes of essentialism and the inevitable deterioration of Indigenous societies.

JESSICA LESLIE ARNETT is a PhD candidate in history at the University of Minnesota.

JOHN P. BOWES

*Gathering Together: The Shawnee People
   through Diaspora and Nationhood, 1600–1870*
Yale University Press, 2014
by Sami Lakomäki

IN *GATHERING TOGETHER*, Sami Lakomäki has written an impressive historical analysis of Shawnee histories over the course of nearly three centuries. From the opening pages he is clear about his intentions to demonstrate the manner in which an examination of Shawnee actions during this extensive chronology have the ability to reveal "how indigenous peoples drew from their culture, creativity, and power to shape the new geopolitical order" (2). More important, Lakomäki argues that the efforts of Shawnees to gather their scattered communities together from the colonial through the American era reveal a drive for nationhood that was based on "indigenous agendas and ideas" as much as they were "powerfully shaped by colonialism" (10). In many ways he wants to develop a more sophisticated analysis of the transition from the colonial period to Indigenous peoples' engagement with the early American republic and its policies. The scope of the effort is ambitious, and at the very least this book provides an argument that deserves and no doubt will provoke a serious conversation about Indigenous formations of nationhood.

Over the course of seven chapters Lakomäki traces the movements and actions of diasporic Shawnee communities and weaves a narrative primarily focused on two divergent actions. The first is that of the Shawnees who chose migration and dispersal as their response to colonial pressures and violence in the seventeenth and eighteenth centuries. The second is that of the Shawnees who by the early nineteenth century began to view and lay claim to the lower Ohio country as a homeland. It is in the actions and recorded statements of the latter that Lakomäki finds the determination of Shawnee leaders like Catahecassa to define "the Shawnee nation in increasingly narrow terms" (143). And it is in the westward migrations of the late 1700s and those relocations led by Quitewepea and Tenskwatawa in the 1820s that Lakomäki identifies "a strategy to assert autonomy from the centralized Shawnee national leadership" (162). Of course nothing is quite so easily defined, and although Lakomäki understands and refers to the complex reality that underlies simplistic categories, he generally assesses the situation as one in which the Shawnees in Ohio were developing an idea of Shawnee nationality and the Shawnees in other areas were outliers in that process.

Lakomäki has an adept handle on the scholarship and the written source materials necessary to write on this particular topic. He often makes use of the linguistic and cultural material produced by well-respected scholars like Carl Voegelin and Erminie Wheeler-Voegelin to develop his points. Yet it is difficult to assess *Gathering Together* without comparing it to another book on the Shawnees published in 2014, *The Worlds the Shawnees Made: Migration and Violence in Early America* by Stephen Warren. Although the latter book covers a shorter time span than Lakomäki's work, the thematic and topical overlap is significant. And despite the cultural analysis that Lakomäki frequently provides, the inner world of the Shawnees is not as developed or apparent as it is in Warren's book. For example, Lakomäki emphasizes vibrant kinship networks and collective decision-making institutions as elements that kept the Shawnees connected despite numerous geographic dispersals from the seventeenth century forward. Yet even that explanation fails to identify what each Shawnee believed it meant to be Shawnee, and therefore does not establish in an effective manner the cultural elements that grounded attitudes toward centralization. And centralization is a key piece to the overall arc of his narrative. His assertion in the concluding chapter that the Ohio Shawnees viewed themselves as a "landed nation" is both critical to Lakomäki's overall analysis and also a catalyst for debate. It raises questions about the extent to which those Shawnees held those beliefs and, more important, to what extent the Shawnees at Wapakoneta and other Ohio villages in the late 1820s might be viewed as representative of the larger Shawnee historical experience.

In the last pages of his introduction Lakomäki reminds his reader that *Gathering Together* presents only one interpretation and that he hopes other scholars will "engage this interpretation, to complement, refine, or contradict it" (11). This monograph undoubtedly provides a great deal of material to discuss and debate, and Lakomäki should be commended for writing a book whose arguments will produce a constructive dialogue that alters the manner in which we think about Indigenous agendas and ideas in the past and present.

JOHN P. BOWES is associate professor of history at Eastern Kentucky University. He is the author of *Exiles and Pioneers: Eastern Indians in the Trans-Mississippi West*, and his latest book, *This Land Is Too Good for Indians: Histories of Northern Indian Removal*, will be available in 2016.

BETH LEONARD

*A Dangerous Idea: The Alaska Native Brotherhood
and the Struggle for Indigenous Rights*
University of Alaska Press, 2014
by Peter Metcalfe with Kathy Kolkhorst Ruddy

METCALFE'S PUBLICATION EXAMINES THE HISTORY of the Alaska Native Brotherhood (ANB) and its influence on aboriginal land rights legislation that eventually led to Alaska Native Claims Settlement Act of 1971. The book's main premise is that "without the Alaska Native Brotherhood there would have been few if any Native claims to settle after Alaska became a state" (xiv). The notion of Indigenous claims as "a dangerous idea" is addressed in the book's introduction, in that aboriginal rights and citizenship rights were thought to be mutually exclusive; that is, if aboriginal rights were recognized, this might circumvent full, "first class" U.S. citizenship rights for Alaska Native peoples.

Chapter 1 begins by exploring the legal concept of "aboriginal title" within the Alaskan context, beginning with a historical analysis of the appropriation of fishing, hunting, and other land use rights in southeast Alaska that provided the impetus for the organization of the Alaska Native Brotherhood in 1912. The familiar phrase "time immemorial" is explained within the context of the Tlingit and Haida Indians suit that validated "exclusive use and occupancy since time immemorial" (8) as related to aboriginal rights.

The second chapter begins with a discussion of Alaska Natives' marginalized, conflicted status in the early 1900s and the influence of Presbyterian and Russian Orthodox principles on the early members of the ANB. The concept of "civilized" as applied to Alaska Natives is explored through a brief case study of Alaska Native leader Rudolph Walton. The influence of William Paul—the first Alaska Native to earn a law degree and serve in the territorial legislature—is examined in some depth.

"Suing the Government" documents changes within and challenges to the ANB as they attempted to meet the provisions of the Jurisdictional Act of 1935. The chapter examines two suits filed by Tee-Hit-Ton Indians, and Tlingit and Haida Indians. The Tee-Hit-Ton suit, filed by William Paul and his sons, pursued compensation for clans, hypothesizing that "Alaska Natives had never been 'tribal members' . . . and, as provided for in the U.S. Constitution, the property of citizens could not be taken without due process and fair compensation" (38). Though this suit failed, the decision by the U.S. Court of Claims confirmed the existence of aboriginal title in Alaska (despite the absence of treaties). In 1959 the U.S. Court of Claims ruled in favor of Tlingit and Haida Indians, finding that southeast Alaska Natives did have uncompensated claims as "aboriginal title . . . had been extinguished by the extralegal action of the U.S. government in creating . . . the Tongass National Forest and Glacier Bay National Monument" (39).

Chapter 4 examines the reservations in Alaska; although Alaska Natives recognized that reservations could provide exclusive title to land and waters and "might be the only opportunity . . . to reclaim land" (51), most Alaska Natives were against establishment of reservations, as these were seen as barriers to self-determination.

Racism in Alaska is explored in chapter 5, including reference to one of the earliest pieces of civil rights legislation in the nation, the Anti-Discrimination Act of 1945. Also examined is the termination movement, which would have abolished "the special relationship between the federal government and Native Americans" (60) with the effort extending to aboriginal claims. "Extinguishment" of aboriginal title that forefronted Alaska Natives' rights to "due compensation" is further discussed in chapter 6. ANB opposition to early statehood legislation that limited their rights to land is also examined in some detail. "Statehood and Native Claims" further discusses the effects of Tlingit and Haida Indians and Tee-Hit-Ton on "unrecognized aboriginal title" and "uncompensated claims" during the statehood movement. Also referenced is William Paul's involvement as legal counsel in the Inupiaq organization of the North Slope Borough, and the "land freeze" that halted state land selection and oil lease sales until aboriginal claims could be resolved.

A Dangerous Idea is a valuable and accessible publication that should interest educators, historians, political scholars, and members of the Alaska Native community. Most recently the ANB's contributions to the 1945 Anti-Discrimination Act are highlighted in the film *For the Rights of All: Ending Jim Crow in Alaska* (2009). However, there are no books to date that focus exclusively on ANB's founders, their relationships with key legislators and the National Congress of American Indians, and their trail of initiatives in aboriginal land and water rights that were crucial to the passage of ANCSA. Readers may be left with questions around how "aboriginal title," "unrecognized title," and "private property" are conceptualized and negotiated legally/legislatively. Approximately twenty-nine pages of endnotes provide additional context with references to key publications and primary sources.

BETH LEONARD (Deg Xit'an Dene) is associate professor of Indigenous studies at the University of Alaska Fairbanks Center for Cross-Cultural Studies.

JENNY TONE-PAH-HOTE

For a Love of His People:
  The Photography of Horace Poolaw
National Museum of the American Indian,
  Smithsonian Institution in association
  with Yale University Press, 2014
  edited by Nancy Marie Mithlo

FOR A LOVE OF HIS PEOPLE is an ode to Horace Poolaw, a Kiowa man born at the turn of the century who photographed his community in southwestern Oklahoma throughout his life (1906–1984). The book combines a selected portfolio of Poolaw's photographs with a collection of essays and is meant to accompany an exhibition of the same name at the National Museum of the American Indian from August 2014 to February 2015 in New York. *For a Love of His People* is a welcome and unique addition to the literatures of Indigenous history and visual culture. The fourteen contributors include members of Poolaw's family and community, art critics, historians, and Native photographers. The combination of family, community, and academic perspectives gives the story depth and connects it in form and method to Barbara Hail's *Gifts of Pride and Love* (2001), a text focusing on Kiowa cradleboards.

For a Love of His People delves into the life and times of a single historic photographer, examining significant topics arising in both Native photography and the Kiowa community. In doing so, it orients the scholarly conversation on the relationship between Poolaw and the people he knew and photographed. Thus it builds on works such as Henrietta Lidchi and Hulleah J. Tsinhnahjinnie's *Visual Currencies: Reflections on Native Photography* (2009) and Tsinhnahjinnie and Veronica Passalacqua's *Our People, Our Land, Our Images: International Indigenous Photography* (2007), which examine Indigenous perspectives on photographers and the images they and others have created. Importantly, this book explores the Kiowa community though the mid-twentieth century, demonstrating the significance of Indigenous citizenship, military service, the connections that Poolaw and his subjects had to other Native people in Oklahoma and to a shared modern America.

Each contributor contextualizes the images with excursions into the history of photography by and of Native people, American Indian and Kiowa art history, women's changing identities, and the Poolaw family. The result is a journey though layers of narratives centering on Poolaw himself, the history of photography, its danger and possibility, and Kiowa and American Indian life at mid-century. He is remembered as a father, great grandfather, an artist, and above all a man of his time attuned to the Kiowa community, which was undergoing a great deal of change during the early twentieth century. The message about Poolaw as a photographer is best articulated by photographer and artist Richard Ray Whiteman, who writes, "He is a participant in his own culture and known to those who appear in his photographs" (146).

The work itself feels like a conversation, and lively exchanges about Native modernities and hybridity thread though the discussion. Art historian David Penney refers to Poolaw's photos and their content as "hybrids" that illustrate "the proliferation of things and their networks that shaped the cultural environment of Oklahoma during Poolaw's day" (62). In contrast, historian Ned Blackhawk eschews the hybrid, arguing for the importance of agency in Poolaw's work by writing that it "subverts the representational power of early American photography, challenging the naturalized and timeless suggestions about Native people" (72). Nancy Mithlo considers the more formal qualities and subject matter of his work. She notes his use of a perspective that allows the viewer to experience a photograph though multiple vantage points as Poolaw saw it (95). David Grant Noble describes "compositional and dynamic elements" that make him "both an artist and documentarian" (112).

Horace's daughter Linda Poolaw and other relatives and community members share what the photographs mean to them as family and as Kiowa people. Linda Poolaw notes that through his photographs, "We can see our ancestors as they really are" (41). Kiowa artist Vanessa Paukeigope Jennings explained his photographs were like "our traditional art: They are a visual record to guide the generations of unborn Kiowa" (151). Additionally, contemporary Native photographers reflect on their own practice in relation to Poolaw and the images he made, emphasizing his significance to later photographers.

For a Love of His People is for anyone interested in the lives of Native people at mid-century, photography, and Native history more broadly. Though the great strength of this book is it multivocality, it is in some ways a weakness. At times the central refrain of the book felt a bit repetitive and a few of the academic voices ran together. However, the layered perspectives, examination of larger issues, and photography itself are powerful and will make this a teachable book that could be used in undergraduate and graduate courses.

JENNY TONE-PAH-HOTE (Kiowa) is assistant professor of American studies at the University of North Carolina at Chapel Hill.

KATHLEEN CARTY

That Dream Shall Have a Name:
  Native Americans Rewriting America
University of Nebraska Press, 2013
by David L. Moore

AS THE MASTER NARRATIVE IS TOLD, America has been viewed as a great frontier, able to be claimed by anyone with the ammunition to subdue it. The space where civilization and barbarity collide, the frontier embodies the imaginary of a nation. In his book *That Dream Shall Have a Name*, David Moore uses this history to guide his readers on a journey of exploration through what he terms "the limits of the frontier." By positioning his book within the context of these limitations of the frontier, Moore presents a fresh perspective on themes central to Native American literature. He reveals to his readers that before our dream can be named we must first understand both the constraints which have been spoken over that dream as well as the ways in which that dream is speaking back, retelling the stories of the past in new voices.

For Moore, these new voices are manifested in what he terms the circle of five themes and five authors, the first referring to five key concepts that speak to the contradictions between Native American and American nationhood: sovereignty, community, identity, authenticity, and irony. Moore opens with analysis, problematizing the history, context, and use of the term under examination. Each chapter links the theme to the five authors under discussion: William Apess, Sarah Winnemucca, D'Arcy McNickle, Leslie Marmon Silko, and Sherman Alexie. Moore develops his theoretical framework for the chapter by engaging with canonical theorists such as Robert Warrior, Louis Owens, Craig Womack, Rennard Strickland, Jace Weaver, and Philip Deloria.

In the first chapter of the book, Moore explores sovereignty within the context of sacrifice. He posits that while American sovereignty and identity require the "vanishing of the Indian," the sacrifice endured by Native peoples is seen as a mark of resilience. In this resilience the good of the people outweighs the good of the individual, ultimately moving the culture toward tribal sovereignty. This idea is the foundation for the second chapter, focusing on community. Moore states that community is the recovering and rearticulating of both identity and sovereignty. As he explores how ideas of community permeate the narration of the five referenced authors, he deems storytelling as a form of community survival. The third chapter, on identity, grapples with selfhood and otherness. The question of who qualifies as Native American is at the heart of this chapter, and Moore problematizes this question in his discussion of "mixed blood." Ultimately he draws more similarities than differences between the narratives of the five authors. In the fourth chapter authenticity is addressed, and Moore highlights how the authors work inside and outside of dominant ideologies. Moore positions authenticity as the foundation connecting all five themes, highlighting the transformative way authenticity redefines and retells America's stories. The final chapter, on irony, captures the vitality of the Native American narrative through its dark comedy. Moore suggests that the function of irony is to create an experience that breaks from all colonial definitions of "the Indian," inventing a new Native voice.

As these themes are drawn together into conversation, their individual perspectives complement one another as Moore weaves the voices of the Native authors throughout the text. Apess employs Enlightenment rhetoric in his call for justice and the humanization of Native peoples. Winnemucca explores the tensions of these themes, speaking from her personal experience of occupying both Native and Anglo worlds. The dialogue of these two authors leads to the perspective of McNickle, who firmly maintains that authentic identity is necessary to healing. Silko takes up the conversation, viewing Native identities as a means of processing change in positive ways, translating authenticity into modern life. Alexie stretches these themes to answer where community, sovereignty, and identity have gone. Beyond a thematic exploration, Moore crafts the broader dialogue of rewriting nationhood and sovereignty. He creates a space for the five themes to engage in dialogue with one another, and with Native communities, and to act as a bridge between Native and non-Native communities.

Moore's *That Dream Shall Have a Name* is the ideal companion for those specializing in Indigenous studies, spanning the scope of audiences from graduate students to established scholars. Beautifully written and artfully crafted, Moore's book unites canonical literary voices with relevant scholarly criticism in an accessible way. *That Dream Shall Have a Name* seamlessly connects central voices from the literature with themes most vital to the field of Indigenous studies. Profoundly insightful, *That Dream Shall Have a Name* may well set a new standard for literary studies in American literature.

KATHLEEN CARTY is a PhD student in the Department of Spanish and Portuguese at the University of Texas, Austin.

NICHOLAS A. TIMMERMAN

*Choctaw Resurgence in Mississippi:
Race, Class, and Nation Building
in the Jim Crow South, 1830–1977*
University of Nebraska Press, 2014
by Katherine M. B. Osburn

THE MISSISSIPPI BAND OF CHOCTAW INDIANS of the twenty-first century poses a historic conundrum to the dominant biracial history of the state. Katherine Osburn's *Choctaw Resurgence* expertly reorients the conversation on race relations in Mississippi by focusing on the marginalized Choctaw and presenting the argument for a triracial history. Osburn skillfully examines the story of Choctaw resurgence from 1830 to 1977, and successfully explains the Choctaw miracle of the late twentieth century. The popular narrative portrays Southeastern American Indians removed to reservations west of the Mississippi River by the mid-nineteenth century, but countless American Indian individuals quietly remained behind, holding tightly to portions of their ancestral homeland. Osburn convincingly argues that the story of the Mississippi Choctaw is one of resilience. In the 150 years since the removal era, the Choctaw struggled to operate within the racial hierarchy of the Jim Crow South, successfully negotiated their relationship between the state and federal government to seek recognition and eventual self-determination, and carefully navigated the volatile civil rights era of the mid-twentieth century to maintain their course of active nation building.

According to Osburn, the Choctaw negotiated Article 14 within the Treaty of Dancing Rabbit Creek of 1830, which offered a path to remain in Mississippi and access to limited citizenship. Combined with Choctaw participation in the Confederate Army during the American Civil War and the rise of Lost Cause ideology, the Choctaw slowly garnered support from white Mississippians and a place within the racial hierarchy. Osburn effectively argues that the Choctaw utilized race to separate themselves from African Americans by establishing connections to popular myths about American Indians. The Choctaw asserted their Indian ethnicity "through crafts, stickball games, dances, and tribal fairs. They acted as anthropological informants and subjects of anthropometric study, spoke with journalists, lobbied for legislation, testified before congressional committees, filed lawsuits, and instituted claims with the Indian Claims Commission" (4). The Choctaw withstood a second removal attempt in 1898 by gaining the favor of local white individuals and adopting federal blood quantum requirements proposed in the Dawes Act of

1887. Osburn persuasively demonstrates that by maintaining distance from African Americans and firmly preserving their "Indianness," the Choctaw attracted the support of unlikely Mississippi politicians. Senators James Vardaman, John Sharp Williams, and Theodore Bilbo diligently lobbied for federal assistance for the Choctaw in the early twentieth century. Choctaw diligence and the work of these senators eventually led to federal recognition in 1945.

Osburn cleverly challenges the common narrative of Mississippi civil rights activity by including conversations about Emmett Till, Medgar Evers, and Fannie Lou Hamer along with Choctaw activism. Osburn demonstrates that the grassroots civil rights activity in Mississippi took place a few miles from the Choctaw reservation. Even though the Mississippi Choctaw maintained their distance from the overt African American civil rights movement, they fought for issues relevant to their people in a "distinctly Indian" manner (183). Activism looked different because their battles were concentrated at the federal level versus the state level. Osburn clearly argues that Choctaw civil rights activity connected them to larger national pan-Indian issues focused on reservation termination, relocation policies, and sovereignty. The Mississippi Choctaw joined national organizations like the Association on American Indian Affairs (AAIA) and the National Congress of American Indians (NCAI), and they established a regional pan-Indian organization known as the United Southeastern Tribes Inc. (USET) that worked toward regional tribal sovereignty.

Osburn's *Choctaw Resurgence* fills a tremendous void in the historiography of post–removal era, Southeastern American Indian studies. The field remains meager; however, Osburn sets the bar high by skillfully exploring the role of the state in mitigating poverty, including American Indians in larger conversations on Southern civil rights, examining tribal resurgence in the American Southeast, and analyzing race and gender constructions in identity formation for the Choctaw in the twentieth century. Osburn could have brought the epilogue further into the future to better answer questions about the Choctaw miracle and how tribal economic investments turned the reservation into one of the top-ten employers in Mississippi by the twenty-first century, but this leaves the door open for further research. This book is meticulously researched and fits well into a graduate seminar classroom or upper-level undergraduate course. Osburn's outstanding study of the Mississippi Choctaw reminds the reader that American Indian history cannot be separated from American history.

NICHOLAS A. TIMMERMAN is a PhD student in history at Mississippi State University.

PENELOPE KELSEY

Sacred Wilderness
Michigan State University Press, 2014
by Susan Power

SUSAN POWER'S *SACRED WILDERNESS* is a tour de force of hemisphere-spanning mythologies of the Middle East and Americas. Set in contemporary Saint Paul, Minnesota, in the Ramsey Hill neighborhood, Power's narrative hinges on the fate of one Candace Altman Jenssen, a Mohawk woman who has lost her way from Kanien'kehaka territory and who inspires the aid of several supernatural beings, including the Virgin Mary and the Hodinöhsö:ni' Mother of Nations.

The granddaughter of Ruby Two Axe, a Kahnawake Mohawk woman who walked away from her community after losing her father to the Quebec Bridge disaster in 1907 and her husband to a freak high steel accident twenty years later, Candace is raised by a secular Jewish father from age seven, after her spiritually bereft Mohawk mother commits suicide. With no anchor to ground her in Mohawk culture, Candace becomes unmoored in non-Native society, excelling at presenting the right fashion and affect and winning the admiration of many men in college, including Barry, a Harvard law student and her eventual husband.

Fast-forward to the present, where Candace is lost in an enormous mansion which is resplendently decorated with imported European furniture and which houses a Native American museum, including an inherited False Face mask that vibrates with palpable rage after decades of neglect. Lost as to how to lessen the emptiness in her life, Candace calls the Minneapolis American Indian Center and asks for help in hiring an American Indian housekeeper. The person who answers this call is Gladys Swan, an Ojibwe-Dakota woman in her sixties, who pities Candace for her angst, which registers even from a distance. Once Gladys arrives in the Jenssen household the action of the novel launches, reaching a crescendo with the advent of Maryam, a supernatural personage who literally beams down from the heavens to the verdant parkway neighborhood where Candace lives. Maryam informs Candace that she has been sent on a mission by one of Candace's ancestors, Jigonsaseh, a clanmother and mother of Ayowantha.[1] Jigonsaseh chooses to send Maryam in her stead, as Candace is more spiritually attuned to her Jewish heritage, having been robbed, in essence, of her Mohawk identity by her grandmother's break from her Kahnawake family.

Candace initially decides to ignore Maryam, being frightened by her presence, and this decision results in blinding migraines and an episode of stigmata that lands Candace first in the ER and subsequently in the psych ward, where she finally fesses up and shares with hospital staff the otherworldly cause of her bleeding palms. While committed, Candace confronts her superficial lifestyle and the ways in which her material obsessions have masked a much graver malaise, and she also accepts Maryam's ministrations and thereby Jigonsaseh's teachings. When Candace returns home, she is able to reunite with her husband and honestly discuss their estrangement from each other, and its source in his dissatisfaction with his career and Candace's intergenerational grief. Together they decide to begin a "new chapter," with Barry leaving day-trading to devote himself to his true passion, acting, and Candace working full-time for foundation boards supporting the arts.

What makes this rather dramatic reconciliation possible is the delivery of Jigonsaseh's message via Maryam. In Power's novel, Jigonsaseh is the Mohawk mother of Ayowantha, a young man who incarnates in the early contact era to renew the Peacemaker's message and who is an unparalleled mediator capable of literally charming weapons from his enemies' hands. Jigonsaseh is mother to twins, Ayowantha and Shawiskara, and Maryam's recounting of Jigonsaseh's narrative confirms both the fated demise of Ayowantha at his brother's hands *and* Ayowantha's timeless message of peace. Power deeply entwines the narrative of Maryam and Jigonsaseh, suggesting a universal urtext of divine mothers and prophetic sons and, thus, portraying Maryam as the perfect medium for the message. The novel, in fact, ends with Maryam's assumption by climbing heavenward up a large white pine presumably (back) to Sky World.

Sacred Wilderness has tremendous value as a novel that bridges differences and intimates the shared fate of Native and non-Native in an increasingly insecure world of climate change and resource scarcity. As cogently as any, Power delineates the fundamental humanity of Indigenous and settler spiritual traditions and makes a provisional peace through the novel's narrative. Where the novel left this reader hoping for greater clarity was in the identification of Jigonsaseh as Mohawk, when most sources confirm she was an Erie or Neutral whose title later entered the Seneca Nation. In fact, there was a Jigonsaseh in the 1650s who mediated during the arrival of the French missionaries, much like Power's character; the last woman to hold the Jigonsaseh title was Caroline Parker Mt. Pleasant (1826–1892), sister to Ely S. Parker. In a related vein, the spelling of Ayowantha's name is somewhat confusing, as "Ayonwatha" is one of several generally accepted spellings, not "Ayowantha." Power also offers a variation of Mary's name, making her "Maryam," so these slight changes might be efforts to emphasize the fictional nature of the work. Nonetheless, these slight historical discrepancies regarding Jigonsaseh are worthy of note.

Overall, this novel is an innovative, groundbreaking work that contemplates Indigenous futurity and writes Native peoples and their stories into those imaginings with impressive facility and literary artistry. Power surely deserves high praise for this visionary novel that both comments on Indigenous storytelling traditions and masters the popular novel genre by bringing tribal literary inheritance and logic to bear on it. *Sacred Wilderness* has the capacity to catalyze a mixed readership of Natives and non-Natives to contemplate what message the Virgin of Guadalupe/Tonantzin might deliver were she to appear again today and how we might reconcile her communiqués with other tribal voices, past and present.

PENELOPE KELSEY is associate professor of English and director of the Center for Native American and Indigenous Studies at the University of Colorado Boulder. She is author of *Tribal Theory in Native American Literature: Dakota and Haudenosaunee Writing and Worldviews* and *Reading the Wampum: Essays on Hodinöhsö:ni' Visual Code and Epistemological Recovery*, and she is the editor of *Maurice Kenny: Celebrations of a Mohawk Writer*.

Note

1. Power's character takes the name of the Mother of Nations, or Jigonsaseh, a traditional title in the Iroquois Confederacy. While some Senecas choose not to use her name, much like the proscription against speaking the Peacemaker's name, the overwhelming majority of Hodinöhsö:ni' use her name in the longhouse and in the popular realm, including naming a prominent Native women's peace award for her.

KATHIE BEEBE

The Power of the Talking Stick:
   Indigenous Politics and the
   World Ecological Crisis
Paradigm Publishers, 2014
by Sharon J. Ridgeway and Peter J. Jacques

THE HISTORY OF HUMANKIND'S USAGE OF NATURAL RESOURCES throughout the world is both rich and often troublesome. For while Indigenous peoples have traditionally remained steadfast in respecting the sanctity of nature by using only the minimal amount of resources that are needed for survival, industrial nations have exhibited an insatiable appetite for Earth's resources. Yet, in recent years, many people have realized that human attempts to harness the riches of nature have significantly depleted the planet's finite resources.

In *The Power of the Talking Stick* Sharon Ridgeway and Peter Jacques employ the contributions of experts in the fields of environmental studies, Native American studies, and political science to systematically demonstrate that economic growth at the hands of industrial nations has led to a worldwide ecological crisis, one that can be mitigated by adhering to the principles that Indigenous peoples have practiced for years. Their approach is designed to inform the reader that contemporary policies are contributing to the destruction of the Earth and that the methods used to reverse this trend by modern scientists are simply not working.

Throughout, the authors demonstrate how social institutions, economic practices, and government hegemony from the beginning of the nation-state to current globalization has created the present state of Earth's ecological decline. One of the biggest contributors to the present ecological state has been the corporate—government alliance that came to fruition at the end of World War II with the creation of the Bretton Woods Institutions such as the International Monetary Fund and the General Agreement on Tariffs and Trade. At the forefront has been the United States, which has enabled corporate elite to gain further wealth at the expense of Third World countries and global ecological systems. Whether specifically discussing policy decisions by American presidents or providing statistics which reveal that most of the food resources in the world are being consumed by the wealthiest nations, Ridgeway and Jacques expertly establish that *industria*'s corporate leaders control world resources at the expense of the planet's ecological life support systems and those who live on the periphery.

Additionally, Ridgeway and Jacques demonstrate that indigenous leaders who have the Earth's best interests at heart are ignored by contemporary globalized culture. In fact, a global Indigenous movement seeks to instill a planetary consciousness in individuals to protect the Earth and enable Indigenous peoples to practice self-determinism. Yet the authors believe these voices are being suppressed by the same few elites who are leading the capitalist charge to reap profits at the expense of Mother Earth. In contrast to these elites, Ridgeway and Jacques cite traditional beliefs of specific tribes such as the Māori, Pueblo, and Lakota who value as well as manage the planet's abundance. As a result, the reader is implored to abandon the destructive ways of the powerful few of *industria* and instead actively join the Indigenous worldwide movement.

Indeed, the authors effectively address the measures needed to be taken by the reader in order to become part of an Indigenous-led global movement that takes on the corporate—government alliances that have placed the world's ecological systems in a precarious state. The authors hope that by reading this work and listening to the Indigenous leaders, people will understand that a greater good comes from only consuming what is required for survival, and not continually seeking to profit at the expense of humanity and nature. While the authors acknowledge that it will not be easy to overturn years of subscribing to a destructive ideology, especially that of enriching a few at the expense of the many, it is vital for the existence of this planet.

Ultimately, *The Power of the Talking Stick: Indigenous Politics and the World Ecological Crisis* persuasively serves as a wake-up call for humankind to understand that corporate greed emboldened by political backers has placed the global community in a situation in which ecological life support systems have been compromised. As a result, this book offers an alternate approach that is suggested in its title—that powerful corporate and political leaders need to be made to pass the talking stick to previously unheard Indigenous leaders as well as others and listen to their insights as to what is best for the Earth's ecological systems.

KATHIE BEEBE is a PhD student in history at Florida State University.

ARTURO ALDAMA

Our Sacred Maíz Is Our Mother:
  Indigeneity and Belonging in the Americas
University of Arizona Press, 2014
by Roberto Cintli Rodriguez

OUR SACRED MAÍZ puts into practice a "decolonial" turn for those who work in Indigenous and Chican@ studies to consider the survival and legacies of cultures and communities grounded in what Dr. Rodriguez calls the "resilience of Maíz cultures," or corn cultures, among Indigenous communities in the United States, México, and the Américas. His book offers six chapters plus an introduction and epilogue. The book is written in a very clear and succinct style, and thus it will be very useful for classroom adoption. As a whole this book will help us in Chican@ studies have an epistemic frame to discuss issues of decolonization, resistance, and persistence of layered Indigenous generative practices that undergird visual languages and sustained cultural practices: food, rituals, dance, and ceremonies. His look at the corn cultures (maize cultures) provides a lens to look at a range of historical events and an interesting way to look at Mexican and Chican@ history, and includes a section on the history of Aztec dance traditions and how they were brought to the Southwest. His book will have a large readership inside and outside of the academic community. The book's design aesthetics are elegant, and the reader is presented full-color illustrations that highlight Maíz cultures from precolonial codices to murals in barrios.

To keep my enthusiastic review concise, I highlight a few points from chapter 3 and the epilogue. Chapter 3 provides an elegant, well-argued, and well-researched look at maps and narratives that represent and discuss origins and pilgrimage of the Mexica peoples from what many call Aztlán. The issue of the origins for Mexica peoples is highly debated among scholars, and is a source of creative and political inspiration for many Chicana and Chicano writers and artists. It also provides a politically charged counternarrative to nativist anti-immigrant views of Mexicans and other Latinos in the U.S. nation-state. This chapter performs an overview of how Aztlán—the homeland of the Mexica peoples—is understood in different political imaginaries, and then it looks at several codices including the well-cited Boturini Codex and several maps to query the location of Aztlán. He provides a discussion on the 1847 Disturnell Map that claims to show the Hopi as having never "surrendered their sovereignty to anyone" and that the "Antigua Residencia de los Aztecas" lay north of the Hopi (81).

The epilogue in this powerhouse and beautifully written book is a must-read for those who are outraged by how the state of Arizona outlawed the teaching of ethnic studies in the Tucson Unified School District and practiced an *auto-da-fé* on creative and scholarly works by and about Chican@s and Native American peoples and nations in the borderlands. Dr. Rodriguez clarifies that the curriculum and pedagogical systems are rooted in Maíz-based concepts and philosophies. He clarifies seven principles of Maíz-based philosophy including *La'kech* (*Tú Eres Mi Otro Yo* or You Are My Other Self) and *Panche be* (*Buscar la Raíz de la Verdad* or To Seek the Root of the Truth) (176). The chapter argues that the battle over the curriculum and the practice of a decolonial pedagogy in Arizona is really about the state trying to "de-Indigenize Mexicans and Central and South Americans living the United States." The chapter posits that this ban attempted to force Indigenous communities to assimilate fully into a Greco-Roman worldview and set of cultural practices and contributed to the "demonization," erasure, and "de-humanization" of communities that are original denizens of the borderlands (178).

In light of the cyclic spectacles of violence directed at Mexicans and other Latin@s in the U.S. nation-state, where human beings are seen as "invaders" and "illegals" and treated as abjects, the political stakes of *Our Sacred Maíz* are resplendent. The consequences for Mexicans and Central Americans, like other Indigenous nations and civilizations in the United States, to realizing that we are the living legacy of a seven-thousand-year-old-plus civilization that predates the establishment of borders by European and U.S. empires are multifold. Rather than seeing ourselves as inferior or vanquished within the U.S. nation-state, we can honor our civilization(s) whose traditions, stories, foods, dance, knowledge(s), and ceremonies persist, and thrive. This decolonial *concienca* (consciousness) that this book offers to its readers both uplifts our resistance and survival, and devours like Coatlicue the arrogance, entitlement, and false knowledges that undergird U.S. nativism and the nation's imperial claims on land, cultures, and space.

ARTURO ALDAMA is associate professor and associate chair in the Department of Ethnic Studies at the University of Colorado Boulder. He is author of *Disrupting Savagism: Intersecting Chicana/o, Mexican Immigrant, and Native American Struggles for Representation*. He has most recently co-edited *Comparative Indigeneities of the Americas: Toward a Hemispheric Approach*.

ROBERT PAHRE

Indigenous Peoples, National Parks,
  and Protected Areas: A New Paradigm
  Linking Conservation, Culture, and Rights
University of Arizona Press, 2014
edited by Stan Stevens

MANY INDIGENOUS PEOPLES live in or near places whose economic underdevelopment leaves them with a relatively intact environment. As central states have begun to value biodiversity, they have also begun to designate such Indigenous spaces as protected areas, such as national parks, conservation areas, or wildlife refuges. These states often remove Indigenous residents or restrict how they can use their customary lands.

Conservationists have traditionally not been sensitive to these human costs, and have tended to trust the state to protect these parks and refuges. They now appreciate better that the state may lack either the capacity or the will to protect wildlife from natural resource extractors. Some also understand that local communities, both Indigenous and non-Indigenous, have developed many practices that effectively manage natural areas in a more sustainable way than do state agencies.

As a result, the time is ripe to reconsider the relationship between Indigenous peoples and protected areas. Editor Stan Stevens's four chapters review the history and summarize a "New Paradigm" for the relationship between Indigenous peoples and protected areas. That paradigm begins by affirming Indigenous peoples' rights. Those rights mean that Indigenous peoples are not just another "stakeholder" among others, but that protected areas can be established on their customary territories only with Indigenous peoples' free, prior, and informed consent. Those rights also mean that Indigenous peoples must take a major role in management.

The New Paradigm believes that Indigenous peoples will often have goals that resonate with those of conservationists. They have been living in their landscapes for a long time and depend on their natural resources. Indigenous peoples have preserved sacred sites and other culturally important areas. In the modern world, they can serve as park managers and as guardians of protected areas' natural and cultural landscapes. Of course, they also have the right to choose economic development of their customary lands.

The book's elaboration of the New Paradigm is thought provoking in many ways. Its claim that states should repatriate preserved areas that were designated without the prior consent of Indigenous peoples has the greatest disruptive potential because this would disestablish almost all protected areas except the most recent. The authors do not confront that politically difficult implication, instead examining more incremental issues such as reclaiming hunting and gathering rights, moving toward comanagement, or repatriating relatively small areas.

This kind of incrementalism often appears in the chapters on developed countries. Australia's Indigenous Protected Areas provides one model for developed countries to start to repatriate some rights to Indigenous peoples. A chapter on three Alaskan national park units provides hopeful accounts of how the Tlingit have repatriated cultural objects and human remains through the Native American Graves Protection and Repatriation Act, have made their heritage visible in a cultural center in Sitka, and have reasserted hunting and gathering practices in Glacier Bay.

The challenges differ in developing countries, where states are still creating large parks, wildlife refuges, and buffer zones, and where Indigenous peoples are more likely to be part of those conversations than they were a few decades ago. However, the New Paradigm's call for greater participation by Indigenous peoples in local conservation would seem to apply equally well to local, non-Indigenous communities—especially since the book does not try to define Indigeneity.

Indeed, Stevens notes that some countries in the Global South define all their citizens as "Indigenous" because they were all the objects of colonialism. Such questions of definition matter in places like post-apartheid South Africa, where the black majority has emerged from colonialism in which it was treated as Indigenous peoples. It now controls a state apparatus that views protected areas in some ways similar to its colonial predecessors. The New Paradigm will need to develop its analysis of such cases.

By focusing on Indigenous peoples as collectives, many contributors also tend to overlook internal disagreements within Indigenous communities. Some chapters hint at differences between "traditionals" and "moderns." Others note some controversy over Indigenous people who choose to work as park wardens, or those involved who produce for the external market versus those who produce mostly for subsistence. Understanding such complexities poses an interesting and important challenge for this New Paradigm for protected areas.

ROBERT PAHRE is professor of political science at the University of Illinois. He is author of *Politics and Trade Cooperation in the Nineteenth Century* and *Leading Questions: How Hegemony Affects the International Political Economy*, coauthor of *Creative Marginality: Innovation at the Intersections of Social Sciences*, editor of *Democratic Foreign Policy Making: Problems of Divided Government and International Cooperation*, and coeditor of *International Trade and Political Institutions: Instituting Trade in the Long Nineteenth Century*.

KIARA M. VIGIL

*American Indians and the American Imaginary:
Cultural Representation across the Centuries*
Paradigm Publishers, 2013
by Pauline Turner Strong

PAULINE TURNER STRONG'S RECENT BOOK *American Indians and the American Imaginary: Cultural Representation across the Centuries* offers a politically and epistemologically engaged approach to analyzing the history of cultural representation of and by Indigenous peoples in the Americas. Strong's aims are ambitious and laudatory. To guide her reader Strong divides the project into four main parts: "Representing History and Identity," "Captivity, Adoption, and the American Imaginary," "Playing Indian," and "Indigenous Imaginaries." In order to first unpack the concept of representation and her ethnographic method, Strong notes in the introduction that this book "employs a theory of representational practice that allows us to consider the ways in which representations are significant parts of power-laden social and cultural processes" (1). This theory is based on Strong's work as an anthropologist and the work of Antonio Gramsci and Raymond Williams as well as Walter Benjamin. Strong views representation as a social practice and frames her research around literary, historical, and anthropological questions. Each of the chapters that follow considers who controls representation, what strategies and technologies of representation are employed, as well as how representations circulate and proliferate given certain limits and boundaries of representation. Finally Strong considers the ways that hegemonic representations exclude and are also contested, and therefore provides examples of Indigenous self-representations that have resisted dominant representations and appropriated representational technologies.

This book builds thoughtfully on the work of Robert Berkhofer, Brian Dippie, Philip J. Deloria, and Jean O'Brien, among others, to offer a well-organized discussion of how representations of tribal, Indigenous, and national identity have changed over time in response to and because of U.S. settler-colonialism. Strong focuses on the intersections between politics and culture to offer a fuller understanding of how white American imaginings of Indian people might shift over time and, perhaps more important, how Indigenous peoples have been able to respond to these imaginings.

Taking a case study approach, Strong considers several different historical figures and events to uncover how various publics have struggled with representations of American Indians in the context of an evolving white American imaginary. She begins with a historical overview of the ways that tribal nations have been constituted by the United States and also negotiated to maintain Indigenous sovereignty. Pointing to crucial legal cases, such as *Worcester v. Georgia* (1835), as turning points in the definition of sovereignty from a non-Native perspective Strong illuminates the challenges faced by Native nations in the past and present. Strong's attention to these dynamics convincingly demonstrates how the United States, as a country founded on protecting the individual rights of its citizens, leaves little room for the general public to understand the collective rights accorded by treaty (and those asserted without this legal "protection") within Indigenous nations. Strong helps highlight the paradox at the heart of numerous legal battles today regarding the political rights of Indigenous nations. She notes, "Native sovereignty, resting as it does on collective rights outside of the Constitution, remains contested even in an atmosphere of increased self-determination" (30). Strong then turns her attention to the trope of discovery and the notion of blood quantum before engaging with captivity, adoption, and the American imaginary. Next Strong considers the "playing Indian" phenomenon, as theorized by Philip Deloria, as well as timely issues such as animated Indians and mascots. Strong concludes with a section on "Indigenous Imaginaries," where she focuses on Native-created and -defined representations within activist ethnographies and Indigenously controlled museums (165).

In chapter 3 Strong describes the different strategies used to represent the Columbian Quincentenary in Spain and the United States. One of the central themes and contributions of the book emerges here in Strong's critique of how dominant tropes like the myth of conquest (most often called "discovery") have been present in public discourses and exhibitions to narrate and celebrate U.S. nation-building practices. Strong offers an insightful reading of the National Museum of Natural History exhibit *Seeds of Change*, and *The West as America: Reinterpreting Images of the Frontier, 1820–1920* at the Smithsonian American Art Museum. The latter exhibit was far more controversial, and revisionist, Strong argues, in its interpretation of frontier art "as ideological justifications of European conquest and capitalist expansion" (35). Both exhibits engaged with contemporary scholarly perspectives to revise how the public might interpret 1492. That *Seeds of Change* resulted in traveling exhibitions, curriculum guides, and magazine features as well as teacher workshops demonstrates the main strength of Strong's book, which is how to teach the public about the pervasiveness and power of cultural representations of Indigenous histories that might reshape current understandings of U.S. history.

KIARA M. VIGIL is assistant professor of American studies at Amherst College and author of *Indigenous Intellectuals: Sovereignty, Citizenship, and the American Imagination, 1880–1930*.

CORTNEY SMITH

*The Gift of the Face: Portraiture and Time
    in Edward S. Curtis's "The North American Indian"*
University of North Carolina Press, 2014
by Shamoon Zamir

BEGINNING IN THE LATE NINETEENTH CENTURY, Edward S. Curtis, a self-trained ethnographer and photographer, began taking pictures of Native peoples living in the American West. Curtis's twenty-volume photographic series, *The North American Indian*, published from 1907 to 1930, depicts more than eighty North American tribal nations. "The Vanishing Race—Navaho," the opening image in the first volume, shows a group of Navaho horseback riders traversing a desolate land toward an unknown destination. While many critics of Curtis's photography argue that this image, and others like it, disavow Native agency, neglect colonial violence, and present Native peoples and their cultures as a "vanishing race," Shamoon Zamir's *The Gift of the Face: Portraiture and Time in Edward S. Curtis's "The North American Indian"* revaluates Curtis's project as an exceptional commentary on cross-cultural encounters. In his revision, Zamir does not dismiss the aforementioned criticisms of Curtis's work but, instead, argues there is a lack of scholarly attention to the aesthetic achievement and epistemological work of *The North American Indian*. For Zamir this aesthetic achievement, found in Curtis's portraiture work, has the potential to "honor the Native American effort to live through the dislocation of culture and time"—a dislocation that was imposed on them by colonialism (9). Zamir argues that it is through Curtis's images of the human face that the crisis of temporal and cultural dislocation is presented. In order to support his argument, Zamir relies on close textual/photographic examination of selected volumes from *The North American Indian*.

For Zamir, critics who argue that Curtis's project romanticizes Native Americans have not properly examined the project's form as a "photobook," which means that the images in *The North American Indian* do not simply accompany the ethnographic text, but rather that the images have an independent role as "argument-making pictures" (235). To support this "argument-making" claim Zamir examines a single image, or a select few, in each chapter. With such careful analysis he demonstrates how a lack of appreciation for the form of the project, as a "photobook," can lead to a dismissal of the value of cross-cultural encounters. Through his reassessment Zamir proposes the existence of a communal participation between Curtis and his Native American models, and that those photographed were "to some degree at least, coauthors of the visual meanings" of the project (3). With over half of the images in *The North American Indian* being portraits, Zamir's analysis invites us to recognize the partnership or collaboration needed for such photography. Zamir acknowledges the possibility of an asymmetrical power relationship between the white photographer, Curtis, and the Native American models, but he argues that even if this is so, we should not be blinded to the agency of the sitter. Due to this relationship, Zamir argues that *The North American Indian* serves as a valuable source for productive discussions on Native American agency.

While there is no doubt that Zamir's reassessment of *The North American Indian* is insightful and persuasive, at times the author diminishes the extent that Curtis's work perpetuated notions of Manifest Destiny and vanishing. This is best exemplified by Zamir's analysis of an image titled "In a Piegan Lodge"—a photograph that Curtis altered by removing a clock. Zamir asserts that the disappearance of the clock does appear to deny agency to those photographed; however, he concludes that Curtis's editing represents an artistic choice rather than a sociopolitical statement. In support of this claim Zamir points to the inclusion of other contemporary objects, like safety pins, in several other photos to attest to Native agency. There may be some artistic reasoning behind the removal of the clock; however, we cannot dismiss Curtis's role in erasing an object that blatantly demonstrated the Native community's relationship with modernity.

The Gift of the Face makes a valuable contribution to several disciplines, including visual cultural studies and Native American studies. But perhaps its most innovative contribution, through the reassessment of *The North American Indian*, is in complicating narratives of cross-culture encounters. For just as Curtis's first image affirms the "vanishing race" myth, "Out of Darkness," a photograph showing a group of Navajo riders (possibly the same men as the first image) emerging from a canyon into the bright sunlight, challenges that myth. And with the existence of these two disparate narratives in the same volume, we confront the cross-cultural complexity of *The North American Indian*.

CORTNEY SMITH is a PhD candidate in the Department of Communication and Culture at Indiana University.

Reviews → WEBSITE

MARISA ELENA DUARTE

American Indian Histories and Cultures
http://www.aihc.amdigital.co.uk/
Adam Matthew Digital, 2015

HOW MANY OF US HAVE SAID, "Boy, I wish that was around when I was a student." Think laptop instead of typewriter, compendium instead of scattered articles, Wikipedia instead of card catalog. I'm feeling some of that browsing through the recently released Adam Matthew database *American Indian Histories and Cultures*, which is best understood as a digital archive with a variety of finding aids, including hyperlinked indices and thesauri, special online collections and exhibits, detailed downloadable records, and cross-searching functionality. The content is rich, comprising a range of manuscripts curated by the Newberry Library. In this review I'll describe the scope of the content, system design, and functionality, and the potential usefulness and key features for scholars and students of American Indian and Indigenous thought, history, and culture.

The collection comprises primary and secondary sources ranging from the early sixteenth to the twentieth century, mostly pertaining to European–Indigenous contact through colonial settlement into the contemporary modern era in North America. A majority of the material is sourced from the Edward E. Ayer collection at the Newberry Library, including artwork, photographs, journals, travel narratives, maps and atlases, speeches, petitions, correspondence, and twentieth-century newspapers. Expertly digitized, the material is searchable by keyword, or by document title, author, tribe, or culture area (e.g., Great Plains). While the search function is helpful, this collection is really best experienced through browsing.

The separate collections of documents, maps, and visual resources have their own browsing and filtering features based on the description within the archival record. There are also finding aids organized around thematic areas such as "American Indians and European Powers" and "Military Encounters: Conflicts, Rebellions, and Alliances." I used the browse by tribe/nation feature in the documents collection to find forty-six documents about my own tribe, the Yaqui tribe, including entire travel journals from early colonial encounters as well as line-item mentions of the work of a Yaqui poet in a 1980s edition of *Akwesasne Notes*, the influential Mohawk tribal newspaper. Each document is also organized into thematic areas; so, for example, records of military encounters between Mexican authorities and Yaqui leaders are also findable in the broader "Military Encounters" thematic area collection. These are digitized documents: the colors are rich, texts include fonts and scripts of the era, and maps and artwork bear the texture of historical documents that inspire scholars to recall the passage of time.

In terms of usability, there are a range of features to assist researchers, including a number of finding aids such as indices to tribal names, place names, and authors, links to popular searches, and special collections of essays by renowned scholars, biographies, and featured art. Visually compelling finding aids include popular searches arranged by word cloud (the phrase "John C. Adams" is quite large) and an interactive color-coded chronology (a lo-fi version is available for interoperability with software for the visually impaired). Documents are downloadable in three ways: through bibliographic managers EndNote and Refworks, as PDF documents, or to an internal MyArchive or MyLightbox account. The systems designers crafted the interface to function with Blackboard for those instructors interested in applying the tool in online learning environments.

I anticipate that Native American and Indigenous studies scholars and students, tribal college students, scholars of U.S. Native law and policy, and archivists and curators of tribal collections will find *American Indian Histories and Cultures* most useful. To me it feels a bit like having a shortcut to a Newberry Library special collection directly through my desktop PC. Comparatively, within the field of Native American and Indigenous studies, it's a sophisticated complement to existing databases *Ethnic NewsWatch*, *eHRAF*, and *America: History and Life*.

Of note, you know how you would exercise caution in allowing your teenaged son to zoom off in your brand-new BMW? (Does any of us HAVE a brand-new BMW? Post-tenure gift? Wild Horse Pass Casino win? In our wildest settler-state reparations dreams?) OK, well, this tool has that fine-tuned engineering that's going to make you want to bring in a librarian to coach your undergraduate students in how to use this bibliographic gem, as well as discern the value of digitized primary source materials. The designers have included a tour on the front page, but it will take some guidance for a neophyte to learn to find documents by browsing through major thematic areas. The scope notes indicate that this collection was curated with the participation of Indigenous scholars and community members. Culturally sensitive material has been removed from this digital collection. The designers view this effort as a work in progress; they are open to recommendations for respectful improvement.

MARISA ELENA DUARTE (Pascua Yaqui) is a researcher with the American Indian Studies Program at the University of Illinois, Urbana—Champaign.

ALTERNATIVE

AN INTERNATIONAL JOURNAL OF INDIGENOUS PEOPLES

www.alternative.ac.nz

AlterNative is an international peer-reviewed interdisciplinary journal. We publish indigenous worldviews and scholarship from native perspectives from around the world.

AlterNative addresses and critically engages with indigenous issues from a scholarly indigenous viewpoint. It spans themes of origins, place, peoples, community, culture, language, history, heritage, colonialism, power, intervention, development and self-determination.

All papers must address and engage with current international and national literature, academic or indigenous theory, and must make a significant contribution to the field of indigenous studies.

We welcome submissions from people who engage and work in areas that are significant to indigenous peoples.

To discuss potential contributions contact **editors@alternative.ac.nz**

NGĀ PAE O TE MĀRAMATANGA

Published by Ngā Pae o te Māramatanga,
New Zealand's Māori Centre of Research Excellence,
The University of Auckland, New Zealand

www.maramatanga.ac.nz

VOICES OF RESISTANCE AND RENEWAL
Indigenous Leadership in Education
Edited by Dorothy Aguilera–Black Bear and John W. Tippeconnic III
$24.95 PAPERBACK · 224 PAGES

Western education has often employed the bluntest of instruments in colonizing indigenous peoples, creating generations caught between Western culture and their own. Dedicated to the principle that leadership must come from within the communities to be led, *Voices of Resistance and Renewal* applies recent research on local, culture-specific learning to the challenges of education and leadership that Native people face.

BRUMMETT ECHOHAWK PAWNEE THUNDERBIRD AND ARTIST
By Kristin M. Youngbull
$24.95 HARDCOVER · 224 PAGES · 8 COLOR AND 11 B&W ILLUS.

A true American hero who earned a Purple Heart, a Bronze Star, and a Congressional Gold Medal, Brummett Echohawk was also a Pawnee on the European battlefields of World War II. This first book-length biography depicts Echohawk as a soldier, painter, writer, humorist, and actor profoundly shaped by his Pawnee heritage and a man who refused to be pigeonholed as an "Indian artist."

UNIVERSITY OF OKLAHOMA PRESS

2800 VENTURE DRIVE · NORMAN, OK 73069
TEL 800 627 7377 · OUPRESS.COM

THE UNIVERSITY OF OKLAHOMA IS AN EQUAL OPPORTUNITY INSTITUTION. WWW.OU.EDU/EOO

University of Minnesota Press
www.upress.umn.edu | www.uminnpressblog.com

The Beginning and End of Rape
Confronting Sexual Violence in Native America
Sarah Deer

How to address the widespread violence against Native women—practically, theoretically, and legally—from the foremost advocate for understanding and change

The Beginning and End of Rape makes available the powerful writings in which Sarah Deer, who played a crucial role in the reauthorization of the Violence Against Women Act in 2013, has advocated for cultural and legal reforms to protect Native women from endemic sexual violence and abuse. These essays point to the possibility of actual and positive change in a world where Native women are systematically undervalued, left unprotected, and hurt.

"This is a compelling and compassionate revelation of the eternal violence against Native women. It is a call to action for all of us."

—**The Honorable Ada E. Deer**, former Assistant Secretary for Indian Affairs and enrolled Menominee

"As a survivor, I am thankful for Deer's insight and theories on creating Indigenous frameworks of justice for victims, their families, and their communities."

—**Radmilla Cody**, singer and advocate for anti-violence

"*The Beginning and End of Rape* documents the brutal history and contemporary reality of how rape has been used and continues to be used against Native women by the federal government to create a cultural implosion of destruction for generations."

—**Charon Asetoyer**, Executive Director, Native American Women's Health Education Resource Center

"An incisive and imperative academic study."

—*Kirkus Reviews*

Sarah Deer, a 2014 MacArthur Fellow, has worked to end violence against women for more than twenty years. She began as a volunteer in a rape victim advocacy program and later received her JD with a Tribal Lawyer Certificate from the University of Kansas School of Law. She is a professor of law at William Mitchell College of Law in St. Paul, Minnesota. She is coauthor of three textbooks on tribal law and coeditor of *Sharing Our Stories of Survival: Native Women Surviving Violence*.

$22.95 paperback | $80.50 cloth
232 pages